Manifestations of

Discontent in Germany on the

Eve of the Reformation

A Collection of Documents Selected,

Translated, and Introduced by

Gerald Strauss

INDIANA UNIVERSITY PRESS

Bloomington / London

Published in Canada by Fitzhenry & Whiteside Limited,
Don Mills, Ontario

Library of Congress catalog card number: 75–135014
ISBN 253–33670–8

Manufactured in the United States of America

C O N T E N T S

Contents

[v i i

Introduction

HEN MARTIN LUTHER sent the manuscript of his *Address to the Christian Nobility of the German Nation: Concerning the Reformation of our Christian Society* to be printed by Melchior Lotter in Wittenberg in June 1520, he must have known that his rousing words would fall on ground well prepared to receive them. For more than a century the voices of protest and reproach had filled the air in Germany, their targets corruption and indifference in church and secular affairs, the arrogance of power and the avarice of wealth, private self-seeking and turpitude, the decline of loyalty to venerable institutions, the slackening of moral vigor and religious zeal. Their grief was for a society gone awry and a time out of joint. If there was hope, it could be found only in a return to principles and customs rooted in a hallowed past, but now abandoned in men's heedless drive for innovation. The voices had grown more insistent in the second half of the fifteenth century. Luther acknowledged them, referring at the opening of his *Address* to the "burdens of pain and oppression weighing on all classes in Christendom, and principally on our German lands, which have moved not me alone, but indeed all men, to give vent to cries of outrage and pleas for redress." Discontent was rising in all quarters of German society, and unrest was endemic. The sources and documents gathered in the present volume are intended to illustrate the manifestations, and show the causes, of the profound social, political, and cultural agitation that stirred Germany in the dawn of the Protestant era.

The Lutheran Reformation lends itself to many explanations, but one thing, at least, would seem to be certain: it occurred and established itself first in Germany because Luther's words and actions responded in some way to the needs of many who had reason to be dissatisfied with conditions as they were. Luther himself supplies a small catalogue of complaints in his *Address to the Christian Nobility*. Apart from the attack on papacy and curia (on which the weight of his militant tract naturally falls) Luther urges that the following shameful abuses be removed by the "true and free council" to be convoked in Germany: usury and speculation; monopolistic business practices by powerful commercial organizations; overconsumption of luxuries, especially common excesses in eating and drinking; the displacement of local customs and privileges by "wordy and far-fetched [i.e., Roman] laws"; university malfeasance (he suggests the establishment of the Bible as the source of all authority, "where we find more than enough information on how to conduct ourselves in all matters"); above all the draining of Germany's wealth into the bottomless vaults of a grasping and wasteful Church. On each of these points Luther repeats the sentiments, and often the very words, of earlier objectors. He might well have included other items: arbitrary rule by strong-armed princes and their officials, intolerable burdens placed upon the peasantry, grinding exploitation in city and countryside, insolence and aggression by foreign powers, and many more. All were of equal concern to the sixteenth-century reformer, for Luther shared with past and contemporary protesters the common view of society as viable only so long as it was animated by Christian principles and carried on in a spirit of Christian love. Opinions differed, and actions diverged, when it came to applying this lofty standard to intractable reality. But a standard it was, made all the more persuasive by its very abstractness and its reference to a lost but nostalgically remembered past.

The grievance literature (as I shall call it) is remarkable for its fusion of high moral sentiment with application to concrete fact. When its authors wrote from a sense of personal injury or defended a vested interest, their strictures and demands were concrete and to the point. Even more noteworthy, however, is another trait, one that explains the homogeneity of the grievance literature and distinguishes it from the political manifestos of other ages: its rearward orientation, its determination to return to beginnings and, if possible, make a fresh start. Expressions such as "in the time of our forefathers," "according to the old customs by which we lived in former times," "as it was done in the good old days and ought still to be done today" abound, indicating the doggedly conservative—or rather restorative—tenor of protest and reform in late medieval Germany. The present is always suspect. "Nowadays" never fails to introduce an assertion of regret or dismay. A sharp contrast is drawn between "then" (good) and "now" (bad). "It has come to this now" opens the way to observations of anger and alarm. "Innovations" (*Neuerungen*) in laws, institutions, ideas, habits, fashions are decried and their abolition demanded with a call for a return to "traditional" (*hergebrachte*) ways. "Ancient privileges" are true and enduring rights; deviations from them constitute violence done to the just social order. To be sure, pleasure is taken in a number of modern attainments: printing, the Portuguese and Spanish voyages, the affluence of urban life, and what was usually called "the flowering of letters in Germany" (a phenomenon which was, along with the art of Dürer, seen as a successful recovery of the excellence first achieved in classical antiquity). But occasional expressions of pride do not mask the general tone of foreboding. The auguries were not favorable. Consolation lay not in the promise of an unpredictable future but in the proven certainties of the past, and often the distant past. Antiquity—biblical, Germanic, and classical—beckoned from across the intervening centuries, holding out the ideal of an established and accepted order (*ordo*). To "set things right" (a frequent admonition) meant nothing less, nor more, than the restoration of this lost order.

Everyone taking notice of events had his special reasons for discontent, but above all local, personal, professional, and class grievances loomed the problem of the empire. In no other segment of public life was the contrast between ideal and reality so pervasive or so apparent. By tradition the first secular state in Christendom, the Holy Roman Empire of the German Nation was, in fact, an anachronism in the political world of the late fifteenth century. Only in theology and history could its bid to be recognized as the *sacrum imperium Romanum*—the world state whose sway would last until Doomsday—and its claims to universal dominion be said to retain a certain validity. In practical politics world empires now commanded no more respect than the claims of another would-be world monarchy, the papacy. Even in jurisprudence the dictum of the *imperator* as *dominus mundi* was meeting effective rebuttal in the contention, first advanced by Italian lawyers in the fourteenth century and then taken up in the chancelleries of national states like France and England, that *rex est imperator in regno suo*. The old idea of a universal state, comprising all men and ruled by one, formulated with great persuasiveness by St. Augustine and accepted as a principle of realistic politics during much of the Middle Ages, had spent most of its force.

At the same time, the empire considered as the German kingdom, the *regnum teutonicum*, was almost equally ill prepared to meet the problems of political survival. Its territories were governed as virtually independent states by a prodigious number of dukes, ecclesiastical princes, counts, and city magistrates, the ablest of whom had, following the example of the imperial electors, succeeded in building a system of effective territorial sovereignty. Few prerogatives remained to the emperor. Apart from the nimbus still adhering to the imperial insignia, the only real powers he exercised flowed from the resources of his own dynastic possessions. He could not tax his subjects directly; he had no reliable army. Even the hereditary principle, long established as a fundamental law in other countries and in the houses of German princes, was lacking to the empire.

Modern historians find some positive features in this imperial disintegration: rising political self-confidence among members of the territorial estates, for example (cf. No. 13), as well as the increasingly competent rationalization of territorial and urban government. But contemporaries did not see things that way. They —or at least the politically literate among them—attributed most of the illnesses of their society to the decline of the empire and to the failure of attempts to shore up its crumbling institutions (cf. No. 1). Their national pride, moreover, suffered as they watched passively while rulers of more effectively governed states flouted the emperor's authority and outdid him in wielding the instruments of power. In its eastern regions the empire stood all but defenseless against depredations wrought by the advancing Turks. Every meeting of the imperial diet saw speakers rise to remind those present of the frightening loss of territories east and west, although none could suggest practical counter measures, and exhortations to unity proved of no avail (cf. No. 2). These being the circumstances, it is not surprising that men should have despaired of the prospects and turned for inspiration to a brighter epoch of German imperial history.

By far the most exciting episode in the imperial past was the age of the Hohenstaufen. Other medieval sovereigns pale beside Frederick I Barbarossa, who left, in literature as well as in the chronicles, the image of what has been called "the ideal type of the medieval Roman emperor." His son Henry VI, who consolidated his power in north and central Italy and conquered the Norman kingdom of Sicily, was a truly mighty ruler. Frederick II had entered the realm of legend while he yet lived, called, even in his own time, "the Lord's Anointed" and "the awakening lion from the tribe of Judah." Seen from later medieval centuries, these twelfth- and thirteenth-century figures appear of heroic size. The literature of their epoch contained much that seemed peculiarly apt in the latter day of a tired empire. The *Ligurinus* (so called from Frederick I's campaigns in Lombardy, the country of the Liguri), a long Latin heroic poem exalting the emperor as the possessor of the *dominium totius mundi,* was first printed in 1507 and republished several times in the sixteenth century. Walter von der Vogelweide and the other masters of courtly poetry of the Hohenstaufen age met in the fifteenth and sixteenth centuries a grateful response to their celebrations of the grandeur of empire and emperor. Otto of Freising and Rahewin, the chroniclers of the deeds of Barbarossa, were read and exploited as sources. A kind of Hohenstaufen nostalgia set in, promoted by men of letters, historians, orators, and publicists whose greatest regret was never to have, in their own time, an occasion to proclaim the lines of an anonymous poet (the so-called *archipoeta*) written in 1162 upon Frederick Barbarossa's victory at Milan:

> Salve mundi domine!
> Caesar noster, ave!
> Cuius bonis omnibus
> Jugum est suave.
> Quisquis contra calcitrat,
> Putans illud grave,
> Obstinati cordis est
> Et cervicis prave.
> Princeps terrae principum,
> Caesar Friderice....
> Nemo prudens ambigit
> Te per dei nutum
> Super reges alios
> Regem constitutum.[1]

In the fifteenth century these sentiments gained considerable point as a result of events on the empire's western frontiers, where King Charles VII of France and his son, the future Louis XI, launched in the 1440's an invasion of Lorraine, Alsace, and Switzerland. Making good sense from the French point of view, a policy of throwing obstacles in the path of the further extension of a practically independent Burgundy was, however, bound to create alarm and lasting resentment in Germany (cf. No. 9), where historical memories were long enough to remember French aggrandizement at the empire's expense during the reigns of Philip III and IV. French pacts with German princes further eroded the emperor's authority and opened the way to a permanent French influence on internal affairs. The culmination of this encroachment came in 1494 with Charles VIII's expedition to Italy, following the defeat of Burgundy in the reign of Louis XI. Never having relinquished title to northern Italy, even though rarely exercising sovereignty over it, the empire, in the person of Maximilian I, could not fail to respond. All who supported Maximilian, writers and publicists in the front ranks, joined in condemning the French move. Public men, especially those with roots in the western regions of Germany, sounded the call for a strong, united, and aggressively led empire, an empire which they tended to see in the image of the realm over which the Hohenstaufens had ruled so successfully.

The rhetorical response to the French provocation, as to so many other challenges, bore the characteristic marks of impotence: appeals, admonitions, evocations of former glories, reminders of present obligations. Among the most interesting, and perhaps not least effective, weapons in this arsenal was the claim to racial superiority, which began its career as an ideological commonplace in the fifteenth century. Pride in Germanic tribal origins became for many a substitute for glory in imperial might and influence. The conviction took root that the Germanic heritage represented a natural and permanent superiority which would, in the end, vindicate the German nation against the *Wälsche*, the Latin races (cf. No. 7). That Germany excelled over the French and Italians in the natural and Christian virtues was taken as axiomatic, although historical proof was also available in recently recovered descriptions of Germanic tribal society by Tacitus and other ancient authors. Needless to say, much comfort was drawn from the heroism exhibited by tribal warriors and from their success against the Roman legions (cf. No. 8). Gloomy speculations about contemporary events therefore drove the German to contemplate

[xv

his past, the heyday of the medieval empire and, beyond that, the uncorrupted and vigorous life of pristine tribal Germania. Reminders of the binding claims of this past upon the present were sounded at every appropriate occasion (cf. No. 6).

Ethnic pride and antipathy to alien ways are strongly marked traits also of German opposition to the Roman Church in Germany. Here, of course, more tangible weapons were at hand. Money could be cut off, jurisdictions ignored, papal bulls could go unpromulgated. But on the propagandistic level, at least, the Church stood excoriated as an alien growth on the German body social, a pack of wily *Wälsch* politicians for whose subtle craftiness the simple German was no match (cf. No. 3). This image of the decent German tricked and browbeaten by a foreign adversary of superior cunning is a remarkably constant one with the writers of the time. It points to another characteristic trait of the grievance literature: its self-pity and tendency to depict Germany as the mutilated victim of unscrupulous foreigners. Luther, too, pointedly reminds the readers of his *Address to the Christian Nobility* of Italian contempt for Germans as crude fools and drunken louts. Plaintive self-pity is, of course, a characteristic attribute of the literature of not only this but also later periods of German history.[2] There are other strains as well. Whenever the objective is limited, concrete, located in a familiar setting, the tone of protest and remonstrance is determined and confident (cf. Nos. 5, 18). But when the alarm is raised on the larger issues—the empire, decline of faith and integrity, corruption in religion and morals, men's disinclination to bear their lot—the voices become shrill and arguments are blurred. So many things were wrong, so few men in authority were willing to make a start toward even the most necessary reforms, that human nature itself seemed at the root of the trouble. Was it not folly to expect a turn for the better? (Cf. No. 34.)

Much in the late medieval grievance literature suggests a mood of distress, if not despair. One senses a society gone adrift, no longer in sight of the direction in which events are proceeding.

Men cannot seem to reconcile the ideal with the possible, or tolerate the many complexities and unresolved ambiguities of an age of swift change. One reason for the bewilderment may lie in an inability to understand objectively what was happening. The absence of informed commentary on the great political and economic problems of the time is certainly conspicuous. Developments in commerce and industry probably touched the ordinary man most painfully, although the impact of administrative centralization in territorial principalities was equally disturbing to large numbers of subjects. Territorial rulers, even if they acted the despots by stripping their subjects of time-honored liberties, could at least be fitted into a familiar frame of reference (cf. Nos. 10, 13). But the symptoms of rampant capitalism were confusing to most men (cf. No. 15). Development of (relatively) large-scale manufacturing in southern German cities had created unfamiliar circumstances: divisions of labor, price rises, conflicts between old artisan elites and a growing new class of wage laborers, a widening division of interest and life style among the rich, the not so rich, and the poor (cf. introduction to No. 17). While vast economic and political power accrued to the merchant barons of southern Germany, the individual saw himself the victim of monopoly, price fixing, social discrimination, and political pressure (cf. Nos. 14, 16). It was a process not confined to the great traders and bankers, but reaching into guilds and town councils as well. To members of a profoundly conservative society, shifts in attitudes and time-honored habits were as disturbing as an economic squeeze. The avid pursuit of wealth, so noticeable now in all ranks of society, was deeply repugnant to men whose sense of value had not kept pace with the changing way of the world. Why was the cobbler leaving his last? Why must weavers and shopkeepers intrude upon each others' livelihood when each man ought to rest content in his own estate? (Cf. No. 29.) Unable adequately to account for what was happening, confused and worried over the direction in which they seemed to be moving, those who thought themselves victimized—and they included all ranks of society—judged events by the touchstone of the familiar and respected past. What was happening seemed a dire violation of the associative nature of traditional Christian society, a threat to its fair distribution of wealth and its clearly established and carefully guarded status system. The cure was simple, though in view of all that had happened it was radical: reverse the movement of events, return to the prescriptive laws of the normative model, abolish ideas, institutions, procedures responsible for the undesirable trends in modern politics and society; make a clean sweep of destructive innovations, from Roman law (cf. Nos. 27, 28) and speculative commerce to scholastic scriptural interpretation and, on the personal level, private ambition and the search for wealth and power.

It still comes as a shock to the modern reader to note the casualness with which so many men of the time were prepared to countenance the disappearance of their civilization. To a single-minded religious reformer like Luther none of the material circumstances of life mattered enough to merit attachment or to deserve grief at their passing. Radical social insurrectionaries viewed the violent destruction of property and institutions as an inevitable and not inappropriate upheaval accompanying the reestablishment of nature's moral equilibrium—although nearly everyone professed abhorrence of rebellion (cf. No. 23), and even firebrand revolutionaries put on the mantle of orthodoxy and conservatism in justifying their actions. Purveyors of apocalyptic visions looked to the crumbling of everything around them as proof that they had read the signs correctly (cf. No. 35). The conviction, shared by nearly all men, that the end of the world was not far away may have enabled them to make sense of at least the most undesirable of current events. Wars, pestilence, shortages and inflation, harsh sovereigns, the havoc wrought by marauding soldiers and rebellious peasants were portents of approaching Armageddon. The gradual fragmentation of the empire heralded the coming of Antichrist, whose reign, it was said, could not begin until the states of Christendom had relinquished their allegiance to the imperial crown. Modern intellects may balk at understanding the workings of an imagination bounded, on one side, by a fixed and ideal past (whether placed in the Garden of Eden, the forests of primeval Germany, or classical antiquity) and, on the other, by the confidently expected approach of the end of the world. But these were the two poles between which the historical thought of the late Middle Ages moved. Only a handful of idiosyncratic thinkers rejected one or both of them. Certain that antiquity had established lasting standards of good and right, and that the final judgment would render a binding verdict on all that had come to pass, men trusted in the permanence of received values and showed neither patience nor comprehension of the fluctuating codes and ambivalent principles of the transitional society in which they lived.[3]

For those who saw themselves as the victims of "innovations" there could be no compromise with the unaccustomed and unconventional; with the princely state, for example, and its impersonal governing procedures and distant bureaucracy (cf. Nos. 22, 25), with gluts and shortages and weird price variations brought on (it was assumed) by unscrupulous and illicit business habits (cf. No. 15), with dissolutions of old ties in town and village, with the social insecurity of an increasingly fluid society, with conflicts and tensions on nearly every plane of national, regional, and local existence, some violent, nearly all acrimonious. Remedies for these ills could be imagined only in accord with what was thought to be ideal. Whether suggested as a palliative or prophesied as the total solution, help for the real and concrete ills of a society in distress could come only through its return to a pristine state of unity, simplicity, innocence of mind, and purity of heart.

This, it should be emphasized, is the intellectual temper in which protest and reform were pondered and argued. It is not explicitly invoked in every list of grievances or charter of demands. Peasants, journeymen, knights, legal reformers, anti-papal pamphleteers were practical work-a-day people and had immediate issues at heart (cf. Nos. 18, 22, 25). But even a cursory reading of the sources suggests that this temper is implicit in nearly every utterance; moreover, frequent specific references are made to it despite its general acceptance, most likely in order to put grievances and demands as persuasively as possible and to demonstrate the place of a particular complaint in the whole network of faults from which society was thought to be suffering. In any case, a turn to the past was sensible pragmatism for many protesting groups, for the imperial knights most obviously (cf. Nos. 24, 25) but also to peasants and journeymen artisans for whom neither present nor future seemed to hold out much hope of an abatement of long-standing grievances (cf. Nos. 17, 18, 19–22).

Needless to say, life in Germany was not all turmoil and distress. In every walk of society men lived and worked in steady pursuit of those ordinary and private purposes which define the plain man's existence in all times and situations. Merchants bought and sold and laid up fortunes. Scholars prepared editions, composed learned commentaries, and lectured at the university. Lawyers drafted briefs for magistrates who governed conscientiously and, by and large, well. Artists portrayed notable contemporaries and painted nativity scenes with sweetly-smiling Virgins. Young men learned a trade and, their apprenticeship completed, produced those marvelous works of skill and artistry for which German craftsmanship in the late Middle Ages was renowned. There was spirit and strength in the German empire, and material wealth enough to sustain it. The country was well-to-do and pleasant to look at with its populous and flourishing cities and neat countryside. But just beneath the surface of this pleasant scene there lay a mood of anxiety and tension quick to rise to the top in moments of stress and confusion, when the perplexities of life seemed too much for men to cope with.

Given the gravity and persistence of the problems, it is not surprising that their resolution often seemed impossible but for the intervention of a superhuman agent. In this respect, too, religious and political ideologies met on common ground. Whether seen as divine savior, as Frederick II *redivivus*, or as the *novus dux* of Joachimite prophecy, the hoped-for redeemer figure entered the human arena with the promise of an abrupt and total end to suffering and privation (cf. Nos. 1, 32, 35). Those who believed in him were offered release from all their anxieties. Forecasts of the blessed realm to be founded by the redeemer varied considerably in scope and detail. National and cultural prejudices colored these prognostications, as well as personal temperament. But common to all was the theme of restoration. The promised reign would bring about the reestablishment of a state of affairs known to have existed at a time when mankind was still free, secure, and happy. As for the immediate future, it must clearly be a time of turmoil and disintegration as things hastened toward their necessary end. Anyone inclined to doubt the fascinated awe with which men anticipated the impending dissolution of the temporal world need only glance at the works of German artists from the late fourteenth century to Dürer and Matthias Grünewald in order to see the common forebodings revealed in all their compelling and morbid force.

As in nearly everything else in this intellectually and culturally eclectic age, we find in the grievance literature of the fifteenth and early sixteenth centuries a dense and usually undifferentiated compound of theories, ideals, convictions, and attitudes. In the resulting mixture the Augustinian historical scheme co-existed with classical ideas of the progressive decay of the world's energy and with eschatologies drawn from the writings of Joachim a Fiore (the twelfth-century Calabrian abbot and most influential of all medieval prophets). Hopes for an improvement in man's condition clashed with the belief that human nature was incapable of self-correction, and these in turn competed with reveries of a blessed golden age and the fervent wish for its restoration. Competent assessment of the work of medieval and recent monarchs coincided with ancient superstitions about healing kings and with visions of a Messiah emperor derived from ideas rooted in Hebrew nationalism and Roman ecumenism. A fresh interest in the data and processes of human history rivaled an obsessive fascination with cosmic schemes as given in astrology, revelation, and soothsaying. Luther himself claimed in 1521 that the old prophecies regarding the reappearance of Emperor Frederick had in his time been fulfilled in the person of his protector, Frederick the Wise. This fusion of religious, political, and poetic traditions, far from being a mere farrago of popular tales and folklore, was the soil in which the culture of the age was rooted. One can ignore it by concentrating on some selected aspects of that culture. But as one pursues the temper of this troubled and expectant society one meets it at every turn.

My purpose in producing an anthology of selections from the German literature of grievance and protest has been two-fold: first, to furnish a survey of the complaints, protests and demands themselves, taking them from the widest, rather than the narrowest, possible chronological spread; second, to provide a sampling of the great variety of sources containing them. In pursuing the latter objective I was not able to be quite as comprehensive as I wished. I should have liked to include examples of other types of source, of the carnival play, for instance, a favorite and effective sounding board for popular grumbling and a good means of assaying moods and tempers. Specimens of tales and novels would have been interesting and made the collection more representative, although they would not have revealed any additional topics of discontent. Theology I have omitted altogether. Some well-known writers could have been included (Erasmus and Luther among them), but I thought it more important to prepare a selection of sources unfamiliar to the general reader and not so easy to get one's hands on.

As regards my translations, I have tended to be rather free, particularly in the rendering of idiomatic expressions. Better to be faithful to the sense of what was uttered and intended than aim at exact verbal equivalents. Where it seemed advisable I have made slight cuts in the texts—indicated by ellipses—but only when this could be done without injuring argument, sentiment, or tone. Brief prefaces to the individual selections establish the context of each. These are also intended to elaborate points touched on in the general introduction and should be read as an extension of it. A few notes identify some persons, places, and other references, but I have not tried to be pedantically exhaustive in these, noting only what seemed worth explaining.

N O T E S

1. "Hail Lord of the world, / Hail our Caesar, / whose yoke is soft / to all good men. / Whoever mutters against it, / calling it heavy, / reveals his obstinate heart / and stubborn mind. / First among the princes of the earth, / Caesar Frederick. . . . / No sensible man doubts that / through God's power / you rule above all other kings."

2. A striking instance of the durability of this trait is Johannes Janssen's famous *History of the German People from the Close of the Middle Ages*, first published 1876, the first volume of which will ring with a familiar echo to readers of this anthology. Janssen portrays a Germany torn apart by internal dissension and assailed by treacherous enemies from without, a people whose indigenous strengths are being sapped by alien ways, whose best hope lies in being true to their most blessed endowment, their religious faith. Like the protesters of the fifteenth century, Janssen castigates monopoly capitalism and the Jews, and idealizes peasants and independent artisans. Only the anti-clericalism of the late Middle Ages is lacking to make the match precise. Interesting examples of the persistence in Germany of visionary ideas about the medieval empire are offered by Friedrich Schneider, *Die neueren Anschauungen der deutschen Historiker über die Kaiserpolitik des Mittelalters*, 6th ed. (Weimar, 1943).

3. See the interesting discussion of classical ideas of the golden age in W.K.C. Guthrie, *In the Beginning* (London, 1957). On millennialism and related ideas, see Norman Cohn, *The Pursuit of the Millennium* (London, 1957), particularly chapters V and XI, but beware of Cohn's irrepressible tendency first to sensationalize and then to deplore.

Manifestations of

Discontent in Germany on the

Eve of the Reformation

[I]

Reform of Empire and Church

1. *The Reformation of the Emperor Sigismund* (c. 1438)*

THE REFORMATIO SIGISMUNDI, the best known and most influential of the many reform treatises produced in late medieval Germany, was written in the late 1430's, most likely in Basel. Its anonymous author was probably a secular cleric resident in one of the southwestern German cities, with connections to individuals close to the Emperor Sigismund (1410-1437), whose reform plans the *Reformatio Sigismundi* claims to represent. It may well be that the author had seen some of Sigismund's reform projects (attempts to strengthen central authority, institute an effective judicial system, regulate coinage, and curtail the independence of ecclesiastical power). Other sources for the treatise may have been a reform plan prepared by Johannes Schele, Bishop of Lübeck, for submission to the Council of Basel; the decrees of the Council of Basel itself; chronicle and prophetic writings; and the Bible in an early German translation. The spirit of the treatise is predominantly religious, a call to re-establish the lost "order" by means of individual purification and social and political restoration. Its influence was extensive. New versions of the original were made beginning in 1440, some of them departing significantly from the earlier text.

* Printed in Heinrich Koller, ed., *Reformation Kaiser Siegmunds* (Monumenta Germaniae Historica: Staatsschriften des späteren Mittelalters, IV [Stuttgart, 1964]).

Seventeen manuscripts survive, and there were eight printings between 1476 and 1522. Everyone writing on the question of reform in the late fifteenth and early sixteenth century was familiar with it. My translation of nearly the entire treatise follows the text of "N" (the version closest to the lost original) in the edition by Heinrich Koller. (For a complete discussion of the various manuscript families, and for bibliography, see Lothar Graf zu Dohna, *Reformatio Sigismundi: Beiträge zum Verständnis einer Reformschrift des fünfzehnten Jahrhunderts* [Göttingen, 1960]). A few condensed connecting passages are inserted in square brackets.

THE REFORMATION OF THE EMPEROR SIGISMUND: This book indicates how spiritual and secular authorities ought to conduct themselves and how they must govern.

Almighty God, Creator of heaven and earth, lend your strength and grace to our endeavor, grant us the wisdom to know and accomplish a true ordering of our spiritual and secular state so that your sacred name and divinity will again be professed everywhere. Your anger is upon us; your wrath has seized us; we are as sheep without a shepherd; without asking your leave we have strayed into the pasture.

> Obedience is dead.
> Justice is grievously abused.
> Nothing stands in its proper order.

Therefore God has withdrawn His grace from us. We ignore His commandments. What He has ordered we do only if it pleases us. We practice obedience without righteousness.

But we ought to realize: matters cannot continue like this. We must undertake a proper ordering of spiritual and secular affairs. . . . Let all princes and lords be admonished therefore, also all knights and all the imperial cities, to proceed to a right ordering of their affairs. . . . And none is to be admonished more earnestly than the imperial cities.

Is it not clear to all that the emperor and king cannot maintain his authority if the electors and other estates refuse to obey him? Our society has become sick and feeble. Be therefore admonished, all you honorable imperial cities, and be reminded, by the blood of our savior—by the rose-colored blood which he has shed for us —and by your Christian faith, to re-examine our ancient charters and privileges and learn from them how we must keep our laws and obligations. Look about you: see how justice has everywhere fallen into corruption and contempt, and how things are growing worse from day to day.

Have you forgotten that imperial cities were founded to be a comfort to the Holy Church, a protecting shield to the empire, a support to justice, and a consolation to the common weal? Do you not know that even today imperial cities are bound by oath and by their honor to help all those who do good, and hinder those who work evil? Think of how things stand nowadays: the sacred Council [of Basel] undertook reform of all that stood in need of reform in spiritual and secular society, from its head to the least of its members. The Council's decrees told the highest personages what needed to be accomplished, what they should do and what they should leave off doing. But are they concerned? Not at all. They show (forgive the expression) their arse to the Council and wish no reformation. Thus simony and greed continue to reign from the thrones of the mighty.

Our lord the Emperor Sigismund, seeking ways and means of preventing such terrible abuses in Christendom, summoned the Council of Constance, which brought about a reunion of the divided papacy. He also charged the Council to undertake a reformation. But the spiritual heads rejected this charge and postponed reform until the Council of Pavia. Nothing happened there either, but a new Council was convoked to meet in Siena, and there they pledged themselves by the most serious vows to undertake a true reformation at Basel and to consider especially three points touching on the gravest grievances of Christendom, namely:

1. to eradicate the heresies that had arisen in many places,
2. to make peace in Christendom,

3. to bring about a proper reformation of spiritual and secular affairs.

The Council considered these three points and issued its decrees. But did anyone obey them? Where were our great lords? Where were the electors? Where were the cardinals and archbishops? They made haste to take their leave. I should have thought that they would be elated by the prospect of a reformation, but no, they refused to pay heed. A reformation cannot succeed in the empire unless it is imposed by force and with the pain of punishment. In thinking about all this, it occurred to me that when Jesus Christ was martyred on the cross, few people stood by him, but those few triumphed. This shows that justice and goodness attract few followers, but in the end they overcome all adversity. The treasury of justice seems to be open only to the few and the lowly. . . .

[WHAT WE NOW SUFFER FROM MOST is simony and greed. Simony arose at the papal court—for more than two hundred years now the papal establishment has not been in good and honest order. Simony touches us most in demands for indulgence payments. "Indulgences—as I love God—are terrible simony and sin. . . . Nothing can be done at the curia nowadays without money. . . . And now the bishops have taken up these same practices, which shows how corruption spreads from the highest to the lowest." Cardinals, bishops, monasteries all profit from financial corruption. As for greed: usury and the lust for riches have been disseminated throughout spiritual and secular society.]

THE HOUR WILL COME for all faithful Christians to witness the promulgation of the rightful order. Let everyone join the ranks of the pious who will pledge themselves to observe it. It is plain that the Holy Father, the pope, and all our princes have abandoned the task set them by God. It may be that God has appointed a man to set things right. Let no one, neither princes nor cities,

6]

make excuses for not heeding God's admonition, for this admonition touches God, our faith, and justice. No one can make excuses for himself before God. . . .

Take note now how each person in the spiritual estate is to conduct himself. . . . I refer to all prelates and regulars, . . . pope, bishops, and secular priests. For if the right order were kept in all things, our spiritual affairs would prosper again, all things would be at one with God, God's wrath would be mitigated, our works would be fruitful, and all things would again be for the best.

Prelates do not relish being reformed, nor do the regular orders, for they are loath to relinquish what they have grasped. But let no one be afraid of the task. . . . If there is to be one shepherd and one flock, we must make a beginning of it. Things have come to their final pass. There must be a new order. . . .

And let all the chief princes and governments be admonished to use the sword against disobedient persons, whoever they might be. An avenging judge is approaching, and he will come among us and judge us, and his judgments will be executed in a spirit of anger. . . .

ITEM: Every government ought diligently to see that copies be made of reform decrees, and that these be posted and promulgated throughout the land so that wrongs may be prevented and the guilty identified and punished. And whoever fails to obey the law, let his body and goods be subject to seizure. Disobedient persons are harmful to us all. This should be understood by all in the land. . . .

HERE IS A TRUE STORY: Not long ago, in the days of our lord the Emperor Sigismund and in the city of Basel where the Council was meeting, a Christian knight entered into a disputation with the Duke of the Turks. The knight said to the Turk: "You are a wise man, my lord, you should see that our Christian faith is a noble faith. All things are well ordered with us, and in our religion you will not find anything amiss. Why not be baptized and become a Christian?" The Turk rejoined: "I see that according to your Bible Christ has redeemed you with His death and chosen you for eternal life. But observing your actions I also see that not one of you truly loves Christ, nor do you desire to live by His word. In fact, you deny Him. You take away your neighbor's goods and wealth; you destroy your fellow man's dignity; you even claim his person for your own. Is this done according to your savior's word and command? Now you plan to come across the sea and wage war upon us, and gain eternal life by vanquishing us. But you deceive yourselves. It would be a far better deed were you to remain at home and do battle with the false Christians in your midst, showing them the way to righteousness!"

Such are the sentiments which we must hear from the infidels! The Turk also said: "If only you had changed your ways, turned to your God and kept your old laws, you would have defeated us long ago!" ...

I should like it known that everything written in this book was translated from Latin into German in order to show how our lord the Emperor Sigismund intended to order and regulate all things for the best. If anyone is wise enough to find items in this book that might be improved according to the ways and customs of his own country, let him do so. If this reformation is adopted, and if the great prelates are obstinate in their opposition to it, its provisions must be enforced with the sword if necessary. Weeds must be rooted out if fruits are to grow in the garden.

CONCERNING OUR FATHER, THE POPE

[The pope is called "holy" because he has charge of holy and sacred matters. He is *servus servorum Dei*, like Christ himself. Precedents for papal conduct were set by the Apostles. No regular orders existed in the apostolic age. "For many years the papal court was maintained according to the regulations of St. Peter." It was when the orders were instituted, and popes and cardinals were chosen from among the regulars, that a change in the character of

8]

the papacy ensued. From then on popes and curia cared neither for the ways of the apostles nor for the decrees for the Councils. "They took possession of the world and let their rules lie asleep."]

No POPES, CARDINALS, BISHOPS should be chosen from among the regulars. If Jesus Christ had intended the orders to play a prominent part in the government of Christendom, He would surely have issued instructions to them, or at least have made mention of them. All the present powers possessed by the orders have come to them from the popes, that is to say, from those popes who were monks. . . . The Emperor Constantine and Pope Sylvester saw to it that churches were well endowed with tithes and other income. But now the monasteries have got hold of it all, and parish churches must go begging. And yet the meanest parish church is worth more than the grandest of monasteries. . . .

THERE IS ALSO MUCH ABUSE done now with papal seals. The Roman curia demands payment for seals, [i.e., for official, sealed documents] which is against all laws. . . . Seals signify right and abiding truth. For this we must now give money! In other words we are compelled to purchase truth, although God himself is truth. This is how it is in all the offices and departments of the Roman curia. Moreover, the bishops and other prelates have now adopted the Roman way because they see in it the promise of great profits. . . . I claim that seals ought to be provided willingly and freely, and without charge; such action would signify true contrition and love. Did Jesus Christ do a trade in seals? He never had any seals other than his five sacred wounds, and these he opened to us without charge, redeeming us with the truth.

Furthermore: No document procured in Rome or elsewhere should cost more than the price of the parchment on which it is written, plus twice that amount as a fee for the scribe.

The papal penitentiary should be staffed by priests only, and the *summus penitentiarius* should also be a priest. . . . If the Roman court were in good and proper state, as it used to be in the old

[9

days, all Christendom would be in better order. When corruption overtakes the head, it must spread to all other members. Once the pope had allowed cardinals to hold plural benefices, bishops followed suit, and after that the monasteries, and following them everyone else in the Church. And today many a cleric holds two or three benefices, though he is not worthy of keeping even one. That is how it goes, and who is the cause of it all?

CONCERNING THE CARDINALS

[No cardinals are to be appointed from the orders. "If an order sees that one of its members is a cardinal, it plagues him with requests for favors, so that the cardinal bends the pope's ear day and night, offering gold and silver in return for privileges, right or wrong, honest or crooked." A cardinal is to be limited in his retinue to fourteen persons, including two chaplains, a chamberlain, a secretary, two nobles, four esquires, a marshal, and a cook. He is to be salaried, not beneficed. When sent out on a diplomatic mission, a cardinal-legate is to have as his first concern the establishment and maintenance of peace. Most of the corruption among the cardinals is due to their drawing their income from benefices which they do nothing to earn or deserve. If the old laws were kept, in this and other points, things would go better in spiritual and secular affairs.]

CONCERNING THE BISHOPS

First of all, no member of a regular order is to be a bishop. I have explained above how damaging it is to Christendom to choose the heads of the Church from the orders. . . . Cardinals and bishops are far guiltier of deception and corruption than the popes; when the pope writes "thus it is" in a bull, and it turns out to be a lie, he himself has probably been deceived.

It ought to be realized that not one of the incorporations[1]

1. *Incorporatio* (or *unio*): the transfer of a parish church to an ecclesiastical institution through a bishop or the pope. The Council of Trent placed severe limitations on this practice.

taking place so frequently now is done according to law. What gives bishops the right to allow Benedictines, Premonstratensians, Franciscans, Dominicans, Carmelites, Augustinians, and other regulars to administer parish churches as though they were secular priests? You can search all the laws and not find this right recorded anywhere. . . . No estate should trespass on the preserve of another; let each estate remain in its proper condition. . . .

TAKE A GOOD LOOK at how bishops act nowadays. They make war and cause unrest in the world; they behave like secular lords, which is, of course, what they are. And the money for this comes from pious donations that ought to go to honest parish work, and not be spent on war. I agree with a remark made by Duke Frederick[2] to the Emperor Sigismund in Basel: "Bishops are blind; it is up to us to open their eyes." . . .

No bishop ought to own a castle. He ought to take up permanent residence in the principal church of his diocese and lead a spiritual life there. He should be an example to the clerics in his bishopric. But nowadays bishops ride about like lords in secular state. Change this wicked practice and you will have greatly increased the chances of peace.

Item: An archbishop's court should be limited to two chaplains, two squires, a notary, a cook, and a marshal. His income ought not to exceed ten thousand gulden *per annum*. Neither archbishop nor suffragan should be allowed to impose extraordinary taxes on his parish priests and churches.

No one is to be beneficed from Rome. All benefices are to be awarded by the bishop in his bishopric for the following reason: only he can make sure that the obligations attending on benefices are being properly fulfilled.

Much evil has come from the practice of permitting individuals to go to Rome to lobby there for benefices. And sometimes it happens that a single benefice is given to two or three aspirants,

2. Probably Frederick IV of Austria-Tirol.

and these persecute and kill each other in order to eliminate competition. Much better, therefore, to let a bishop control all benefices in his diocese. At least he will know who is worthy of holding a benefice, and who is not.

No bishop should assign a priest to a parish church unless the priest has brought him a diploma from a university testifying to his learning. This diploma, and nothing else, should qualify him. The parish priest must be, at the very least, a *baccalarius;* a cardinal should be a doctor of laws and of Scripture; a bishop should be a doctor of Scripture and a scholar in theology and canon law. A worthy person who offers himself as a candidate for benefice should first be examined and, if found acceptable, confirmed in his post in return for the payment of one gulden and not more. The wicked custom of demanding the first year's income from every church should be brought to an end. Every beneficed person should have his fixed annual income. He should not be allowed to take gifts, donations, bribes, or whatever else you call it.

We all know what pain and harm have been occasioned by the practice of beneficing unlearned, unqualified priests. Such men cannot preach the Gospel, nor can they administer the sacraments. We call such men "blind guides." Follow them and you fall into a ditch.

Here is what goes on nowadays: A man sends his son to school to study; the son is graduated. As soon as he becomes a master he applies for a post as a member of a cathedral chapter. If he gets it, he is not satisfied until he obtains a parish church as well. To administer this parish he hires a priest for as little money as he can. He does not ask the priest whether he knows anything; he merely wants someone to hold down the job. Thus all the learning he acquired at school is lost to the world. He does not serve God; he serves only pride and arrogance. . . .

The blame for such goings on must be placed on the bishops, for it is they who provide dispensations from residence requirements, knowing full well what evils must follow. . . . No one should have more than one benefice. And if a man has studied, and is learned in Scripture, he ought to be compelled to become a parish priest. As for cathedral chapters, let them be filled with men who can read and sing, which is learning enough for that job....

Item: Every bishop is to have a gaol or dungeon where priests guilty of malfeasance are to be held. Unless his crime is so severe that it is punishable by death, the guilty priest is to be deprived of his benefice, imprisoned for a month, but then allowed to return to his place. If he transgresses a second time, let him be held for two months. If a third time, he should lose his benefice for good....

Item: There should be one or two men, to be called "presidents," in every university whose responsibility it is to award baccalaureate and master's degrees to worthy men. They ought to swear by God and the saints that they will advance no one who is not worthy of and prepared for the duties of the post for which he is an applicant....

Item: Bishops must hold annual synods with the prelates and priests of their bishoprics. At these meetings the bishop should read the statutes and ask all present whether or not they obey them. He should see that no ill will or other disturbance exists among his prelates and priests.... Disobedient persons should first be admonished, then banished from the diocese. Serious crimes should be reported and transmitted to secular courts....

... Parish churches ought to be governed by a unified rule, so that one place does not observe customs strange to another. The liturgy, too, should be uniform, which is not the way things are now. No two bishoprics share the same rules and prayers....

ITEM: Each bishop should have a visitation to every church in his diocese carried out once a year by his vicar and his judicial officer. These officials should be priests; no layman ought to be entrusted with such responsibilities. And the bishop himself should participate in visitations when he can. Visitations are to be financed partly from parish funds and partly from episcopal funds. . . .

ITEM: A bishop is to conduct himself piously and honestly and to have no worldly concerns. He must be an example to all men in his bishopric. . . .

HOW PARISH CHURCHES OUGHT
TO BE REFORMED

Next to the bishop, the parish church is the most important member of the Church. Here is what ought to be done to restore parish churches to proper order: each parish is to have at least two priests. If it produces too little income to support two priests, it should be merged with another parish. All priests ought to have the same income and perform the same tasks.

One of the causes of the ill will that has come between bishops and priests is the bishops' practice of taxing priests illegally and intimidating them with lawsuits if they fail to pay. They make it a special habit to threaten priests who live with concubines, because these men are afraid of being placed under the ban and usually pay up willingly to escape the bishop's wrath. Thus the bishop gets his money while he permits illicit practices to continue. . . . To put a stop to such dishonesty, would it not be better to adopt the customs of the orient and Spain[3] and allow priests to take wives? Christ himself never forbade marriage. It seems to me that great evils have arisen in the western part of Christendom since Pope Calixtus imposed the rule of celibacy. It may be a good thing for a man to keep himself pure, but observe the wickedness now going on in the Church! Many priests have lost their livings because of women. Or they are secret sodomites. All the hatred existing between priests and laymen is due to this. In sum: Secular priests

3. It seems to have been a widely held notion in the fifteenth century that Spanish priests could marry.

ought to be allowed to marry. In marriage they will live more piously and honorably, and the friction between them and the laity will disappear. But note that no priest should be compelled to take a wife. If he wants to keep himself pure, let him be free to do so, as long as he is honest. If, however, he is found guilty of fornication, he is to be banned from saying Mass until he has spent three months in jail on bread and water. Should he transgress a second time, let him be stripped of his benefice, defrocked, and live the rest of his life as a layman.

A priest who has taken a wife—who must be a virgin—is to set aside a week for his clerical duties, the two parish priests alternating in regular rotation. During this week he may not lie with his wife. On the Saturday on which his week begins he must purify himself with confession and washing his body in the bath. On Sunday he should put on his clerical habit and go piously to church. In alternate weeks he and his wife can have their marital relations, and, as long as they conduct themselves honorably, they are to be held in esteem. . . .

Adulterous priests should be thrown into a dungeon and left to atone there until the time of their natural death. . . .

Item: Every priest should have an income of 80 gulden *per annum*, to be paid in two installments. He should have no business with tithes or interest. Every church is to have a resident curator to take care of the practical needs of church and parish. This curator is to receive all rents and other income due to the parish church, and for his work he should be given a wage. Once a year he renders an accounting before a board consisting of the two priests, an official designated by the bishop, and two or three honorable laymen of the congregation. . . .

Item: Let an estimate be made of the rents and other income of every parish, and, where this income is larger than what is needed to support two priests, the excess is to be used for benefices. Where the income is insufficient, wealthy parishes should be required to help out. . . .

ITEM: No priest shall receive tithes, interest payments, or any kind of rent and income. . . . A priest has only one office, and that is to conduct the divine service and to study, read, write, preach, and protect his flock.

When a new bishop is invested, the priests in his diocese are to make him a gift of half a gulden each and not more. If this were done, all parish churches would fare well.

You may ask: How can this new order be introduced? Are bishops not powerful and monasteries not mighty? No one can compel them against their will. True, but you must know that wrongdoing cannot forever prevail against the determination to set things right. Refuse to bow to their threats, reject their claims to be your judges, and they will become powerless. And the poor, the common folk, must show faith in those who fear God. They will surely overcome, as you shall hear in the last part of this book. You will see: one will arise who will establish the better order by means of force. Join him, one and all. The new order must come, for it is the will of God. The time is near as you shall learn. . . .

CONCERNING BENEDICTINES AND BERNARDINES

Now I come to the Benedictines and Bernardines, two exceedingly miserly orders. If you forced these two orders to live in observance of the rules originally drawn up by their founders, they would be good and righteous. But nowadays they have utterly abandoned their ancient regulations, observing only those that bring them gain and advantage. They ought to be locked up within their cloisters and not allowed to roam freely about the world. But as things are, they are free to come and go; they travel all over the world on foot and on horseback, they lead wanton lives, gamble, take part in worldly affairs; they threaten and punish like secular rulers. They purchase dominion over lands and men, and, as soon as they discover that they are lords, they make good use of their powers. The founders of their orders—holy men such as Saints

Gregory, Bernard, Augustine, Benedict—knew that heaven cannot be bought with material goods. . . . But their followers have turned everything upside-down. They purchase parish churches and procure papal confirmation with bare-faced lies, saying that there has been war in their lands and properties have been burned—and not a word of truth in all of this. . . .

Monasteries should be locked and the monks kept shut within the walls to observe their rules. No monk ought to be seen abroad. If a monk is found on a city street or country road—unless his father or mother be desperately ill and he has permission from his superior to visit them—let him be thrown into prison and left there. . . .

ITEM: A monk should possess no more than forty gulden and these he should hand over to his order. None is to own more than his brother. They should hold everything in common. An abbot may have eighty gulden. He should take his meals with the convent and see to it that rules are observed. He must live in the monastery and go abroad only when appointed visitator when called to a chapter meeting. . . .

ITEM: There are far too many monks in some monasteries. Where there are sixty, the number is to be reduced gradually until only twenty-four are left; where there are twenty-four, let the number be cut down to eight, or even six. The smaller the number, the more likely they are to live a pious life. . . .

ITEM: Monks should not hear confession or conduct burials, nor should they preach without special permission granted by a bishop. As a general rule, no monastery is to perform duties that a parish church can do better. . . .

CONCERNING ALMS, I wish to say the following: four kinds of men may take alms in Christendom. First, pilgrims, be they rich or poor, may ask for aid as they travel in foreign lands. Second, the four mendicant orders, Augustinians, Franciscans, Dominicans, and Carmelites. Their prayers and other good works help all those folk in Christendom who fall short in their godly duties, and for this service they are entitled to alms (though nowadays Franciscans and other mendicants break the laws . . . and do many things that are forbidden to them by their rules). Third, lepers, who are scorned by the whole world. Fourth, all those who are crippled or otherwise handicapped in earning their daily bread, also those who lie in prison. . . .

CONCERNING THE REFORM OF SECULAR ESTATES

Having shown what reforms must be undertaken in the spiritual estates, let us now turn to secular affairs.

First and foremost we must establish a new order for our lord the emperor, or the king when there is no emperor. And what is this new order to be? Spiritual and secular princes of Germany know full well how the Emperor Sigismund used to complain that the electors have deprived the empire of properties and of tolls, so that the empire has become enfeebled. Not that the kings are free of guilt in this; they pledged and sold so much of the wealth of the empire that they have barely anything left of it for themselves. The emperor should now issue a mandate that all properties and rights are to be restored to the empire. Whenever an alienated property or privilege is discovered, whether it be in the lands of an elector or of a lesser prince, let it be recalled to the empire.

What can a king do nowadays? He cannot stop wars; no one obeys him; the imperial cities, seeing that there is no sovereign in the land, do as they please. Thus, the empire falls sick. . . .

Only a learned person should be chosen emperor, a doctor of laws and a man experienced in legal affairs. . . . If he were also an ordained priest, so much the better. . . .

Listen closely, now: Melchisedec[4] was made a king in Jerusalem.

4. On Melchisedec, see Genesis 14: 18 and Leviticus 25: 10. The ascription of the revelation of the fifty-year cycle to Melchisedec, rather than to Moses, is a confusion.

He was an anointed man and a priest, and he celebrated God's sacrifice in the sacrament of bread and wine. He built the great city of Salem (a name he got by dividing the word of Jerusalem in two), and God granted him many revelations. God made known to him the order of governing heaven; namely, that every fifty years, from the time of God's first creation, there has been a new beginning in its government and order. And this was revealed to him for the reason that, since the renewal of all created things must begin in heaven, the same fifty-year period should be established on earth, all things on earth being renewed every fiftieth year. And thus it came to pass that King Melchisedec decreed that upon the advent of every fiftieth year each man is to purify himself of his sins, so that he may become as new as when first created. This order was also established by the holy Council [of Basel] and it is called the Jubilee Year during which men may have indulgence of the pain and guilt of their sins, so that they be made wholly new....

This is what God has decreed and ordered for us, but we reject it in our ignorance. Let us now bring about the establishment of God's order, or we shall not last....

ITEM: The emperor must be stern in the exercise of his authority. He should punish severely and suppress without flinching all persons who resist justice in the state. Toward those who obey and advance the interest of the empire, on the other hand, he should be lenient. Such people should be endowed with benefices and raised to the nobility. For that man is truly noble who places his life and belongings in the service of public order.

[Brief history of emperors, from Ninus, "who instituted knighthood as an instrument," to Constantine, who, with Pope Sylvester, founded the imperial cities, "so that knights and cities together might guard the empire against destructive invasions. It is for this reason that they have liberties and immunities; and where it is discovered that they do not fulfill the obligations to which they have sworn, their liberties should be rescinded."]

[19

CONCERNING TOLLS AND CUSTOMS

Concerning tolls, it must be said that all countries are now so burdened with them—there is hardly a village without its toll—that no country can supply the needs of another, nor can anyone sell his goods at an honest price; and of this the tolls are the main cause.

It is interesting to learn how tolls first came into being. The first to institute and grant tolls was the Emperor Constantine. . . . The empire was covered with steep mountains across which men had to travel, and (as the old chronicles tell us) some provinces petitioned the emperor to grant them the right to build roads through these mountains. The emperor agreed to do what was asked of him and ordered every merchant traveling on this road to pay a tax of a penny per journey. . . . This was a slight toll, not burdensome to anyone, and all payments went to pay for the construction and repair of these roads.

But as time went on, it came to pass that tolls were levied everywhere, until the whole world had been corrupted by tolls and customs duties. He who demands toll payments in one place and takes the money away to another is a public usurer and no better than a highway robber; for robbers deprive people of their belongings, while those who levy tolls for any purpose other than building or maintaining roads are equally guilty of theft, though they claim to be honest men. . . . Some tolls are necessary, in mountainous regions, for example, or where a torrential river cuts a road. But all other tolls should be abolished, and those that remain should be lowered to cover construction costs and nothing else. . . .

TOLL RATES are to be examined every fifth year to determine whether they should be raised or reduced, so that justice might be done to all and no one fall into sin. Two men should be chosen in each city, and they must swear before the saints to keep an honest eye on road and river tolls. . . . And as it is done in the cities, so shall it be done in the countryside and in all princely territories. If this were the practice everywhere, we would soon have good roads and highways to travel on, and we would not have a toll station in every suburb. And the two citizens in charge of collecting the toll must have no connection with any council or court. They are to perform their bounden duties on their oath and on their honor.

CONCERNING GUILDS

Guilds were invented in the imperial cities. Whoever first allowed them to be introduced cannot be saved by prayers or alms, for they are a great evil in society, as you shall hear.

First of all: Guilds have grown much too powerful. In every city three or four members of each guild are placed in the council and this would seem fair enough. But what happens is that the common interest and public weal—which these councilors should protect and advance—is forgotten as each guild councilor seeks to favor his own trade. Let a baker reduce the size of his loaves, or a butcher sell his meat too dear, and what will the councilors do? Will they punish the malefactors? Not at all. They will say: "If I punish you today, you will punish me tomorrow. Leave us alone and we will let you be." Thus the common good has to go begging, oaths are forgotten, truth is extinguished, justice dies, and souls go straight to hell. . . .

NOWADAYS a man going to a city to buy or sell will come away saying "They have cheated me." Everything in the city is sold at too high a price; this is why knights and country people show so much ill will towards burghers. If all things were shared in the city, if people associated to own and do things in common, all these evils would disappear. If no man tried to injure the interest of his neighbor, if all men worked together for the common good, there would be no struggling and no strife, and each would live in equality with his neighbor. . . .

CONCERNING VARIOUS TRADES

Another evil prevalent in our cities—and in the country, too—is that everyone seems to want to carry on more trades than is fitting for him. One man is a wine merchant by trade but deals in salt as well. Another is a tailor but sells cloth on the side. A shoemaker does his own tanning. Look at any of our crafts and trades: you will see that not a man is content with his lot. He goes after whatever he thinks he can get. In many cities four or five individuals control so much trade that twenty men could easily make a living from it.

Do you want to know what the old imperial laws[5] say on the subject? Our forefathers were not fools. Crafts and trades were instituted for one purpose only: to assure every man of the opportunity to earn his daily bread. No one was allowed to trespass on another man's trade. In this way society takes care of its needs, and every individual may earn his livelihood. Whatever trade a man has learned, that trade he should practice. There ought to be no exceptions to this rule. All the imperial cities should enforce it, on pain of forfeiting forty marks of gold to the imperial treasury if the city is shown to have overlooked an infraction. No person must deprive another of his daily bread.

Another cause for complaint nowadays is the deception commonly practiced by merchants who carry on overseas trade in Venice and other places. Here is what they do: Having taken on a supply of goods—cloth or spices or whatever it is—they agree among themselves on a selling price profitable to them all, so that a merchant in Vienna will know how much is being asked for a certain article in Basel or Strassburg. And if people complain about the high price, the merchants reply that they have suffered great losses on the sea. This is how they defend their wicked profit making.

But there is an effective way of putting an end to such tricks. Let the imperial escutcheon be mounted alongside the port sign in every seaport in Germany, and let every piece of merchandise brought in be inspected there, to ascertain that spices and herbs are of good quality and to determine the price originally paid for

5. The expression "imperial laws" in the *Reformatio Sigismundi* usually means the *Schwabenspiegel*, a German law code edited in the late thirteenth century and widely used in southern and western Germany.

the article. This price must be recorded by two sworn inspectors, who should be elected to their posts, in a sealed official document which the merchants are required to carry with them as they travel overland. When they enter a city they should go at once to the merchants' hall. There the mayor and two members of the city council should examine the document, inspect the articles offered for sale, consider the expense, toil, and risk incurred in transit, and then set a fair price at which the articles may be sold locally, so that the same price will be paid by all, rich or poor. If this were done, merchants would once again be held in honor and esteem and would not be sinning against God. And poor folk would never again be cheated of their own.

Item: There have now arisen great merchant companies whose members collaborate in far-flung trading ventures. It matters little whether their merchant luck goes well or ill; they arrange things in such a way that they come out ahead. They can lose nothing. They work all sort of deceit, and cities and countryside are ruined because of them. There should be laws made against the incorporation of such companies, whether founded by nobles or by burghers. And where they exist already, we command in the name of the empire, and hereby give authorization, to put them down, abolish them, and strip them of all their goods and wealth until they are destroyed. Such commercial fraud is not to be permitted, for it does great harm in all countries. Let every man see to his own trade and leave others alone; in this way each one of us will earn his daily bread. The plowman shall cultivate his field, the vintner his vineyard; thus it shall be in all trades. . . .

CONCERNING JUSTICE AND PUNISHMENT

Matters of jurisdiction and punishment are to be observed according to the old imperial laws. The great territorial princes of Germany have kept, at least in part, to the old laws; but many counts, barons, and knights who are noble and possess privileges of jurisdiction and punishment have established proprietary rights over their subjects, calling them their own, taxing them, and levying excessive dues for the use of wood and produce.

It is an incredible outrage that there should be in Christendom today a state of affairs where one man may say to another, before God, "You are my property!" as though we were pagans. As if God had not redeemed us all and made us free! God himself has removed all bonds from us, and no one should be so bold as to claim ownership of a fellow being. And this is proven to us by Jesus Christ. Some of his disciples were nobly born; others were of common origin. Where there arose a struggle among them to determine which of them should be recognized as the greatest, Jesus said: "He that is greatest among you shall be your servant." To God we are all the same. Nobility, power, wealth avail a person nothing before God, for the least may become the greatest. In heaven no one has more freedom than the next man. For this reason we know that whoever says to his neighbor "You are my own" is not a Christian. . . .

Nowadays even members of the clergy own serfs. And these are men who ought to be God's shield, and show the rest of us the right and truthful way! I say it plainly: whoever calls himself a Christian and holds other men in bondage, let him either emancipate them voluntarily, or else be stripped of his goods and chattels and made to do penance. And if it is a monastery, let it be destroyed. If this were done it would not be displeasing to God. . . .

Monasteries are not satisfied with saying "Such and such is our property." They exploit widows and orphans, and if a father dies they acquire his children. In what book have they found this? Who gave them license? Not the emperor! The pope permits it, . . . but in doing so he consigns them all to hell. . . . Monks rule and govern nowadays as though they were secular lords. This is not to be tolerated. Let us rediscover our true interest and live by our conscience. That is the godly way.

Item: Many a good estate in the country has been so burdened with dues and interest payments that it has been confiscated by the creditor, and its pasture and wood and field interdicted to the peasants, even though they are taxed and driven mercilessly to do excessive work and made to serve day and night. . . .

Now I maintain that neither forest nor pasture nor field should ever be closed to peasants, except that lumbering may be restricted if building timber happens to be scarce. . . . Nor should the use of waterways be interdicted. Rivers and streams flow freely, as God made them. They serve many countries, and if they are navigable no one should control traffic on them, except that a modest ferry toll may be levied, and also a bridge toll. Small streams should be free of all toll burdens. It has now come to this: if the ground could be closed to free traffic, as rivers can be closed, they would surely do it. . . . Even the dumb animals, could they speak, would say to us: "O you pious Christians, heed the warnings that have been addressed to you, look into your hearts and undo the wickedness in your midst." It is high time! God will avenge our evil deeds on us! . . .

CONCERNING JUDGES

Concerning courts of law and legal matters of property, inheritance, and blood, the following ought to be said: first of all, a person—be he noble or common—who has been appointed judge and charged with the administration of justice must be a man of unblemished reputation, a good Christian, not a usurer, not an adulterer nor a speculator. No man who has led a blameworthy life should ever sit on a judicial bench. If it should happen that a defendant is convicted by a corrupt judge, his case should be appealed to another court. The same is true of arbitrators: if they are guilty of any of the above transgressions, their findings shall have no validity. A plaintiff against whom such corrupt judges have given a verdict may reject their findings and go before another court. . . .

Item: The chief courts of our country ought to insist that only the old imperial law be used as the fount of justice in the empire, and that every judgment be based on the written law as contained in the imperial lawbooks. . . .

No secular court shall judge spiritual matters; secular and spiritual justice must-be kept separated. If a clerical person has a claim to press against a secular man, let the case be tried before a magistrate. In the same way, if a secular person has litigation with a cleric, they should go before a spiritual judge. But if it should happen that one or the other party feels wronged by the verdict rendered, the issue can be appealed to a learned cleric and a learned secular person who shall be appointed for this purpose. . . .

CONCERNING SEALS

. . . It ought to be known that in secular and spiritual affairs all transactions are affirmed and acknowledged with a seal, which is meant to be a guarantee of truth. In the old days none but the highest persons at the papal and imperial courts could use the seal. But as time went on, and the business of government became heavier, notaries and lawyers were appointed and given the right to issue notarial documents . . . which nowadays count for more than seals. . . . Today it seems that everyone must have his own seal. First princes and counts acquired them, then the imperial cities. Even bishops now employ notaries and seals. And it is a disgrace that in our day a seal—that is to say, truth—is obtainable for money, which is a kind of usury. . . .

CONCERNING PEACE AND ORDER

Regulations ought to be made concerning peace and order in territories, cities, and countryside. We all know how much discord there is among us. Let there be four vicars in the empire, each with imperial authority and the insignia of the empire as symbols of the power vested in him. These vicars are to allay discord and guard the faith. They shall have their seats in the four principal parts of Christendom, one in Austria, the second in Milan, the third in Burgundy, and the fourth in Savoy. Wherever trouble arises, the nearest vicar shall deal with it. Whenever possible the vicars should attempt conciliation and give each man his due. But when a man infringes the right of another, or assaults him, the offender is to be deprived of his own rights. . . . And if it is a city that has transgressed and been guilty of an attack on the privileges of another, the nearest vicar must punish the city and strip it of its freedoms. . . .

CONCERNING BUYING AND SELLING

We all know that Christendom must be supplied with necessities such as wine, salt, grain, lard, meat, and so on. These activities are carried on by means of buying and selling. Now it may happen that the harvest in one country is better than the harvest in another; and a merchant will hear of this, go into the country of plenty to buy up the supply, and sell elsewhere at a higher price. We call this speculative buying [*Fürkauf*]. Merchants who engage in this kind of trade defraud the world and exploit the poor. This and other kinds of deception which men carry on against one another in our society bring disasters upon us all, tempests, floods, hailstorms, bad harvests. And we ourselves are to be blamed for these, for our sins have offended God.

Nature itself renders judgment on us. We expect a good harvest but get a drought instead; we should enjoy warm weather but must suffer cold. These are the just verdicts and punishments of the four elements. Sudden death, discord and strife in our midst are the fruits of our guilt. In most of our towns church bells are rung when a bad storm threatens; this is done as a reminder to say our prayers and ask God for help. Instead we should toll our common sense and good reason, and recognize the gravity of our sins—that would be resonant ringing indeed! . . .

I say this emphatically: Whenever you take something from your fellow man by means of dishonest buying and selling, you will not be able to use or enjoy it. It will burn, or be destroyed, or you will consume it in sickness and agony. And this will happen because of the ill faith we show toward each other. . . .

To put an end to all this, let us banish those merchants who roam from country to country, buying up surplus grain and meat and other necessities. Let us force them to stay at home and not journey about to seek their profits. And let no one sell grain or wine in another country. Grain and wine may be brought to local markets, but no one ought to be allowed to buy more than he can use in his own home, saving only landlords and tavern keepers. . . .

A uniform price should be set in all imperial cities on wine and grain, meat and salt, and on all of the necessities that come to market. Four honorable men should be chosen in each place to fix this price, which should be posted in public so that no one will pay more for what he needs than is right. . . .

One might object: What happens when there is a hailstorm or a bad harvest? Will products not be dearer in some years and in some places than in others? I answer: If you hold to the procedures I have suggested, peace and honesty will reign among citizens, no man will deprive another of anything, and all will lead a common, equal life. The air will become pure, the elements will be kind to us, and nature will be bountiful. God will be well disposed, usury and crooked selling will disappear, the golden age will return. . . .

CONCERNING THE RIGHT TO
ACCEPT NEW CITIZENS

Imperial cities should be free to adopt new citizens, but those who become citizens of a town should swear an oath of obedience to the Holy Roman Empire, and promise to keep its laws in good faith and preserve imperial institutions. Along with this oath the citizen shall give a pledge of his good faith, which is to be recorded in a pledge book. . . .

IT WILL COME to pass that the lowly are raised up and the mighty humbled, as Jesus Christ says in the Gospel. Our prelates, cardinals, and bishops have been blinded; as it is written: "Their sins have made them blind." It will come as St. Augustine prophesied: the ignorant will rise and touch heaven, and the learned and spiritual will descend to hell. This is God's own warning. God wished it said through Augustine and other prophets that we should be mindful of the future.

St. Paul speaks as follows: "Quench not the spirit. Despise not prophesyings." By such writings we are admonished, and yet we care not. Our teachers and prophets say only that which God has put on their tongues, so that we men in the world might know.

In the fourth book of Ezra we read:[6] "In the year 1439 there will arise a small consecrated man [*sacer pusillus*] who will govern and punish the people. And he will rule from sea to sea. His feet shall suppress sin. All that are harmful shall be destroyed and burned. All people will be joyous. Justice will rise again." This is not wrongly prophesied. We sense that the time is near. Our lord the Emperor Sigismund has foreseen it. The time of fulfillment is at hand, as God has willed it to be. . . .

"There will arise a small consecrated man." This is to be interpreted as follows: there shall come a humble and just man, a man consecrated to be a priest. No one should be surprised to hear this. Christ himself was a priest, and Melchisedec was both king and priest. Our emperor should be at least a deacon; if he were also a priest, so much the better.

There is another prophecy that applies to our days, Deuteronomy 11: 22–25: "For if ye shall diligently keep all these commandments which I command you, to do them, to love the Lord your God, to walk in all His ways, and to cleave unto Him; then will the Lord drive out all these nations from before you, and ye shall possess greater nations and mightier than yourselves. Every place whereon the soles of your feet shall tread shall be yours. . . . There shall no man be able to stand before you: for the Lord your God shall lay the fear of you and the dread of you upon all the land that ye shall tread upon, as He hath said unto you."

6. A very free version of the apocryphal fourth book of Ezra 16: 53.

This prophecy will be fulfilled. God will not abandon the just, for he is the Lord of Justice. Therefore I speak to you, all you true and faithful princes and lords who hold benefices of the empire: how long has it been since you were mindful of the empire's good name? Be admonished now and warned, and be reminded of your sacred oath. All you knights of the empire: be reminded of your knightly honor. And all imperial cities: be likewise reminded of your honor and your duty to God. When you see the approach of the just ones, enlist in their ranks, join them, and help destroy all those inequities and iniquities which now cause the whole world to be plunged into despair. All you nobles: rally to the cause, and do honor to your nobility. Justice shall be the reward of the noble. When you see the standard of God being raised alongside the standard of the empire, be in the vanguard of the campaign for God and for justice.

REVELATION OF THE NEW ORDER

Be it known that it is God's will to have a new state and order come into being appropriate to the Christian faith.

In the name of God and of the Lord Jesus Christ, we Sigismund, unworthy servant of God and Protector of the Holy Empire, make known what has been revealed to us, causing us much sadness in the thought of how small we are in the sight of God. Though placed at the head of the empire, we are not meant to achieve the holy blessed new order, as you will hear. We affirm by our soul and by the passion of Our Lord Jesus Christ that what we are about to divulge was revealed to us in the year 1403 in Pressburg in Hungary. Toward dawn of Ascension Day, as the morning star appeared in the sky, a voice came to us saying:

Sigismund arise, profess God and prepare a way for the Divine Order. Law and justice languish neglected and scorned. You yourself are not destined to accomplish the great renewal, but you will prepare a way for him who will come after you. He who will come after you is a priest through whom God will accomplish many things. He will be called Frederick of Lantneuen. He will raise the standard of the empire to the right of his own standard, and between them he will raise a cross. He will rule sternly and with severity. No man shall be able to stand up against him. He will establish God's new order. Princes and cities shall obey him. . . .

As we heard these words, we were grievously saddened. . . . But upon reflection we understood that we had been chosen to prepare a way for the new order, and this thought renewed our good cheer and confidence. From the very day on which we became the empire's servant we have striven with all our thoughts and efforts to establish and maintain the right order in Church and empire. We have reunited the papacy, convoked a council, and brought order into the estate of the Holy Church. . . . However, the spiritual princes are opposed to the divine order. And yet this may be a good sign, for we may come all the sooner into a reformation, seeing how their name and honor grow daily more despised. . . .

BUT NOTHING can be completed until he arises whom God has chosen for the task. . . . Therefore when the time arrives and you hear of the coming of the appointed man, join this cause, help him to whom all wrongdoing is abhorrent. Would God that we might soon see the day. Let us be faithful and loyal Christians and go with the priest king even unto death. . . .

HIS NAME shall be Frederick [Friedrich], and he shall bring peace to the empire and all its lands and regions. . . . His work will go speedily. Though stern at first, his rule will grow mild; he may appear strange to us but will become familiar. Eternal life lies before us. Whoever craves it must join his cause. King and emperor do not admonish you: it is God, our Creator, who utters the prophecy. For the wicked, hell is always open, but the faithful are called to heaven. Let us but bring order and obedience to our land and we shall soon overcome the heathens. This will happen. All men await his coming. The time is near. It shall be fulfilled.

2. *Berthold von Henneberg's Speech to the Diet of Worms* (1497)*

ALTHOUGH THE ZEAL FOR IMPERIAL AND CHURCH REFORM never flagged, successes were meager. The following selection suggests the profound pessimism which occasionally overtook its most energetic proponents. Berthold von Henneberg (1441–1504) was a distinguished ecclesiastical and imperial diplomat before his elevation to the Electoral See of Mainz in 1484, a post that also made him chancellor of the Holy Roman Empire. He enjoyed wide renown as a strict and scrupulously honest administrator of his territory and as a vigorous clerical reformer. His historical fame rests mainly on his unremitting attempt to bring about the political and administrative reorganization of the empire, a struggle which came to a culmination at the Imperial Diet of Worms in 1495, where the Emperor Maximilian was his principal adversary. The address translated below reveals the gloom with which Berthold himself viewed the prospects of reform only two years after the Diet of Worms.

AT THIS POINT, a small number of delegates still being gathered together, my gracious Lord of Mainz commenced to speak as follows:

O my gracious lords, how slowly our affairs do proceed! How little resolution there is among the estates of the empire, from the highest to the lowest! We are indeed to be pitied. Must we continue in this way, seeing how the empire has declined and still declines from day to day? The King of Bohemia is, and should be, an elector of the empire; but what aid or comfort does he lend to the realm? Not long ago, the lands of Moravia and Silesia separated themselves from the empire, although by rights they pertain

* Printed in Johann Joachim Müller, *Des Heiligen Römischen Reichs Teutscher Nation Reichstagstheatrum . . . unter Kaiser Maximilian I . . .* , II (Jena, 1719), 144–145.

to it. In the reign of the great Emperor Charles the Holy Roman Empire still comprised territories and communes in Italy, to wit: Lombardy, Milan, and their rulers. Even in Emperor Sigismund's reign a good many domains in Italy were still loyal to us. But now they have defected and feel no further obligation toward the empire. All the heavier, therefore, the burdens placed on the remaining estates, who must now shoulder the weight of the entire empire.

It has come to this, that if we continue in our present path, we may soon see a foreigner appear in our lands, ruling us all with iron rods. But no one listens to warnings, no one looks to his own motives, and each goes his own way. If we do not come to our senses, we will one and all go to our destruction.

Not many years ago, a diet held in this very city of Worms deliberated at length upon measures to be taken when important domains appertaining to the realm fall vacant and revert to the empire. We agreed that, in the case of such vacancies, no new investiture should be made, save with the advice of the electors. But everyone knows how things have been done in actuality. The Duchy of Milan fell vacant and nearly at once was enfeoffed again. Since our departure from Worms some years ago, the Duchy of Savoy has fallen vacant and reverted to the empire; and to whom did our Lord King Maximilian grant it, but to Duke Philip,[1] who in all matters is a loyal partisan of the French and an enemy of the empire. If this is how we intend to sustain and strengthen the empire, may the Lord help us! There has come to us recently a letter sent from Prussia by the Grand Master of the Teutonic Order, who writes that the Duke of Muscovy has reconquered the fortified towns which had been taken from him and has rebuilt them, making them stronger than ever before, and that he has attacked Christians and oppresses them grievously. This is the same Duke of Muscovy who used to side with the Christians and who helped us against the Turk. And now he has turned against

1. Philip of Bresse, called *Senza Terra*, Duke of Savoy, 1496–97.

us![2] Must we struggle against two enemies at once? Lord have mercy on us. It is high time we worked more resolutely at keeping the empire in state and character. Events have been so discouraging and the general situation so calamitous that we ought now to look into our hearts and resolve earnestly to attend to matters and affairs so that unity may at last be restored to the empire. It displeases me much to know that when I say these serious things and when I issue sealed instructions and orders, I find that no one hurries to comply and that many refuse altogether to listen to me.

2. Ivan III, Grand Prince of Moscow, who was negotiating with the Ottoman Turks in the late 1490's as part of his extensive diplomatic preparations for the Russo-Lithuanian War.

[I I]

The Grievances of the German

Nation against Rome

3. The Debate with Enea Silvio Piccolomini
(1457–1515)*

T HE Gravamina nationis germanicae are German national
complaints against the practices of the Roman Church and its
agents, and frequent remonstrances made to Rome in hopes of abolishing some, and alleviating all, of these complaints. First formulated
at the Council of Constance in 1417, the *Gravamina* remained a rallying cry for anti-Roman resentments among the German clergy and for
the reform movement within the German Church. Few other titles
appear as frequently in the political literature of the century before
the Lutheran Reformation. The three following selections are representative examples of this extensive grievance literature.

In the winter of 1457 Enea Silvio Piccolomini, a prolific and widely
known literary man, humanist scholar, secretary, diplomat, church-
man, memoirist, and—from 1458 to 1464—Pope Pius II, addressed a

---

* The texts translated here are most conveniently available in Latin in Adolf
Schmidt, ed., *Aeneas Silvius, "Germania" und Jakob Wimpheling "Responsa
. . ."* (Köln-Graz, 1962) and in German in the same editor's *Enea Silvio
Piccolomini, Deutschland, Der Brieftraktat an Martin Mayer . . .* (Köln-Graz,
1962).

[35

lengthy treatise on the state of German society and the German
Church to Martin Mair, the chancellor to the Archbishop of Mainz.
Mair, who was one of the ablest of German statesmen in the fifteenth
century and an energetic proponent of imperial and ecclesiastical
reform, had sent a congratulatory message to Enea on his elevation to
the cardinalship, using the occasion to deliver a forceful reminder of
the many complaints of the German nation against the Roman curia.
Mair's letter has not survived, but Enea placed a condensation of it
at the head of his reply. This reply, the so-called *Germania*, an expan-
sion of an actual letter sent some months earlier, aims at far more
than a refutation of Mair's charges. Enea saw himself as a candidate
for the papacy, and he wished to be known as an advocate of doc-
trinal orthodoxy and papal absolutism, especially in view of his own
past association with, and defense of, the Council of Basel.[1] Hence
his spirited apologia for the entire papal establishment. The *Germania* set him on the way to the famous sentence he uttered when
confronted with the contradiction between his earlier advocacy of
conciliarism and his later condemnation of it in the bull *Execrabilis*:
"Forget Aeneas, follow Pius."

The *Germania* had an interesting history in the empire. Its
second book was universally admired as a model for geographical and
historical descriptions of country and people, and for useful comparisons of ancient and modern Germany. On the other hand, its
defense of papal centralization, fiscalism, and misgovernment continued to be resented. A rebuttal was called for, particularly in the
early years of the sixteenth century when the influence of the descrip-
tive part of Enea's treatise was at its height while demands for a
change in the relations between Rome and the empire were more insistent than ever. In response to these demands the Alsatian publicist
Jacob Wimpheling (1450–1528), lecturer, preacher and writer in
Heidelberg, Strassburg and Schlettstadt, friend of Sebastian Brant
and Geiler von Kaisersberg (see below, Nos. 11 and 30), wrote his
Responsa et replice ad Eneam Silvium in 1515. Wimpheling, on commission from Maximilian I in 1510, had drawn up a memorandum

1. For this defense, see his *Commentaries on the Proceedings of the Council of Basel*, ed. and trans. Denys Hay and W. K. Smith (Oxford, 1967).

on the *Gravamina nationis germanicae*, which contained suggestions of remedies and a draft of a pragmatic sanction for the empire on the model of the French Pragmatic Sanction of Bourges of 1438. Thoroughly familiar with the entire grievance literature, he was the obvious man to set readers straight on Enea's assertions.

I have translated Mair's letter (in Enea's version) in its entirety, summarized the *Germania*, and translated about two-thirds of Wimpheling's response, shearing it here and there of Wimpheling's rhetorical excrescences.

MARTIN MAIR'S LETTER

MARTIN MAIR, chancellor to the Archbishop of Mainz, sends warmest greetings to the venerable Father Enea, Cardinal of Siena.

Letters from friends have brought me the news of your elevation to the cardinalship. My congratulations go to both of us: to you because a fitting reward has now been bestowed upon one of your ability, and to myself whose friend has attained a position and dignity which may upon occasion be useful to me and to those close to me.

One thought alone clouds my joy in your elevation. It is that you have been born into a time fraught with dangers for the Holy See. The Archbishop, my master, receives daily accusations and complaints against the Roman pontiff [Calixtus III, 1455–58], who, it is charged, keeps neither the decrees of the Council of Basel nor the agreements made by his predecessor [Nicholas V]; who, moreover, despises the German nation and seems bent on sapping it of its strength and substance. To wit: Elections of prelates are set aside. Benefices and incomes of all kinds are reserved[2] to cardinals

2. Papal reservation: the pope's right to reserve to himself nomination to certain benefices. Originally confined to posts of clerics dying at Rome, this right was greatly expanded in the thirteenth and fourteenth centuries. In Germany, opposition to papal reservation gained force from the attempts—unsuccessful—of the Council of Basel and the Vienna Concordat to restrict the practice.

and protonotaries; you yourself are the holder of reservations of benefices in three German provinces. Expectancies[3] are granted in unlimited numbers. Annates or semi-annual revenues are collected without thought of respite, and everyone knows how much more is squeezed out of us than we owe. Clerical positions are given not to those best qualified to hold them but to the highest bidders. New indulgences are approved day after day for one purpose only: their profits to Rome. Turkish tithes are levied without so much as a by-your-leave to our own prelates. Law suits that should plainly be heard in our own courts are summarily transferred to Rome. A thousand subtle tricks are invented to cheat us "barbarians" out of our money.

As a result of these abuses, our proud nation, once renowned for the ability and courage with which it gained the Roman imperium and became lord and master over the world, has been reduced to beggary, subjected to humiliating exactions, and left to cower in the dust, bemoaning its misery. Now, however, our leaders have been, so to speak, awakened from their sleep and have begun to ponder what means they might take to oppose their misfortunes, shake off their yoke, and regain the ancient freedom they have lost. Consider what a blow it will be to Rome if the German princes should succeed in their design! Thus, joyful as I am in the thought of your new dignity, I am saddened that your service as cardinal should come at so troublesome a time. God's plan may be otherwise, however, and His will is sure to prevail.

Be of good cheer, then, and let your wisdom reflect on the measures that must be taken to keep the raging stream safely in its bed. Farewell!

From Aschaffenburg, August 31, 1457[4]

3. Expectancy: the appointment to an ecclesiastical post before it falls vacant, assuring right of succession. The practice had been forbidden by canon law but gained currency in the fourteenth and fifteenth centuries, particularly through the papal custom of appointing coadjutors to bishops with rights of succession.

4. Enea Silvio's date. Mair's actual letter must have reached him before then.

Enea Silvio's *Germania* (1457)

Enea's reply to Martin Mair is usually entitled *De ritu, situ, moribus et conditione Germaniae*, or simply *Germania*. The following is a brief synopsis.

Book I: The grievances and burdens catalogued by Mair either do not exist or are trivial. Each of Rome's alleged violations of conciliar decrees can be explained. Papal arrogation of rights formerly possessed by chapters was necessary for the better and independent administration of Church and society. Papal fiscal practices, though universally maligned, are in fact efficient and, by and large, honest. Abuses do exist, but popes and cardinals are men, after all, and will occasionally fall victim to human failings. If you observe the conduct of secular rulers, Rome will come out well in the comparison. Take law courts, for example. Everyone knows that common people find no justice before German judges; Roman courts are their only recourse. As for indulgences, their purchase is voluntary; why should this be condemned? You are jealous of the money going to Rome; there you have the root of your accusation. "All your lamenting is about money!"

Book II: Mair contends that Germany used to be rich and mighty and has been reduced to beggary by Rome. The very opposite is the case. Caesar, Strabo, and Tacitus portray a barbarous and uncivilized society. By contrast, look at Germany today: larger than in antiquity, dominated by superb cities [Enea describes more than twenty of them and mentions several others; they are, according to him, the finest in Europe.], highly developed natural resources, abundant mercantile wealth. The Germans themselves are a pious, industrious, resourceful people. "This then, is the present appearance and might of your country. If you call it contemptible, there is no lack of observers who would rather deem you to be contemptible and lacking in judgment." True, the empire can no longer boast the universal dominion it enjoyed under Charlemagne and the Hohenstaufen emperors. But who could claim this to be Rome's fault? If the empire is weak today, the cause must be sought in the divisiveness of the Germans themselves. No one obeys the emperor; there are too many rulers, each bent on achieving his own "freedom." Germany's political history is one of contention, feud, and civil strife. Face this fact, and do not blame Rome for your own troubles.

Book III: Contemplating rebellion against Rome is folly. Who are these "leaders" you say are making preparations to "oppose" Rome? [Enea supplies a roster of German princes and prelates, loyal sons of the Church all of them.] It is only the rabble, the mob, that craves "innovations" and talks revolution. What ingratitude! Where would you be without the Roman Church, the "Mother of the German people"? You would be heathens still. As for papal and curial "opulence," remember Ecclesiasticus 13:23: "When the rich man speaks all are silent: . . . when the poor man speaks they say 'Who is this fellow?' " How could a poor shepherd undertake to accomplish all that the pope must do? Why not demand that secular rulers and city magistrates also return to the humble circumstances of their origins? In any case, no change in Church organization can be contemplated unless it emanates from the pope. Nor may there be a council except under papal auspices. There is no denying that popes do, on occasion, fall into error, but men have no recourse beyond them. Only God can judge the pope.

JACOB WIMPHELING'S RESPONSE TO ENEA SILVIO (1515)

DEDICATION TO ALBRECHT OF BRANDENBURG, ARCHBISHOP OF MAINZ

Most venerable father and noble prince! Martin Mair, chancellor to your predecessor in the archdiocese of Mainz, wrote a letter of complaint to Enea Silvio, a man whose popularity in Germany, aided by the intervention of His Majesty the Emperor, won him his elevation to the cardinalship. Martin's complaint noted a number of oppressive and intolerable burdens weighing on our German society. Enea, as an Italian and acting from the fear that the copious flow of German money into his country might one day be stopped, sought to refute Martin's charges, heaping honeyed praise upon our nation, her cities, churches, people and, especially, her noble families. . . .

On the advice of friends I have now undertaken a task which Martin, were he still living, would no doubt want to assume himself. As a German and on behalf of Germans, . . . as a son of the empire and on behalf of the empire, I reply to Enea as he responded to Martin. It is my conviction that to no person could this reply more fittingly be dedicated than to you, most venerable father and prince, so that as the grievances of our people formulated by Martin Mair issued from Mainz, my refutation may return there; for regardless of how its merits may be judged, my treatise's sole sources are Scripture and the canon law. . . . It is not my purpose to instigate a rebellion. Far from it, I have always abhorred disobedience, knowing that it destroys order in church and empire, creates factions, and enfeebles discipline. Nor have I undertaken my task in order to denigrate the Holy See. . . . No lover of the Gospel and the Holy Fathers will feel stung by the criticism I make of Enea's views; on the contrary, I am confident that all partisans of the right doctrines and the true faith will find themselves in agreement with me. . . .

Written in solitude, May 19, 1515

RESPONSES AND OBJECTIONS TO ENEA SILVIO

Rightly does Enea Silvio praise Germany as the source of his elevation [to cardinal]. Because he is an Italian, however, and loves the land of his birth, he would not enjoy seeing the flow of money from our country to his own slowed to a trickle. He therefore flatters us with stories of the translation of the *imperium* from the Greeks to the Germans, though we all know that our ancestors

[41

had to win this imperium with their courage and their life's blood. He goes on to laud the ample treasures to be found in our churches and homes. But even if Germany really did possess so abundant a store of hard-earned and frugally managed wealth, how much of it would remain to us after we had taken care of our daily needs, had seen to the maintenance of our churches, cities, streets, and public institutions, assured our country's protection from its enemies, provided for orphans, widows, and the victims of plague, pox, and French disease, and comforted beggars, as Christian piety demands?

Enea makes much of the fact that we Germans received our Christian faith from his compatriots. "Rome," he writes, "preached Christ to you; it was faith in Christ, received from Rome, that extinguished barbarism in you." We concede, of course, that missionaries from Rome brought the saving message of Christ to our land. But by the same token Rome herself was, like Germany, converted to the Christian faith, and Rome should therefore show no less gratitude than Germany for the reception of her faith. For was it not Peter, a Jew from Palestine, who preached the Gospel of Christ in Rome? If Enea's argument were applied to the Romans themselves, they would now be obliged to send annual tributes of gold and silver to Syria. . . .

It is not that we deny our debt to Rome. But we ask: Is Rome not also indebted to us? Have not two of our compatriots, clever and skillful men hailing from Strassburg and Mainz, invented the noble art of printing, which makes it possible to propagate the correct doctrines of faith and morals throughout the world and in all languages? . . . Do we, who have been true and industrious in our service to religion and to the Holy Roman Church, who are steadfast in our faith and even—as Enea admits—prepared to shed our blood for it, who willingly obey orders, buy indulgences, travel to Rome, and send money—do we who perform all these duties deserve to be called barbarians? . . . Despite this slanderous label, Enea speaks with lavish praise of our fatherland, of our cities and buildings. For what purpose? For one only: to make our ears more receptive to the demands coming from Rome dressed in Christian garb but serving Italian interests; in other words, to put us in the mood for wasting our fortunes on foreigners. . . . As it is, our compatriots crowd the road to Rome. They pay for papal reservations and dispensations. They appear before papal courts—and not always because they have appealed a case to Rome, but rather because their cases have been arbitrarily transferred there. Is there a nation more patient and willing to receive indulgences, though we well know that the income from them is divided between the Holy See and its officialdom? Have we not paid dearly for the confirmation of every bishop and abbot? . . .

Thus we are done out of fortune, and for no purpose other than to support the innumerable retainers and hangers-on that populate the papal court. Enea himself gives us a list of these papal lackeys, the number of which increases daily. True, if the pope must furnish court rooms for all the legal business in Christendom, he requires a huge staff. But there is no need for this. Apart from imperial courts, there exist in our German cities learned and honorable judges to whom appeals from lower episcopal courts could be directed. It is in the highest degree objectionable that Rome bypasses courts of higher resort—often on trivial pretexts or out of pique—and compels our compatriots, laymen included, to appear in Rome. No one will deny that intricate and weighty matters should be appealed to Rome as the seat of highest power and of greatest wisdom and justice. But the rights of imperial and episcopal jurisdiction must not be infringed. If these rights had remained intact, the Apostolic See would not today stagger under an unmanageable weight of legal and administrative business. . . .

The Council of Basel pointed out that our sacred church fathers had written their canons for the purpose of assuring the Church of good government, and that honor, discipline, faith, piety, love, and peace reigned in the Church as long as these regulations were observed. Later, however, vanity and greed began to prevail; the laws of the fathers were neglected, and the Church sank into immorality and depravity, debasement, degradation and abuse of office. This is principally due to papal reservations of prelacies and other ecclesiastical benefices, also to the prolific award of expectancies to future benefices, and to innumerable concessions and other burdens placed upon churches and clergy. To wit:

Church incomes and benefices are given to unworthy men and Italians.

High offices and lucrative posts are awarded to persons of unproven merit and character.

Few holders of benefices reside in their churches, for as they hold several posts simultaneously they cannot reside in all of them at once. Most do not even recognize the faces of their parishioners. They neglect the care of souls and seek only temporal rewards.

The divine service is curtailed.

Hospitality is diminished.

Church laws lose their force.

Ecclesiastical buildings fall into ruin.

The conduct of clerics is an open scandal.

Able, learned, and virtuous priests who might raise the moral and professional level of the clergy abandon their studies because they see no prospect of advancement.

The ranks of the clergy are riven by rivalry and animosity; hatred, envy, and even the wish for the death of others are aroused.

Striving after pluralities of benefices is encouraged.

Poor clerics are maltreated, impoverished, and forced from their posts.

Crooked lawsuits are employed to gather benefices.

Some benifices are procured through simony.

Other benefices remain vacant.

Able young men are left to lead idle and vagrant lives.

Prelates are deprived of jurisdiction and authority.

The hierarchical order of the Church is destroyed.

In this manner, a vast number of violations of divine and human law is committed and condoned. . . . "It is the pope's special mission," writes Enea, "to protect Christ's sheep. He should accomplish this task in such a way as to lead all men to the path of salvation. He must see that the pure Gospel is preached to all, that false doctrines, blasphemies, and unchristian teachings are eradicated, and that enemies of the faith are driven from the lands of Christendom. He must heal schisms and end wars, abolish robbery, murder, arson, adultery, drunkenness and gluttony, spite, hatred and strife. He must promote peace and order, so that concord might reign among men, and honor and praise be given to God."

So Enea. My question is: Does a court of ephebes and muleteers and flatterers help the pope prevent schism and abolish blasphemy, wars, robbery, and the other crimes mentioned by Enea? Would he not be better served by men learned in canon law and Scripture, by men who know how to preach and can help the faithful ease their conscience in the confessional? The Council of Basel was surely inspired when it decreed that a third of all benefices should go to men versed in the Bible. . . . If I am not mistaken, the conciliar fathers wished to see the true Gospel of Christ preached everywhere. They wished honor and glory given to God. We ourselves want nothing else. We would rejoice if many men were to praise God, if every priest in his sufficiently endowed benefice were to serve God and celebrate the Eucharist, if popes and emperors, if the whole Church were to draw rich benefit from this holy work, the most efficacious office of them all. . . .

Let therefore the Holy Apostolic See and our gracious mother, the Church, reduce at least the most severe of the taxes she has placed on our country. Let her show herself mild and considerate to the successors of our present archbishops and bishops when these shall have been called from this world. For the sums of money our prelates must send to Rome are taken from the pockets of poor burghers, rural clerics, and impoverished peasants, and many a husband and father cannot nourish his family for the taxes he must pay. Such a reduction of our tribute might well prevent the outbreak of a violent insurrection of our people against the Church. My own ears, God be my witness, have overheard the grumbling, muttering, and threats of popular discontent. It would not take much for the Bohemian poison to penetrate our German lands. . . . The taxation of twenty thousand or more gulden recently imposed on the people of Mainz is surely excessive, the more since the election of a new archbishop will require payment to be made a second time, even though the first sum has not yet been fully met. We cannot forget that in the old days the pallium fee was never more than ten thousand gulden. But when one incumbent failed to make payment, his successor owed not only his own ten thousand gulden but his predecessor's as well, and this double fee was then entered into the rolls and became the standard pallium fee of twenty thousand gulden.[5]

Let our gracious mother, the Church, also consider that while Rome's need for money increases daily through the proliferation of offices, the income of German electors and princes is reduced by war and lawlessness in their lands. Let her not forget that German fields lie uncultivated, and that formerly rich veins of precious metal (located in mining regions described with clever flattery by Enea) have become exhausted. . . . Let her lighten the heavy burden of reservations placed on our tired land. Let her desist from granting numberless expectancies to a single collator, a practice condemned not only by the Council of Basel but by Enea himself. . . .

Would that our nation were able to accomplish other much needed reforms in the Church. To wit: Candidates for benefices should not with impunity pass themselves off as the pope's familiars. Such people must not receive preferential treatment in the assignment of benefices, for this practice works to the disadvantage of the sons of our own princes. Sixtus IV explicitly forbade the custom of granting expectancies to German benefices to non-Germans. Furthermore, incumbents of wealthy clerical livings should not, when they grow old or infirm, become the victims of

5. An exaggeration. In 1420 Martin V doubled the *servitia communia* of the archdiocese of Mainz from 5000 gulden to 10,000 to make its tax equal to that of Cologne. But to the *servitia communia* must be added *servitia minuta*, pallium tax, and various special fees and gifts. The total may therefore well have been in excess of 20,000 gulden.

vicious law suits intended to drive them from their posts, to be replaced by cunning rogues who have no right or claim to the benefices in question. . . . Well-to-do canons should not be allowed to acquire expectancies to additional benefices through the intervention of influential personages. No one ought to hold two or three prebends at several collegiate churches in the same city, as well as the vicariate of the cathedral church, thus excluding learned and able candidates from nearly all positions, dignities, parish posts, and pensions.

Law suits, often concerning trivial or capricious matters, consume more money than would be required to appoint a new parish priest or to purchase properties with which to support a learned cleric. This should not be so. Some of the richest priests spend their lives and employ what money they can squeeze out of the poor in competition or litigation for new and more profitable posts. . . . If I were to record all the intrigues that people of this sort carry on against one another, I should require as many pages as are contained in the Old and New Testaments.

I need say nothing of indulgences here, except to point out that the many conflicting interpretations of penance and indulgences given in sermons must confuse the faithful, while the prolific distribution of indulgences is likely to incline people to immoral lives. We all know how heavy a burden on our nation these indulgences have become, to say nothing of confessional letters which, by the way, are not available for small change, as Enea contends, but will cost a man a week's household money or more.

The wise Archbishop and Elector of Mainz, Berthold von Henneberg, learning with pleasure of the election to the apostolic throne of Francesco Piccolomini [Pius III, nephew of Enea Silvio], a man most generously inclined toward our nation, set down all the above-mentioned and other complaints of the German nation against Rome, having long and carefully pondered each item. He hoped to gain from the Holy Father a moderation of at least the worst of these abuses. My sympathy with the objectives and aspirations of this noble prince has prompted me to undertake in the place of Martin Mair the composition of this reply to Enea Silvio. Other motives urging me on were my love of empire and nation, my devotion to Holy Scripture, also my compassion for our wretched peasants, plagued by Jews and oppressed by tyrannical princes, . . . and the affection I hold for my Christian neighbors, which impels me to protest against the neglect of pastoral duties by ignorant and careless priests. . . .

I have not attempted to rebut here all of Enea's assertions. Most of them are, in any case, easily refuted. Because of my preoccupation with other tasks I have had to write hastily and keep to generalities. Nothing I have said is intended to hold anyone up to scorn or to cause harm. My only purpose has been to caution the prospective reader of Enea's treatise to arm himself, like Odysseus against the sweet song of the sirens, in order to resist Enea's honeyed flattery of our German people. I have also tried to persuade him to do as much as lies in his power to remedy the steadily deteriorating condition of our country and raise the welfare and dignity of our German nation and the honor of the Holy Roman Empire.

4. A German Clergyman's Criticism of Rome (c. 1451)*

THE FOLLOWING STATEMENT of grievances was compiled on the occasion of Nicholas of Cusa's mission to Germany in 1451–52 and forwarded to the Cardinal, perhaps at the Synod of Mainz in 1451. Its aggressive and outraged tone suggests that its author was a member of the lower clergy, or perhaps a monk. The document may well be a memorandum intended to acquaint the Cardinal-Legate with the mood prevailing among German churchmen as he traveled about the

---

* Printed in Latin in Christian Wilhelm Walch, *Monimenta medii aevi* . . . , I (Göttingen, 1757), 101–110 and in German translation in Bruno Gebhardt, *Die Gravamina der deutschen Nation gegen den römischen Hof* . . . , 2nd ed. (Breslau, 1895), 5–9.

country organizing provincial synods and outlining programs for reform.

MOST VENERABLE FATHER,

I submit the following grave matters for consideration at a holy council:

1. The authority of general councils should not be destroyed or weakened by the decrees of the Cardinal-Legate. The Cardinal-Legate has been introducing, on the authority of his legation and as though they were his own decrees, certain decrees issued by the Council of Basel which have not yet been accepted by the German nation. If our nation were now to accept these decrees on the authority of a cardinal's legation, the legate's power would appear to be superior to that of the council, which is contrary to the truth. Furthermore, it does not seem advisable to begin special and particular reform of one province without reforming other provinces at the same time. Practices vary widely in the Church, and faithful observance of divine laws would vary from province to province if they were to be reformed separately. For the same reason, both a general council and a national council for Germany must be called into session, so that the German nation, if reformed, will not deviate in its ways from the practices of other nations.

2. The Cardinal-Legate has come to us in order to reform our nation. But how shall he succeed in this reform? If the head is sick, the limbs also feel the pain. If reform is to be accomplished, it must begin with the pope and the Roman curia. It is the pope and the cardinals who daily commit the most fearful transgressions and abuses, carrying on a cursed and detestable simoniac trade in ecclesiastical benefices as though they were taking pigs and cows to market. Such wicked transactions bring a hoard of gold and silver to Rome, and the pope, in his haste to fill his money bags, is heedless of what the rest of us know, namely, that the higher a man's place, the graver his sins.

[49

3. Another much-needed papal reform concerns inflated fees for apostolic letters. These used to cost seven or eight gulden. Now they cost twelve to fourteen. It is the same with awards of expectancy.

4. Day after day the pope and his advisers use their cunning to squeeze money out of the German people. I could cite many examples to prove this. In the first year of his papacy, the pope [Nicholas V] showed himself gracious and benevolent and awarded expectancies to all who applied to him. Rich men and poor therefore hoped to receive benefices, to which they felt entitled by the expectancies they were holding. Having in this manner drawn a good sum from Germany, the pope began in the second year of his reign to offer more favorable expectancies, issued *motu proprio*,[1] to all and sundry. Once again, both the rich and the poor sent their money, thinking they would profit thereby. But in his third year, seeing that no more money could be made from expectancies issued *moto proprio*, the pope proceeded to interpret *motus proprius* as a device to abolish the fraudulent acquisition of benefices. And so the poor wretches who had hoped to acquire something desirable by means of the pope's *motus proprius* were cheated of their money. The pope also began to grant reservations to benefices not yet vacant, a previously unheard-of practice. Such a reservation was worded as follows: "We desire that you have as your prebend or dignity the first that shall become vacant in such-and-such a place. To this end we suspend any and all expectancies, however and to whomever we may have issued them in the past, until you shall have received the first prebend or dignity." I ask: Is it just or holy to hold people in such contempt?

5. The curia, too, needs reform in many respects. Cardinals move about in pomp and splendor, accompanied by a retinue of 160 or 170 horses. Their familiars wear silken garments embroidered in gold and silver. Even in the days of Boniface IX, Innocent III and John XXIII [1410–15, deposed by Council of Constance]

---

1. *Motu proprio:* a papal disposition or ordinance issued "from his own motive" and without the formalities of a bull.

they did not live in such ostentation. It is not unknown for a cardinal to hold three metropolitan and cathedral churches *in commendam*² and to have ten abbeys, six priories and archdeaconates, and four parish churches as well. As for the number of monks remaining in their monasteries, the cardinals could not care less. A monastery where, in the old days, six or ten monks celebrated divine service has only one or two now, because the place has been stripped bare of income sufficient to support sixty monks. And this is done so that cardinals may live in greater style than the pope himself.

6. Bankers and usurers have free access to the curia and the pope. Pope and cardinals invest their money with them. God alone knows whether this leads to good or to evil.

7. The worst crooks, however, pimps and prostitutes not excepted, are to be found among the familiars of cardinals. Such riffraff used never to disgrace Germany, but the pope tolerates them now. The pope and the Italians are not satisfied with the enormous sums brought to Rome during the Jubilee Year; they now send us a cardinal empowered to take what remains of our fortune through the sale of Jubilee Indulgences. How, under such circumstances, can the faithful believe in the good intentions of the pope and Rome? Have they not been cheated innumerable times before, paying out good money for the conversion of the Bohemians and the restoration of the Greeks, neither of which events ever took place? Furthermore, why should Germans be victimized when Italians make huge profits by pocketing the proceeds from the Jubilee Year and by not contributing anything themselves? Is this how the legate plans to reform German clerics and German millers, butchers, and cooks? To be sure, if pope and curia were to reform themselves, or if a general council were to bring about a universal reformation of the Church, there would be no difficulty in reforming every Christian in his own estate. It is therefore most sensible, as well as most necessary, for the pope to

---

2. *In commendam*: enjoyment of the income of a benefice by someone who cannot or does not take charge of the duties connected with it.

decide that he must forthwith convoke a general council of the entire Church, as he is sworn to do.

5. *The Statement of Grievances Presented to the Diet of Worms in 1521**

READERS OF THE PRECEDING SELECTIONS will by now be familiar with most of the points made in the following list of complaints. But the statement of grievances translated below is, as it were, official. At the Imperial Diet held in the city of Worms in 1521—the first meeting of Charles V with the German Estates and the occasion of Luther's appearance before the emperor—the Estates pointedly reminded Charles of the popular support enjoyed by Luther and urged the emperor to recognize the need of going beyond anti-Lutheran mandates to an attack on the "oppressive burdens and abuses imposed on and committed against the Empire by the Holy See in Rome." Charles, in his reply, invited the Estates to submit an itemized catalogue of these burdens and abuses. A committee of spiritual and secular electors and princes proceeded to draw up a list of grievances for presentation to the emperor, probably using material submitted by individual members of the Estates. No formal action was taken at Worms, but at the Diet of Nuremberg in 1523 the Estates insisted on revising the grievances once more for transmittal to Rome.**

My translation is of the first version, the Estates' report submitted to Charles V at Worms. I have made a selection from among the 102 gravamina, eliminating duplication and emphasizing the most important points. I have retained the numbering used in the edition of the gravamina in the Acts of the Imperial Diet.

HIS ROMAN IMPERIAL MAJESTY desiring the electors, princes, and General Estates of the Empire to acquaint him with the burdens

---

* Printed in *Deutsche Reichstagsakten, Jüngere Reihe*, II (Gotha, 1896), 670–704.

** This formal version of the grievances is printed in *ibid.*, III (Gotha, 1901), 645–88.

placed on the German nation by His Holiness the Pope and other ecclesiastics, and to make known to him our counsel and opinions as to how these burdens might be lifted from us, we have in all haste set down the following points, beginning with matters touching His Holiness the Pope.

1. *Secular Cases Are Transferred to Rome for Trial in the First Instance.* Our Most Holy Father the Pope, heeding the clamor of his priests, causes numerous persons to be summoned for trial in Rome in matters of inheritance, mortgage and similar worldly concerns, a practice conducive to the curtailment of the competence of secular authorities. We ask that Your Imperial Majesty undertake to ensure that no person, spiritual or worldly, be summoned to Rome for first trial in any matter, spiritual or worldly, but that he be allowed instead to appear in the first instance before the bishop or archdeacon of his province or, if he is a layman and the matter at issue is secular, before the prince, government, or ordinary judge with appropriate competence.

2. *Concerning Conservators and Papal Judges.* Ecclesiastical princes and prelates have obtained papal appointment of certain abbots or prelates of their own dioceses as judges with jurisdiction over all their legal affairs. Such judges are called "conservators," and they summon laymen, nobles as well as commoners, to appear before them in order to answer charges in secular matters, notwithstanding the competence of secular courts where the cases in question should be heard. If a man refuses to go before such a conservator, he is excommunicated; many examples of this practice might be given. Thus it happens that secular authorities and secular cases are tried before ecclesiastical courts, which are, needless to say, biased in opinions and judgment. And thus the constitution[1] of the empire is violated, for our laws state categorically that no person is to be deprived of the right to trial before his ordinary judge and court.

3. *Concerning Papal Delegates and Commissioners.* His Holiness the Pope bestows upon ecclesiastical persons who so petition

1. I have generally translated German *Ordnung* as constitution.

him special powers to act as judges delegate or commissioners. Armed with such powers, these clerics undertake to summon before them lay persons of every estate and, in the case of failure to comply, compel them through threats of excommunication. . . .

5. *Concerning Ecclesiastics Who Die in Rome or on the Way to Rome.* His Holiness has decreed that whenever a cleric dies in Rome, or while enroute to Rome, whether or not he was a familiar of the pope, his offices and benefices, large or small, shall fall to the pope. As a consequence of this practice spiritual and worldly patrons and liege lords have been deprived and robbed of their rights.

7. *Rome Often Grants Benefices to Unworthy Persons.* Rome awards German benefices to unqualified, unlearned, and unfit persons such as gunners, falconers, bakers, donkey drivers, stable grooms, and so on, most of whom know not a word of German and never assume the duties connected with their benefices, shifting them instead to worthless vicars who are content with a pittance in pay. Thus the German laity receives neither spiritual care nor worldly counsel from the Church, while a hoard of money flows yearly to Italy with no return to us, least of all gratitude. We think that German benefices should be awarded to native Germans only and that beneficed persons ought to be required to reside in the place to which they are assigned.

8. *There Should Be No Tampering with Ancient Freedoms.* A person who holds a papal privilege entitling him to invest others with benefices or offices should not be deprived of this right, nor should he be subjected to legal pressure to give it up. Papal letters or mandates setting aside these ancient privileges ought to be declared null and void.

9. *Concerning Annates.* In former times emperors granted annates to Rome for a limited term of years only and for no purpose other than to enable the Church to hold back the Turk and support Christendom. In the course of time, however, the payment of annates grew into a regular custom, and, as is generally known, the German nation has been excessively burdened with them. . . .

10. *Annates Are Constantly Increased in Amount.* Not only are annates almost daily raised in amount, but they are also being extended from archbishoprics and bishoprics to abbeys, priories, parishes, and other ecclesiastical prebends. . . . Although the old regulations placed a pallium fee of not more than ten thousand gulden upon the bishoprics of Mainz, Cologne, Salzburg, and others, the pallium cannot now be fetched home for less than twenty thousand to twenty-four thousand gulden.

11. *Concerning New Devices Employed by Rome.* The main reason for the constant rise in the cost of episcopal confirmations and pallium fees is the proliferation of offices in Rome, such as chamberlains, shield-bearers, and others, for whose emoluments our bishops' subjects must pay taxes and tributes. Furthermore, Rome obtains money by means of a number of cunning and novel devices, especially the following: a certain newly elected bishop has been given papal leave to pay his pallium fees not in cash but instead in the form of a pledge from certain sponsors to make payment at a given time. Suddenly, and for no reason, these sponsors are excommunicated and, almost at once, absolved again, for which absolution the bishop-elect must pay from three to five hundred ducats. It has been made known to us that His Holiness has this year created several new offices and is now personally served by more than 150 retainers who make their living off the proceeds of ecclesiastical benefices, for which the German nation furnishes the money.

12. *Concerning Commendation and Incorporation.* It should be understood that a great many abbeys, monasteries, and other ecclesiastical houses have fallen under the control of cardinals, bishops, and other prelates or, as they say, have been "commended" to them or been "incorporated" by them. As a result of this practice, imperial and princely endowments fall into ruin and the divine service is curtailed, since monasteries formerly housing forty or fifty monks are now reduced to a much smaller number. The cardinals act on the principle: the fewer the monks, the higher the profits.

13. *Concerning Regulations of the Papal Chancellery.* These regulations are trimmed to the advantage of Roman courtiers. They are frequently altered or reinterpreted so as to bring ecclesiastical benefices, especially German benefices, into Roman hands and to compel us to buy or lease these benefices from Rome, a practice which is against both statutory law and the dictates of justice.

14. *Concerning Reservations, Regressions, Incorporations, Unions, and Concordats.* When it comes to such procedures, His Holiness is insatiable. Day after day he invents new devices to enable him to squeeze money out of the German nation and further to destroy the divine service. . . .

18. *Concerning the Pope's Prevention of Episcopal Elections.* The pope takes it upon himself to prevent, restrict, or set aside the free election of bishops, priors, deans, etc., in our cathedral churches. Instead he distributes these offices as he pleases, eliminating a canonically elected bishop and replacing him with another *per confirmationem consistorialem*.[2] . . .

19. *Concerning Papal Dispensation and Absolution.* Popes and bishops reserve to themselves certain sins and offenses from which, they say, only they can absolve us. Whenever such a "case" occurs and a man wishes absolution, he discovers that only money can procure it for him. Nor does Rome give out a dispensation except on payment of gold. A poor man without money will not see his matter despatched. A rich man can, moreover, for a sum, obtain papal letters of indult, which entitle him to priestly absolution for any sin he might commit in the future, murder, for example, or perjury. All this shows how Roman greed and covetousness cause sins and vices to multiply in the world.

20. *Concerning the Depredations of Papal Courtiers.* The German nation also suffers exceedingly from the greed of papal and curial hangers-on who are bent on occupying ecclesiastical benefices in our land. These courtiers compel honorable old clerics,

2. *Per confirmationem consistorialem:* confirmation by the consistory, i.e., the College of Cardinals.

long established and blameless in their offices, to go to Rome, where they are subjected to humiliating chicaneries. There they must wait until Rome gets what it wants through reservations and pensions obtained by means of so-called Chancellery Rules, setting aside old agreements and replacing them with new ones. In this way, honorable old clerics who are not schooled in courtiers' tricks are defrauded of their benefices *lite pendente*,[3] no matter what the outcome of their case will be.

21. *Under the Pretext of Papal Familiarity, Many Benefices Are Acquired.* Excellent remunerative benefices come into the hands of motley persons who claim to be officials or familiars of the pope. They gain the right to hold prebends or offices *in commendam* or "provisionally," or through "regression," "reservation," "pension," or "incompatibility," which causes benefices in our country to decrease and decline as more and more of them fall into Roman hands.

22. *Concerning Indulgences.* We also regard it in the highest degree objectionable that His Holiness should permit so many indulgences to be sold in Germany, a practice through which simpleminded folk are misled and cheated of their savings. When His Holiness sends nuncios or emissaries to a country, he empowers them to offer indulgences for sale and retain a portion of the income for their traveling expenses and salaries. . . . Bishops and local secular authorities also get their share for helping with the arrangements for the sale. All this money is obtained from poor and simple people who cannot see through the curia's cunning deceptions.

23. *Concerning Mendicants, Relic Hawkers, and Miracle Healers.*[4] These riffraff go back and forth through our land, begging, collecting, offering indulgences, and extracting large sums of

3. *Lite pendente:* pending judgment. A case in litigation but not yet decided.

4. The German word used to describe these is *Stationierer*, from Latin *stationarius*, a trader or salesman, but referring particularly and derogatorily to itinerant monks exhibiting relics for cures and indulgences.

[57

money from our people. We think these hawkers ought to be kept out of our country....

31. *How Some Clerics Escape Punishment for Their Misdeeds.* If an ordained cleric going about in the world on secular business and in secular clothes is brought before a secular court on some charge and is detained by it, he need only say "I am ordained" and demand to be transferred to an ecclesiastical court, and he will go free. His bishop will support him, notwithstanding the fact that the man was apprehended without tonsure and wearing worldly dress. And if the secular court does not release him within twenty-four hours, its judges are excommunicated. Are not such practices bound to encourage clerics to wicked acts, the more since ecclesiastical courts let them go scot-free, no matter what their offense? . . .

32. *How Secular Property Comes into Ecclesiastical Hands.* Seeing that the spiritual estate is under papal instructions never to sell or otherwise transfer the Church's real estate and immobilia to the laity, we think it advisable for His Roman Imperial Majesty to cause a corresponding law to be made for the secular estate, to wit, that no secular person be allowed to make over any part of his real property to any ecclesiastical person or institution, and that this proscription apply to inheritance as well. If such a law is not introduced without delay, it is possible that the secular estate will, in the course of time, be altogether bought out by the Church . . . and the secular estate of the Holy Roman Empire eventually be entirely beholden to the Church.

37. *Ecclesiastical Courts Give Support to Jewish Usury.* Everyone knows that the Jews' usury in Germany pauperizes and corrupts Christian society. But whenever a secular authority sets out to curb the Jews, the latter call upon an ecclesiastical court for help and cause the Christians to be excommunicated. For although the debtors swear that the money owed the Jews was not procured on terms of usury, the court knows that Jews do not lend except usuriously and that the poor, in their great need, perjure themselves. Canon and civil law forbids the rendering of judicial or

other aid in matters of usury, but bishops and prelates permit it nonetheless.

39. *Sinners Are Given Fines to Pay Rather Than Spiritual Penance to Do.* Although spiritual penance ought to be imposed upon sinners for one reason only, to gain salvation for their souls, ecclesiastical judges tend nowadays to make penalties so formidable that the sinner is obliged to buy his way out of them, through which practice untold amounts of money flow into the Church's treasury. . . .

43. *Excommunication Is Used Indiscriminately, Even in Trivial Matters.* Notwithstanding the original and true purpose of spiritual censure and excommunication, namely, to aid and direct Christian life and faith, this weapon is now flung at us for the most inconsequential debts—some of them amounting to no more than a few pennies—or for non-payment of court or administrative costs after the principal sum has already been returned. With such procedures the very life blood is sucked out of the poor, untutored laity, who are driven to distraction by the fear of the Church's ban. . . .

47. *Concerning Improper Interdicts and Suspensions of Divine Service.* If a priest is injured by a layman, or done to death by him, an interdict is generally laid upon the town or village where the deed occurred, even if it was done in self-defense or in other legally extenuating circumstances. This interdict remains in force until the guilty party, or else the council or commune of the town, declares himself responsible. Moreover, interdicts are imposed for debt and other monetary matters, although the Church's own laws prohibit this; but the Church evades this prohibition by claiming "insubordination" as the real cause of the interdict. . . .

50. *They Demand Their Share of Pilgrims' Offerings.* In some bishoprics the clergy demand a third or fourth part of all offerings collected from pilgrims who come to visit a shrine or holy place. There is no basis in canon law for such a demand.

54. *There Are Too Many Vagrant Mendicants in Our Land.* The poor in Germany are sorely oppressed by the extraordinary

number of mendicant monks, especially by begging friars maintained by mendicant orders in violation of their own rules. Some villages and towns have two, three, or four of these begging brothers going about with hands outstretched, and the alms that should go to old and indigent householders who can no longer support themselves fill the monks' pouches instead. Bishops condone this practice in return for a portion of the collection.

56. *Too Many Priests Are Ordained, Many of Them Unlearned and Unfit.* Archbishops and bishops have been ordaining base and uneducated persons whose only claim to the priesthood is that they are needy. Such people, either because of their low estate or because of some native inclination to wickedness, lead reckless and dishonorable lives, bringing the whole spiritual estate into disrepute and setting the common folk a bad example. Before making ordination, the bishop is obliged to consult six witnesses on the candidate's fitness for the priestly office; but as things are now, the witnesses have, likely as not, never seen or heard of the candidate. Thus our Christian laws are nothing but pretense and sham to them.

58. *Bishops Ought to Hold Frequent Synods.* All the above shortcomings would doubtless be alleviated if bishops fulfilled their obligation to meet in synods with their prelates and ecclesiastical subjects in order to seek the aid and counsel of all the clergy present, as the law of the Church obliges them to do.

62. *The Common Folk Are Forced to Give Money for Processions and Prayers for the Soul.* Priests have become accustomed to burdening their flock with special payments for processions and displays of the holy sacrament. The amount of these payments is left to the priests. They even molest the poor, who cannot afford to have special prayers offered on the anniversaries of their friends' and relatives' deaths, shaming them into paying a few pennies to have a mass sung, or at least to have one read, though they know that their benefices oblige them to say anniversary masses whenever required. Thus, with a single mass, a priest may take in two or three salaries at once.

63. *Priests Demand Payment from Parishioners Who Leave*

the Parish. If a man or woman marries outside the parish, his or her priest demands a gulden as a leaving fee. The parishioner has no choice but to pay it, for if he refuses, the sacraments are withheld from him.

64. *In Some Circumstances Gravesites Must Be Bought for the Dead.* Persons who have been found dead under questionable circumstances, such as drowning, murder, and so on, but who did not necessarily die in mortal sin, are refused proper burial by the Church unless their friends or next of kin accommodate the priest.

66. *Certain Clerics Behave Like Laymen and Are Even Seen Brawling in Taverns.* The majority of parish priests and other secular clerics mingle with the common people at inns and taverns. They frequent public dances and walk about the streets in lay garments, brandishing long knives. They engage in quarrels and arguments, which usually lead to blows, whereupon they fall upon poor folk, wound or even kill them, and then excommunicate them unless the innocently injured parties agree to offer money for a settlement with the offending priest.

67. *Clerics Set Bad Examples by Cohabiting with Their Serving Women.* Most parish priests and other clerics have established domestic relations with women of loose morals. They dwell openly with the women and with their children. It is a dishonest, detestable life for priests and a wretched example to set for their parishioners.

69. *Many Clerics Have Turned to Tavern Keeping and Gambling.* Clerics can frequently be seen setting themselves up as inn keepers. On holidays, in places where they have proprietary rights, priests put up tables for dice, bowls, or cards and invite people to play. Then they take the winnings, shamelessly claiming that these belong to them by rights of sovereignty. . . .

70. *Concerning Regular Clergy, Monks and Mendicants.* It is well known that rich monastic orders, such as Benedictines, Cistercians, Premonstratensians, and others, have succeeded in wresting secular properties from lay hands, growing daily more wealthy and powerful. In return for the lay properties thus acquired they offer no other services to His Imperial Majesty or other secular

authorities, pay no higher taxes and shoulder no greater burdens than those they had assumed in days gone by when very much poorer. . . . Our welfare as a country requires that the orders be prevented in future from taking any more real property out of lay hands, whether by purchase or by any other means of acquisition. . . .

71. *They Prevail upon the Old and the Sick to Withhold Their Estate from Their Rightful Heirs.* Priests and monks hover about a man in his final illness if they know him to be rich in gold or land. They attempt to persuade him with cunning words to leave his property to them, though more often than not the estate should go to the man's heirs, offspring, or close friends.

77. *Even Clerical Servants Can Cite Poor People before an Ecclesiastical Court.* It ought to be known that not only do the priests themselves drag laymen into ecclesiastical courts, but their administrative officials, bailiffs, retainers, and even their women servants can do it.

85. *They Try to Gain Exclusive Jurisdiction over Legal Matters, Which Should Be Heard in Secular Courts.* Much legal business that, according to law, may be settled in either ecclesiastical or secular courts, has in fact been usurped by the clergy. For when a secular judge claims a case, it often happens that a spiritual judge steps forward and threatens the other with excommunication unless he lets go of the case. Thus the clergy take over what they wish. According to our laws, offenses like perjury, adultery, and black magic may be handled by either spiritual or lay courts, depending on who first claimed the case. But the clergy make bold to grasp all such cases, thus undercutting secular authority.

88. *How They Take Over Secular Jurisdiction by Falsely Pleading Prescription.* Some experts hesitate to call attention to the Church's practice of acquiring rights by possession, that is, by pleading prescriptive rights to gain legal jurisdiction over lay matters, though His Imperial Majesty's and the empire's highest dignities and jurisdictions are thereby being steadily eroded. But we know it to be according to right and law that no one may prescribe, or claim to have acquired by possession, against the high

sovereignty of pope and emperor, no matter how many years he has held on to something or used it without interference.

91. *Money Can Buy Tolerance of Concubinage and Usury.* If a man and a woman cohabit without being married, they may pay an annual fee to the clergy and be left to live in shame and sin. The same is done with usurers. . . . A married person whose spouse has disappeared but might still be living is, without any further search for the missing partner, allowed to take up cohabitation with another. This they call *"toleramus,"* and it serves to bring contempt upon the holy sacrament of marriage.

95. *Innocent People Who Happen to Live Near an Excommunicated Person Are Themselves Excommunicated.* In some towns and villages ten or twelve neighbors of an excommunicate are placed under the ban along with him, although they have nothing to do with his offense. And this is done for no reason other than the clergy's eagerness to establish its authority and to have it obeyed. Because of this practice, poor and innocent people are forced to buy their way out of the ban, or else to remove their families and belongings from their homes. No distinction is made in these indiscriminate excommunications. No one asks: Is the man poor or not? Did he associate voluntarily with the excommunicated sinner? And even though their own canon law forbids declarations of interdict for debts or other money matters, they impose the ban on whole towns and villages, alleging disobedience as the cause in order to mask their illegal and unjust action.

97. *They Demand a Weekly Tribute from Artisans.* In many places the clergy demand a weekly tax or tribute from millers, inn keepers, bakers, shoe makers, smiths, tailors, shepherds, cowherds, and other craftsmen. If this tribute is refused, they enforce their demand with the threat of excommunication.

101. *They Withhold the Sacraments for Trivial Offenses.* If a man owes a small debt to the priest or to the parish, and if he is too poor to repay it on time and asks for a short extension of the loan, the priest often withholds the sacraments from him and nags and intimidates him, although the matter ought by rights to be brought before a secular judge.

[I I I]

Wounded Pride in Nation

and Ancestry

6. Heinrich Bebel's Oration in Praise of Germany, Given before Maximilian I (1501)*

AMONG THE MOST NAGGING of grievances voiced in pre-Reformation Germany was the complaint that the German people as a nation were not being accorded the respect and admiration they deserved to hold in the international community. Although largely confined to the circle of humanist intellectuals (whose pointed comparisons of Greek and Roman antiquity with ancient German history and civilization bore the authority of their expert classical scholarship), these grudges, accusations, protests and demands for redress were voiced with increasing stridency in the latter decades of the fifteenth and the early years of the sixteenth centuries. Bitterness was most vehement and aggressive in the border areas, particularly in the west, where the struggle with France inflamed tempers and aroused patriotic sentiments. But there was hardly a humanist writer who did not at one time or another charge that Germany's past history and pres-

* *Oratio Henrici Bebeli . . . ad . . . Regem Maximilianum, de eius atque Germaniae laudibus,* printed in Simon Schard, ed., *Rerum germanicarum scriptores varii,* I (Giessen, 1673), 95–104.

ent achievements were being shamefully concealed and flagrantly falsified by malevolent and covetous foreigners.

Heinrich Bebel's oration before the Emperor Maximilian, the major portions of which are translated below, gives summary expression to these widely held convictions. All the self-pity, the suspicions, the boastful exaggerations of the patriotic grievance literature are there, as well as its search for a heroic past—including a vindication of medieval history—its claims to racial purity, and its quest for a national identity based on the possession of Christian virtues in which Germans are said always to have been superior to all other peoples. The age of Maximilian I is seen as the fulfillment of long-cherished hopes of the restoration of the German nation to a position of influence and honor in the world.

Bebel was a prolific scholar, educator, and poet, who studied at Cracow and Basel, taught at Tübingen, and published works on philology, history, and education, as well as polemical writings and verses. His oration was given before the emperor at Innsbruck upon the occasion of Bebel's coronation as poet laureate in 1501. My translation omits the wealth of quotations with which Bebel larded his speech.

I KNOW, exalted emperor, that those who appear before you as orators tend to admonish you in long speeches and with great prolixity, circumlocutions, and learned citations to be mindful of your responsibility for the restoration of peace to empire and Church, and for the conduct of campaigns against the barbaric nation of the Turks. . . . I, for my part, believe that you, our emperor, know only too well all that is beneficial and all that is harmful to the German nation. Indeed I am certain that you have before your eyes a clear picture of what needs to be done. When I see how our German princes neglect the public weal in favor of their private interests, and how they waste their days in feuding and pleasure-seeking—a mode of conduct responsible for the disintegration of many cities and realms in the past—I should be fearful indeed of our future as a nation were it not for you, exalted emperor, who, having already saved the empire from certain disintegration, give promise of using your native wisdom and skill to rescue our state, built through our forefathers' courage and retained with their blood, from the brink of annihilation to which sloth and lassitude have brought it. . . .

Not many nights ago I beheld in my dream a woman, imposing in stature, with greying hair, clad in torn and threadbare garments, so wasted by poverty and privation that all those who saw her were seized by feelings of terror and pity. But from her fine head shone a golden radiance so bright as fairly to blind my poor eyes. She bore a laurel wreath in her hair. Had she not taken me by the hand and uttered consoling words, I should have fallen senseless to the ground, so overwhelmed was I by the sight of her. When, at last, she addressed me as her son, I recognized her as Mother Germany. Offering salutations, I inquired after the cause of her pitiful appearance and feeble state. For a long time she could not answer for the pains that racked her body. Then she spoke, tears moistening her cheeks: "Quickly, Bebel, go before my king and dear child, Maximilian, a monarch who never refuses audience to the humblest of men. Relate my condition to him. Tell him of my misery, of my tears, and of the melancholy that consumes me. Say to him that he is his grieving mother's only refuge and consolation, having been my hope since the time I carried him in my womb. Of all my sons he is the most flourishing; all the other members of my body languish in sickness and decrepitude. Tell him to be hopeful, not to surrender himself to despair. His strength and vigor will restore the health of those of my children who now lie ill. But let him have no pity on men whose condition has deteriorated to the point of putrefaction. They must be cut from my flesh if my body is to be saved. Tell him of my displeasure at the sight of princes and nobles joining in pacts and agreements the better to escape their obligations to the empire. Make him reflect on the decline of mighty states like Persia, Macedonia, Greece, and Rome, the cause of whose destruction is to be found in license given to personal greed and ambition, in the search for private gain and advantage, and in internal dissensions resulting from these—afflictions, all of them, from which our own nation now suffers. . . ."

But let me come to my theme, noble emperor. All I have to say touches on the glory of our country and on the paucity of writers who might give fitting praise to it. Let me add my voice to the laments over the destiny of our valorous forefathers, among whom we find innumerable doers of heroic deeds but not a single man who took it upon himself to record them for posterity. This fact I bemoan here in your presence, noble emperor; over this I shed my tears. For had we possessed able authors to commemorate acts of German bravery, were the achievements and virtues of our emperors Charles, Louis, Lothar, Friedrich, Otto, Henry, Konrad, Rudolf, and Albrecht fresh in the memory of our own people and the world, we would not today be disgraced by lying Greek historians who set up Theseus, Themistocles, Pericles, Militiades, Epaminondas, Pausanias, and Alcibiades as models of all virtues; nor by the mendacious Romans who eulogize their Fabians and Caesars and Scipios—men to whom our own citizens were not only equal in magnitude of achievements but whom they excelled, not least because we Germans were spurred by ideals of justice and virtue, while Roman conquerors were driven by nothing more than the lust for power and dominion. Our ancient German rulers faced hardship, perils, and death in order to serve God and extend the Christian faith and the sway of our religion. . . .

The books of rhetoricians, poets, historians, and philosophers are replete with the deeds of Romans and Greeks, whom they hold up as very paradigms for posterity. But who speaks of Frederick, of Charles, of Otto? No one does, and yet no finer examples could be given, and none worthier of emulation. For this neglect there is no reason except the oblivion into which the deeds of our ancestors have fallen. Whoever wishes to praise Germany as she should be praised will find that our history has no shortage of praiseworthy and virtuous deeds. Indeed he will realize that the German past can hold its own not only with attainments considered excellent in our own day but also with the greatest of the feats of antiquity. Whatever qualities the nations of the world count as their proudest, our people will be seen to possess them, so that we may say with justice: Germany contains within herself all the excellent and praiseworthy things claimed by other peoples. . . .

To come to the point: What other nation on this earth has such well-born princes and so high-minded a nobility as ours? What people can boast braver knights and more self-sacrificing warriors? No other land is as populous and as well endowed with courage and vigor. Even the most distant peoples on the earth know this about us. . . . What other nation has extended its borders as far as we have pushed ours? Long ago, as we learn from the ancients, the limits of Germany were the Vistula and the Hungarian frontier in the east, the Rhine in the west, the Danube in the south, and the ocean in the north. Now, however, we have gone far beyond these ancient confines, not in predatory expeditions but to occupy and to hold, so that the peoples we have conquered can no longer recall the time when they belonged to another master. In the east we have vanquished the Hungarians and occupied Transylvania. . . . In the south we own the former lands of the Rhetians, Vindelicians, Bavarians, the Alpine peoples, Austria and Styria. We have advanced deep into Italy; we hold Croatia, Carniola, and Carinthia. Even Lombardy, Liguria, Tuscany, Sicily, and the Greek regions of southern Italy have fallen into our hands.

The sainted Jerome referred to the Germans when, writing to Heliodorus, he described his feelings of terror as he observed the traces of destruction and ruination in his age. "For twenty years or more now," he laments, "Roman blood has been spilled in the region between Constantinople and the Julian Alps. The northern tribes sweep through Scythia, Thrace, Macedonia, Thessaly, Dardania, Achaia, Epirus, Dalmatia, and Pannonia. Wherever we observe Goths, Sarmatians, Quadi, Alani, Vandals, and Marcomanni, we see them victorious." The Lombards, too, were Germans. Everyone knows what they accomplished in Italy and Gaul. Hungary is said to have belonged to them as a result of their expulsion of the mighty Huns from that country.

And in the west how far have we Germans advanced the glory of our name! Switzerland is ours, for we have driven out the Gauls. Ours, also, the lands of [all the Gallic tribes] conquered by us. England is ours, the country that got its name from the Angles mentioned by Tacitus. . . . Picts and Scots were Germans as well, and if we were to say nothing of the Franks and the Burgundians —Germanic peoples, both of them—we would be expunging the entire history of France. . . . And what shall I say of Spain, a country that felt all too painfully the effects of German strength and courage? . . .

Looking toward the north, finally, we see that Prussia is ours, the land whose ancient inhabitants . . . we saved from the grip of heathenism and made into civilized, Christian men. Thanks to us, Danes, Swedes, and Norwegians are Christians today, as are the peoples residing on the most distant borderlands of Germany. All this is borne out by the most learned cosmographers and historians. . . . In sum: Few peoples in the world have not, at one time or another, felt the sharpness of German swords or have at least trembled at the terror of our name. It is true we have upon occasion been defeated by the armies of Rome, mistress of the entire earth. But we never gave the Romans an easy victory, nor did we allow them to return to their homeland without bloody losses. And often we vanquished them and subjected them to humiliating defeats. . . .

Therefore, most august emperor, my claim that our people does not lack for a past of glorious deeds. We miss only the historians who should have recorded these deeds. [There follows a lengthy attempt to piece together what scraps of German history may be culled from the ancient authors.] If the older Pliny's twenty books on the Germanic-Roman wars were still extant, we would, I am sure, find in them ample material for the elaboration of our fame.

But, alas, they have disappeared in the destruction wrought by time. . . .

I do not wish to speak as an historian, noble emperor, and fill your ear with a long catalogue of events. Let me therefore pass from the German wars—the proper telling of which requires a stout volume rather than a brief address—to other matters. I see that many states and peoples boast of their ancient origins, but in antiquity of descent, as well as in valor, we Germans can hold our own with any nation under the sun. We may say of ourselves what the Athenians claimed for their own: our renown rests not only on what we have made of ourselves but also upon our roots and our first beginnings. We were not immigrants into our land; we are not an amalgamation of nomad groups. We are an autochthonous people, born from the soil of the land on which we now make our home. Where we live today are our ancient origins. Cornelius Tacitus, the great Roman historian, is witness to this fact. . . . Our best claim to honor and glory, however, is founded upon our superior virtue, a trait in which we excel all the other nations of mankind. What people, pray, shows greater devotion to justice? What people is more steadfast and sincere in its faith? Observe the magnificent churches, monasteries, convents and altars standing in our land; where may clearer evidence be found of a people's love and respect for divine worship and the Christian religion? Where are signs of greater devotion than the wars we have fought for the protection and propagation of our faith? Have the rulers of other countries done as much for the Roman Church and the Catholic faith, indeed for the salvation of Christendom itself? . . .

But before continuing, let me say a word on behalf of those of our emperors who have been the victims of censure and excommunication by the popes. Not for any fault of their own were they placed under papal ban but because they had been bold enough to challenge the popes' excessive greed and ambition. Had our emperors not contended with them for dominion over Italy, they would never have incurred papal anger and excommunication.

Flavio Biondo gives us proof of this in his history, though he is a writer normally partial to Rome. [There follow references to the deeds of Charlemagne, Henry I, Frederick I and the other Hohenstaufens in the service of the Church and religion.] If I were to tell it all, I should be writing a book instead of pronouncing a speech. But who can doubt our people's merits, considering that it was in recognition of our service to the Christian Church that the Roman imperium was transferred to us? Assyrians, Medes, Persians, Greeks, and Romans usurped the imperium through violence and lust for power. As they gained their rule shamefully, so they lost it again, falling back into the servitude from which they had risen. Our race, on the contrary, was judged worthy of the imperium because of its innate virtue and because of the perseverance with which we took the labors of God upon ourselves. May we, under your aegis, noble emperor, long continue to be worthy of exercising the Roman rule. As virtue and faith are superior to vice and oppression, we who possess virtue and faith are greater than all other nations.

Notwithstanding this, history records not our deeds but those of other peoples. Our past is shrouded in darkness and lies hidden in obscure corners. When an occasional foreign writer does mention us, he is moved by antipathy, fear, or the need for flattery to alter historical fact or to leave out much that should be said. Do I need to cite examples of my charge? [He mentions Robert Gaguin's *De origine et gestis Francorum* of 1495.] But now, at last, God has begun to look with favor upon our condition. He has given you to us, noble and august Maximilian. Under your auspices and leadership our people's magnificent exploits will shine forth in renewed brilliance, having lain neglected all these years, hidden in rust and squalor. Learning flourishes again, men's minds have become active once more, and poets respond to your munificent encouragement, for you love men of letters and are gracious in supporting them. And not in vain, for authors and scholars return their thanks by celebrating you and your glorious accomplishments. Among the ancients those men were counted happy whom the gods had chosen either to perform great actions or to record them. Those, however, they judged happiest of all to whom it was given to do both. You, noble emperor, may therefore be called happiest, for not content with performing great deeds in the daily pursuit of affairs of state, you read history and express the desire to hear tales of memorable feats done in the past. They even say that you yourself are engaged in the writing of history and that you are planning a description of Germany to rival that of the great Julius Caesar, who won the admiration of all Rome because, while fully occupied as governor and general, he was also a devotee of arts and letters. . . .

7. *"Germans Are Not Barbarians": Three Chapters from Irenicus'* Exegesis Germaniae (1518)*

THE MOST GRANDIOSE attempt to provide Germany with a heroic ancestry was undertaken by a young scholar and theologian, Franz Friedlieb (1495–c. 1559), called Irenicus, who published in 1518 a long and exhaustive work entitled *Exegesis Germaniae*. Adopting the gushing style of the patriotic sentiments for which he considered himself advocate, Irenicus treated his readers to a passionate eulogy of every aspect of Germanic tribal culture and history. An enormously learned production, an anthology of everything said about the ancient Germans by every writer its author could get his hands on, a fierce polemic, and obviously a labor of love, the *Exegesis* provided a generation of Germans with facts to refute doubters and detractors. The book is too prolix and shapeless to lend itself to effective excerpting (there are in all 488 chapters plus an alphabetical encyclopedia of subjects relating to Germany), but the following three chapters— somewhat shortened in translation—will indicate Irenicus' objective and the spirit in which he pursued it.

* Franciscus Irenicus, *Germaniae exegeseos volumina duodecim* (Hagenau, 1518), Book II, chapters 33, 34; Book IV, chapter 3.

Whether the Germans are Barbarians, and What Barbarians Are

According to the Greek use of the word "barbarian," only those who cannot speak Greek fluently and well should be called by that name. Homer believed that the inhabitants of Caria were barbarians, Greeks though they were. After the Trojan war the word was used only to describe non-Greek peoples. The early Romans were called barbarians; Cato, for example, designates them as such. But once Rome had gained the imperium, Italians and Latins tended to be exempt from the application of the word. Following the birth of Christ, a barbarian was one who was neither Greek, nor Roman, nor Hebrew. More recently, the name has been given to all those people not subject to the Roman empire.

Many writers have calumniated the Germans by labeling them barbarians. When the imperium had been ceded to the Germans, and the Germans could no longer be called barbarians according to the Roman use of the term, and writers had little cause to malign us except from motives of envy, they still attached the name of barbarians to us. Today the word should not be used at all except to describe the enemies of the Christian faith. It ought never to be applied to Germans, for—I cite Enea Silvio as witness, writing in his letter to Martin Mair [cf. No. 3 above]—the Christian religion has utterly extinguished all traces of barbarism in Germany. This is what Enea says, and he is an Italian, not a German.

Against Hermolaus Barbarus and Joannes Campanus Who Persist in Calling the Germans Barbarians

Italians to this day speak of Germans as an unformed and rude people, an opinion they could only have derived from writers altogether ignorant of German society. They call us rough and uncultivated; see, for example, the remarks of Hermolaus Barbarus in a letter to Pico della Mirandola. Hermolaus writes: "Among Latin writers I do not number the Germans, whose works do not survive nor, indeed, did they ever live, or, if they live, they live in contempt. The whole world calls them uncouth, rude, uncivilized barbarians."[1] Upon what other nation, besides the German, does Hermolaus heap such abuse? This man, who traveled in Germany and wrote on German affairs, goes out of his way to say unpleasant things about us. Joannes Campanus brands us with similar words, claiming that we all, without exception, are uncultured barbarians; indeed, there is no subject in Campanus' letters which seems so to engage his interest and talents as the depreciation of the name and glory of our German people. . . .[2]

WRITERS ALWAYS DISPARAGE GERMANS WHILE EXALTING THE ROMANS

IT is altogether wicked and deplorable that ancient writers saw fit to deprive our German ancestors of the glory due them for their bravery and success in war. No mention of German deeds is made in their fawning accounts of Roman history. Not a word about German virtue and valor was allowed to detract from the glory of Rome. On the other hand, every sort of perfidy and dereliction was attributed to the Germans. They were portrayed as devious and wily fighters who favored attack from ambush, while the deeds of Roman emperors were told in such a way as to make the Romans appear altogether admirable. There is no other ex-

1. Ermolao Barbaro, 1453–93, was a noted classical scholar, theologian, poet—he was crowned by Frederick III—and diplomat. The reference is to a letter to Pico, written in 1485, on the importance of Greek for a sound knowledge of Latin.

2. Giovanni Antonio Campano, bishop, ecclesiastical statesman, and scholar was best known for the collection of his letters in nine books, published in 1495. He saw diplomatic service in Germany, hated every moment of it, and gave vent to his feelings in letters to friends. In fact, Campano's letters (republished in 1707) can serve as a digest of the sophisticated Renaissance Italian's attitude toward, and prejudices against, Germany and all things German.

planation for these lies than their desire to flatter and please Roman readers. The true facts about the Germans remained hidden in silence. . . .

8. From Ulrich von Hutten, Arminius: A Dialogue Taking Place in the Underworld (c. 1518)*

THE SEARCH by German humanists for an admirable past received a tremendous boost from the publication in 1515 in Rome of a new edition of Tacitus, including the recently discovered first books of his *Annals*. These contained the story of Arminius, a chieftain of the Cherusci, who led the anti-Roman uprising of A.D. 9 and inflicted humiliating defeats on the Roman army. Tacitus draws a vivid portrait of the German leader (*Annals*, I: 55–68; II: 9–17, 44–46, 88), but the real beginning of the German cult of Arminius is Ulrich von Hutten's dialogue, written within three or four years of the publication of the *Annals* but not printed until 1529, six years after Hutten's death. Hutten, scion of an old family of Franconian knights, a brilliantly gifted poet, scholar, and polemicist, was Germany's most effective propagandist in the tug of war with Rome. Though he never formally became a Lutheran, he supported Luther's struggle, seeing it through the distorting lenses of his own aggressive and romantic nationalism. Charles V's edict against Luther caused him to abandon the confidence he had originally placed in the emperor, and from 1521 on he advocated increasingly violent means of ridding his country of the rule of priests. His association with Franz von Sickingen (on whom see below, No. 24) led to his persecution. Diseased and reduced to beggary, he died a fugitive in Zurich in 1523.

Apart from presenting Arminius as the ideal German—selfless, idealistic, and unflinching in his determination to overcome obstacles—and his age as the seedbed of Germanic virtues of courage, honesty,

---

* Printed in Eduard Böcking, ed., *Ulrich von Hutten, Schriften*, IV (Leipzig, 1860), 409–18.

candor, simplicity, and the love of liberty, Hutten's dialogue expresses its author's and his colleagues' resentment of Latin claims to cultural and political superiority, and their exultation in the discovery of a German who had taught his haughty enemies a lesson in valor and determination. Although the parallel is not made explicit, the dialogue contains the unmistakable hint that Hutten's Germany is more than ready to receive a new deliverer in the style of Arminius.

ARMINIUS: Your verdict, Minos, is unjust, and I protest against it.

MINOS: Softly, Arminius Do not accuse the all-wise and all-just Minos of having given an unfair verdict. Which verdict do you mean?

ARMINIUS: Let me first crave your forgiveness for the aggressive tone of my words. As you know, we Germans have it in our character to abhor bland speech. We speak openly and to the point, avoiding cant and phrases. My complaint is the following: When awarding accolades to the great military commanders of history you, Minos, passed over me as though I had never lived. Not so long ago you proclaimed Alexander the Great of Macedonia as the first among soldiers, and after him the Roman Scipio, followed by Hannibal of Carthage. Of me you made no mention. . . .

MINOS: Here in the underworld we base our decision upon the claims of the departed themselves. Each shade is entitled to address us on behalf of his own merits. . . . You have yourself seen how overburdened we are with business. Unless a deceased man take it upon himself to persuade us of his fame, we are apt to overlook him. I should gladly have heard you, had you been here to speak on your own behalf.

ARMINIUS: Will you not, then, listen to me now? Bring back those to whom you have recently given the palm so that they may hear.

MINOS: Why not? Go, Mercury; summon the commanders to attend us. . . . Gentlemen, we are in the company of Arminius the

German, a valiant soldier, leader of his countrymen in their struggle for freedom against the Romans. He claims to have been unfairly passed over when honors for distinguished generalship were recently announced. He desires to prove to us that his is the best claim to excellence.

ALEXANDER: Let him give his evidence then.

SCIPIO: I agree.

HANNIBAL: So be it.

MINOS: Speak, Arminius.

ARMINIUS: Before I begin, I should like Cornelius Tacitus, a Roman, to be called to speak as witness to my achievements. . . .

MERCURY: Appear, Tacitus, appear. . . .

ARMINIUS: Tacitus, will you repeat before this assembly the words you have written in your history concerning my abilities and my character? . . .

TACITUS (reading): "Arminius, however, did not long survive. The Roman army being withdrawn from Germany, . . . he had the ambition to aim at the sovereign power. . . . A civil war ensued. Arminius fought with alternate vicissitudes of fortune and fell at last by the treachery of his own relations: a man of warlike genius and, beyond all question, the deliverer of Germany. He had not, like the kings and generals of a former day, the infancy of Rome to cope with: he had to struggle with a great and flourishing empire. . . . He died at the age of thirty-seven, after twelve years of fame and power. In the rude poetry of the barbarians his name is celebrated to this hour, unknown indeed to the annalists of Greece, who embellish nothing but their own story. Even among the Romans the character of this illustrious chief has met with little justice, absorbed as the people are in their veneration of antiquity. . . ."[1]

ARMINIUS: Tell me, Mercury, was not this Tacitus a man of honor and integrity? . . .

MERCURY: Indeed he was, Arminius; honest above all others

1. Tacitus, *Annals*, II: 88. Arthur Murphy translation.

and possessed of greater love of truth than any rival historian. He had, moreover, some acquaintance with Germany, having observed the country with his own eyes and written a description of the lives and customs of its people. . . .

ARMINIUS: What need, then, of words from me when a spokesman for my former enemies has, in his writings, erected this monument to me? He calls me "the deliverer of Germany," and not wrongly, for it was I who tore the German land from the grip of Roman armies, restoring freedom to my countrymen who had grown accustomed to their slavish yoke. I also deserve the title because I attacked Rome not when she was in her feeble immaturity, as did Pyrrhus, Antiochus, and Hannibal but—Tacitus is my witness—at a time when her power stood in its zenith. I challenged her not in self-defense against Roman assaults but of my own free will, provoking battle and fighting to the end. Indeed, I was the only one of Rome's enemies to do so. . . . Inasmuch as everyone admits that no greater might than Rome's ever existed on the earth, and seeing that I succeeded in vanquishing this might at the moment of its apogee, I believe to be entitled fairly to the name of greatest general of all times. . . . If I speak here of my own accomplishments, I do so without malice toward others, motivated solely by my innate love of virtue. I have never pursued fame for its own sake. The consciousness of the merit of my deeds was glory enough for me. . . .

MINOS: We are content to hear you out, Arminius. Continue.

ARMINIUS: Let me begin with you, Hannibal, who are praised above all others because, as they say, you rose from insignificant origins to exalted heights. If this is the source of fame, then I deserve it more than you, . . . for whence could I have derived my power, Germany being in a desperate situation, near the brink of annihilation? . . . Young as I was—not yet twenty-four years of age —I had not the stature of my person to rely upon as I advanced to the head of an army that was still unorganized; it was considered highly doubtful, in view of the dissension among my people, that an effective striking force could ever be created. Do not imagine that money helped me in my task. Money did not then exist in Germany. Despite these and other obstacles, impeded on all sides, bitterly poor and lonely, armed with nothing but my own resolution, I built a secure foundation for the establishment of liberty in Germany and inaugurated a new epoch in the history of my country. . . . As you know, it was I who began the war against Rome. . . . I began it at the head of an undisciplined army that knew nothing of the art of war, was practically unarmed and so short of equipment that the very iron for the arrows was lacking. But for all we lacked I substituted the sagacity and resourcefulness of my mind. . . . Nor did I face an unworthy opponent. Three legions stood against me, . . . equipped with all the refinements of Roman military science, disciplined and experienced in warfare. . . . These I defeated in my first battle. At that moment the very existence of my fatherland depended on the actions of a single person: myself. Even Scipio cannot claim to have saved his republic from so hopeless a situation. . . . And even you, Hannibal, cannot boast of having put Rome to such a fright as I, separated though I was, in my obscure corner of Germany, from the land of the Romans by mountains, marshes, and river; such a fright, I say, that the great Augustus, most formidable of all the Caesars . . . vowed to dedicate new and lavish games to Jupiter if this mortal threat were to be lifted from Rome. . . . All this I accomplished at a time when Germany was in a state of utter prostration and fragmentation, and Rome stood at the very summit of her power and fortunes. . . .

After this I healed the divisions within my own country and ended the civil strife among our tribes. I punished those who persisted in their rebellion, while forgiving all who craved pardon for their destructive acts. I purified my people of their vices. No one, I decreed, was worthy to be called a German who paid tribute to an alien ruler. I declared it to be a national disgrace that Roman fasces and togas had ever been seen between Elbe and Rhine. Having in this way inflamed the spirits of my countrymen with the love of liberty, I made them a solemn promise that within a short time every trace of the Roman yoke would be extinguished from

Germany; indeed that the very name of Rome would not be remembered among our people.

The Romans, for their part, in an attempt to hold on to the country, sent the flower of their youth to Germany. Tiberius Nero came, and his brother Drusus, and many others. They warred with me and then went home to celebrate their triumphs, while I maintained Germany's independence and sovereignty. I withstood the onslaught of the valiant Germanicus and his dreaded legate Caecina, who, as though bent on a second Trojan expedition, sailed against me with a fleet of 1000 ships. On all I inflicted humiliating losses. . . . You, who are shades in the underworld, know better than I how many brave Romans I despatched to these regions, how ruthlessly I dealt with the traitors among my own people, and how extensive and violent were my military operations. . . . Thus it happened that the Romans were driven from German soil, nor have they, to this day, succeeded in reestablishing their dominion over us.

Although he may try to convince you of the contrary, Alexander could not have vanquished the Romans as easily as he conquered the effeminate peoples of Asia . . . and the defenseless nations of India, whom, carousing all the while, he overwhelmed with his drunken army. . . . My own ambitions were always directed to the attainment of virtue, never to fame and possessions. I own no trophies to testify to my victories. I fought neither for riches nor in order to rule over others. One goal alone spurred me on my course: the love of freedom and the wish to restore it to my enslaved fatherland.

It is for you, Minos, to consider whether or not others have earned more glory than I, either by struggling to fame and victory against even greater odds, by fighting fiercer wars for holier causes and against mightier opponents, or by adhering more steadfastly than I to the ideals of good and right.

MINOS: A noble speech, Arminius, worthy indeed of a great commander. I know that what you say corresponds to the facts, and that you do not embellish the truth. . . . Unfortunately, however, my decision was made some time ago, . . . and I am afraid that the order of things must stand. But seeing that you are Germany's deliverer, that you remained undefeated in your wars of liberation, that you braved innumerable dangers, and that in everything you did, you aimed at the common good, I shall assign you to a place beside Brutus and call you first in rank among the great defenders of their countries' freedom. Be it your task, Mercury, to let forum, streets, and temples resound with the name of Arminius the Cheruscan, the most freedom-loving, most victorious, and most German of all heroes. This I have resolved and ordered, and let no one dare gainsay me.

ALEXANDER: One moment, Minos. Was not Arminius once a slave, while I have always been a king, and free?

ARMINIUS: In spirit, Alexander, I was never subject to any man. The fair image of liberty was ever before my mind's eye, one fervent wish filling my soul: to bring liberty to my fatherland. . . .

SCIPIO: Among the Romans Arminius stands accused of breach of faith and is charged with having abused his victory over Varus by excessive cruelty.

ARMINIUS: If that accusation were to stand, Scipio, all tyrannicides and liberators would be judged faithless, most notably your own patriots who drove out the Tarquins and assassinated Julius Caesar. And yet these heroes enjoy fame and glory among you. I, for my part, call those men faithless who trim their sails to the winds of good fortune, who offer their loyalty for sale to the highest bidder. I myself was driven by the sacred merit of my nation's cause. From it, also, I derived the strength to resist the blows of adversity.

HANNIBAL: One more question, Arminius. It is charged that you, who boast so loudly of love of country and freedom, were in fact ambitious to seize the supreme power over your people. Once the alien yoke was shaken, it is said, you intended to replace it with that of your own authority. . . .

ARMINIUS: . . . Never, Hannibal, did I feel the least desire to become ruler over my country and people. My enemies' jealousy

is responsible for the invention of this malicious calumny. . . . I
am not the first to be thus slandered, nor will I be the last. . . .
   MINOS: Truly spoken, Arminius. Has there ever been a great
man without envious detractors to count his very virtues as crimes
against him? We who know Arminius love him with all our hearts.
. . . On your way, then, Mercury, and carry out my instructions.
   MERCURY: Follow me, Arminius.

9. The Lady from Brittany (1491) *

THE FOLLOWING verses preserve the memory of an incident widely
resented in Germany as a shameful national insult and retold as a spur
to national regeneration. Maximilian, King of the Romans and emperor to be, had been betrothed to Anne, heiress of Brittany in 1487,
a year before the death of her father Duke Francis II, whose duchy
was the last of the great French fiefs to resist unification with France.
The marriage took place by proxy in 1490, Maximilian assuming the
title of Duke of Brittany. In the meantime Charles VIII of France
had invaded the duchy, and Maximilian, short of cash and occupied
elsewhere, could do nothing. Resolved to settle the Breton question
once and for all, King Charles, supported by Breton nobles who
sought an end to the unceasing rivalry with their powerful neighbor,
occupied Brittany and compelled Anne to cancel her marriage to
Maximilian on the ground that she, as Charles' vassal, had failed to
ask his permission to marry. At the same time he packed off his own
betrothed, Margaret of Austria, Maximilian's daughter by his first
wife, Mary of Burgundy, returning her to her humiliated father.
Whether or not he actually abducted Anne while she traveled
through France on safe conduct is not clear. This, at any rate, was
the story told in Germany, where it was moralized as a paradigm of
French perfidy and German national impotence. It was a subject
made to order for balladeers and didactic rhymesters; the poem trans-

* Printed in Rochus von Liliencron, *Die historischen Volkslieder der
Deutschen*, II (1866), 292–99.

lated below is one of several on the topic. Its otherwise unknown
author identifies himself in the last line.

O Holy Spirit, love sublime,
Extend your blessing to this rhyme
Which I, an artless man, shall make
For Mary, Queen of Heaven's sake.
Lend to my halting speech your ear,
Mother of God, our woe to hear.
Ave regina caelorum,
O mater regis angelorum,
O Maria flos virginum,
Give us strength *in mundum.*

. . . . . .

In the year of our Lord and your son
Fourteen hundred and ninety-one,
I fell to musing how our sovereign,
The much-beloved King Maximilian,
Had been brought low and put to shame
By the King of France, Charles by name,
Through his contempt for the sacrament
Of marriage, in deed and intent.
All Christian princes I implore:
Learn this sad tale, and evermore
Remember France's treacherous act,
And how a lawful, sacred pact
Was broken, and a noble maid
Humiliated and betrayed.

. . . . . .

Encamped in Nuremberg our King
(Of whom this sad lament I sing,
Maximilian, noble and fair,

[83

The Emperor Frederick's son and heir)
Announced the happy news that he
Would wed the Duchess of Brittany,
Make her in holy wedlock wife
And dear companion in his life.
From Brittany Bishop Raymond came
To sign the deed in his own name,
And was received most graciously
In honor and civility.
'Til late at night, in the castle's hall
High above Nuremberg's ancient wall,
They sat and studied the domument
Which had from Brittany been sent.
All favors Duchess Anne demanded
King Maximilian freely granted;
No other man but him she chose
For matrimony's sacred oath,
While he toward Anne was much inclined;
And so the deed was drawn and signed,
To bring about with all despatch
The consummation of this match.

King Maximilian, with delight,
Summoned a well-born, noble knight
Of stainless honor, untouched by blame,
Herr Wolf von Bolheim was his name,
And sent him off on embassy
To claim his bride in Brittany,
And, in King Maximilian's stead,
In Church and in the marriage bed,
Accomplish with the least delay
The marriage, as is princes' way.
The knight sped on his journey and
Soon found himself in Breton land;
Rode straight to Rennes, such was the plan,

Where he was met by Duchess Anne.
That night together lay the bride
And Maximilian's faithful knight,
A sword between them on the bed,
His body clad from toe to head
In steel, only one foot left bare—
It's royal usage everywhere.
Custom and law thus satisfied,
Into the church went knight and bride,
There to exchange the sacred vows
To make Anne Maximilian's spouse.
And all this was done fittingly
With grave and seemly dignity.

Now Anne, considering how she
Might swiftly travel to Germany,
Thought of King Charles and deemed it best
To send him a polite request
For transit rights and escort bands
To journey safely across France.
The King was quick to grant her wishes;
Anne had no cause to be suspicious;
He sent two royal dukes to guide her
Through French domain, and ride beside her,
Bearing safe conducts, which the King
Had signed and sealed with his own ring.

When all were ready for the start,
She gave the signal to depart
From Rennes and presently came upon
A stone bridge on the river Oudon.
There, drawn up on the other bank,
Were soldiers, standing rank on rank.
Alarmed, the duchess called her knight:
"Herr von Bolheim, tell me, what might

This troop of soldiers there portend?"
He answered: "Gracious duchess, send
For your servants, bid them hurry,
You have become King Charles' quarry."
No sooner had retreat been sounded,
Than the duchess found herself surrounded;
Useless to fight, to flee no chance;
A prisoner of the King of France.

When she was taken to him, he
Received the duchess royally.
That evening, after they had dined,
Charles went to her and spoke his mind.
He said, "I do not wish you ill,
But you must now obey my will;
You shall become my wife because
I cannot risk Brittany's loss;
No foreign prince shall rule your land,
None else but France shall claim your hand."
The duchess, shocked and mortified
To hear the king speak thus, replied:
"My gracious liege and sovereign, such
Proposals honor me too much.
I beg your lordship to recall
That I have been betrothed with all
The sacraments of our Church,
Which no good Christian may besmirch,
To Maximilian, mighty lord
Of the Roman scepter, crown, and sword.
No other spouse but him I'll know;
I pray your majesty let me go."
In vain, alas, this speech so brave;
The King dealt with her like a knave.
Faithlessly he deceived and lied,

Two marriage covenants defied;
Yes two, for he was bound to wed
The noble Princess Margaret,
Who had been pledged his wife to be
In fourteen hundred and eighty-three.[1]
Two crimes and sins extraordinary
Against our Queen, the Virgin Mary.

O that these verses might extend
My cry to Rome and Pope Innocent.
The pope can excommunicate,
Can threaten foes with a crusade,
He can send legates, emissaries
To bring to heel his adversaries.
Let him urge every priest to prayer
That we may see a new age where
No Christian man need be afraid
Of neighbor's envy, malice, hate.
O Emperor Frederick, do you see
That my lament, complaint, and plea
Concerns your very flesh and blood?
Do not spare goods and money, but
Bestir yourself to help your son
That right and justice may be done.
Rally the princes and electors,
Suffer no shirkers or defectors,
Call on all Christian kings abroad
To join with us in the name of God.
O highborn dukes, I summon you,
Counts, barons, knights and nobles too,
All who have power and jurisdiction,
Let none be charged with dereliction,

1. Margaret was betrothed to Charles in 1482 when she was three years old. They were married in 1483.

Discontent in Germany on the Eve of the Reformation

Let every pious Christian soul
In our righteous cause enroll.

Mary, our lady, hear my cry;
You never wittingly deny
Your gracious aid to one whose prayer
Is fervent and whose cause is fair.
Auxiliatrix, hear my voice,
Reparatrix, in you I rejoice,
Illuminatrix, hope of our nation,
Adjutrix, our consolation,
We crave your help in these troublesome times;
And thus Hans Ortenstein ends his rhymes.

[IV]

Oppression and Exploitation:

Political

---

10. *How the Mighty Rule: Three Chapters from* Reynard the Fox (1498) *

EYNARD THE FOX is the best known and most interesting example of the animal epic, a type of literature much in vogue during the Middle Ages. With their roots in the classical fable, medieval animal epics seem to have arisen in learned clerical circles in northern France and Belgium around the turn of the millennium. Carried through Europe by itinerant clerics and minstrels, turned into regional vernaculars and dialects, and equipped with moralizing glosses, these epics became repositories for much social comment and criticism. The epic of Reynard the Fox exists in many forms, verse and prose, of which the French *Roman de Renart* and the Dutch *Reinaert* are the most famous. (A prose version of the latter was translated into English by William Caxton and published in 1481.) A Low German verse redaction, *Reynke de Vos*, published in Lübeck in 1498, became the foundation of all subsequent German versions. The translation below of three chapters from Books II and IV of *Reynard*

---

* *Reineke der Fuchs . . . , nach der Ausgabe von 1498 ins Hochdeutsche übersetzet, . . . von Johann Christoph Gottscheden* (Leipzig and Amsterdam, 1752).

[89

was made from the eighteenth-century German translation by Johann Christoph Gottsched.

Thoroughly and objectively human in his cunning and in his self-seeking drive for advantage and success, Reynard is a kind of folk hero inviting self-identification, especially from common folk, whom he initiates into the sly machinations and brutalities with which the game of life is played. The excerpts given below record Reynard's apologia and final triumph. Having once before talked himself out of the hangman's noose, Reynard again falls under the lion king's wrath by killing Cuwart the hare and shifting the blame for the act upon Bellin the ram, whom he has despatched to carry the hare's head to the king. Grimbert the badger goes to warn his uncle Reynard, but the fox decides to brazen it out and go before the king. The following conversation takes place as Reynard and Grimbert journey to the lion's court.

Reynard Continues His Confession and Defends His Sins by Citing Examples of Misdeeds Done by the Mighty of the World
[Book II, chapter 7]

Grimbert replied: "Your sins are grave, Reynard, but what is dead is dead. I shall forgive you, now that your enemies are close upon you. I absolve you of your sins, though I fear that Cuwart's death will make things difficult for you. You should not have sent his head to the king. Such acts of bravado will surely bring you to grief."

"It will not," said Reynard, "of that I assure you, dear nephew. If you wish to make a success of life in this age of ours, you cannot put on a holy face, as the monks do in their cells. Cuwart excited me. He jumped up and down before me, and he was exceedingly fat. And so I put aside the love I normally bear my fellow creatures and killed him. I did the same with Bellin. They have come to harm and I have fallen into sin. Why should I make great ceremonies over their deaths? I have no taste for that. I ought to love my own kind, I admit it. But, although I cannot oppose goodness, I pay little attention to it. As you say: dead is dead. Let us speak of other things.

"We live in a perilous time. Lords and prelates set examples for us to follow—everyone can see that. Lesser folk notice what the mighty do. Who does not know that the king himself is a robber and a conniver? What he does not eat himself, he leaves for the bears and the wolves. And he claims it as his right that things should be that way. No one tells him the truth; neither his chaplain nor his father confessor says to him, 'You have done wrong.' Why don't they? Because they like to enjoy their share of the loot. If a poor creature should come and present his grievances he might just as well flap the air with his tongue. He is wasting his time. What they've taken from him is gone. No one heeds his complaints, and when they get tired of listening to him, they throw him out.

"Moreover each of us knows that the king is much too powerful to be resisted. The lion is our lord and master, and what is more natural than that he should grab what he can get? He says to us, 'You are my vassals, all of you,' and thinks we ought to be thankful that he deigns to do us harm. If only I could speak freely, nephew, I should say much more. Our king is a noble prince, but he loves best him who offers the most and dances to his tune. No law compels him to go to council with the bear and the wolf, but he goes just the same, and much damage these fine councillors will do us all. Victims will keep their peace in any case, for it hardly matters who steals what.

"Thus our king the lion has sitting in council with him a select band of robbers, whom he holds in great honor and makes the greatest among his nobles. But let the poor wretch Reynard take a chicken, and you'll see them pounce upon him and scream, 'To the gallows with him!' Little crooks are hanged; big crooks govern our lands and cities. I grew wise to this long ago, nephew, which is why I seek my own profit in life. Sometimes I think that, since everybody does it, this is the way it ought to be. At other times I am mindful of my conscience and of God's judgment, for I know that goods acquired dishonestly ought to be returned. And thinking such thoughts I feel great contrition. But then I observe the potentates of this world and note the rules according to which they live *their* lives, and then I thumb my nose at contrition. . . ."

MORE OF REYNARD'S CONFESSION, AND HOW THE WICKED ARE PUNISHED
[Book II, chapter 8]

"Now, Grimbert," Reynard continued, "a person who wishes to make his way in the world and who observes how our potentates live, some well, some ill, falls into sin even as he observes. Many a prelate is good and just, but this does not keep scandal from touching him, for people have a passion nowadays for sniffing out wrongdoings, and where they don't find any they invent them. The common mass of our fellow men are an evil-minded lot and scarcely deserve to be governed by good and just rulers. They are quick to come forward with detractions and calumnies, but if they know something good about a man they keep it to themselves. How, then, shall things fare well in this world?

"Our world is full of slander, lies, bad faith, thievery, treachery, perjury, robbery, and murder. We are deceived by false prophets and hypocrites. The common man observes his superiors, some of whom are good, others bad. He follows the examples of the wicked, and thus inflicts the most damage on himself. If punished for having sinned, he argues that sins are not as serious as the learned teach and the priests preach. 'If it were really dangerous to be in sin,' say the wicked, 'priests would not be quite so lighthearted about sinning.' Men excuse their own wrongdoing by citing the bad examples of the priests, whose lives they emulate.

"There is hardly a parish where the priest does not have a concubine, living in sin and shame, producing children like husbands in normal wedlock. Such priests are solicitous for their offspring and advance them as best they can, over and above children of legitimate origin. Their children strut about proudly, as if they came from a noble house. When, in the old days, did priests' children have such preferred standing? Nowadays money calls the tune, and a priest's bastard is dubbed lord or lady. Show me a country where the priests do not levy the toll or run the village mills. Spreading wickedness by their own examples, they pervert the whole world! . . .

"Is it any wonder, therefore, that the few good priests who do their work piously and conscientiously find themselves without a following? Hardly a soul attends to them; none emulates them. But evil is aped, and wickedness magnified. How, then, shall things be well in the world? . . .

"A pious and learned cleric is to be honored, but a wicked one can do infinite harm by his bad example. He may preach an inspiring sermon, but his congregation will say, 'Is he asking us to mark his words and ignore the shiftless, immoral, wicked life he leads?' He invites us to give our money to help build and maintain the Church in exchange for indulgences, and all the while he himself tears it down by the ill repute brought on the Church by his unsavory life. He would never put his own money into the collection pouch, knowing that the Church is in decline and has little life left in it. His ideals are sumptuous garments, pretty women, rich food and wines, and giving as much thought as possible to worldly affairs. . . .

"As for those who go about in cowls and spend their time begging and pleading, my view of them is no different. Monks would far rather hang about the rich and mighty than spend their time with the poor. They are masters of the shifty argument and are easily bribed. . . . The brashest among them attain highest standing in their orders, are made lectors, priors, and guardians. Less aggressive ones take the back seat. They rise at all hours of the night to chant, read, and walk about the graves, while their fat colleagues eat a belly full of fancy food and lie the whole night snoring.

"And what about papal legates? What about abbots, priors and other prelates, Beguines, nuns—whatever their names are? They all say, 'Give me what is yours, and I'll keep what is mine.' You cannot find three out of ten among them who live according to the rules of their orders. This is how corrupt the spiritual estate has become."

The badger replied: "Uncle, what good does it do you to confess other people's sins? Confession isn't worth a penny unless you admit your own transgressions. What is the clergy to you? Why worry about monks and nuns? Each must carry his own burden and justify his conduct as best he can. . . . But you speak of so many things that I fear greatly to fall into error by listening to you. You know the condition of the world, and how everything stands on earth. You really ought to be a priest so that I might confess to you and profit from your advice and be turned to piety and wisdom."

Saying this, they had arrived at the king's court. Reynard felt his courage leave him, and his knees began to shake with fright. But he said: "Well, we are here. Let us take our chances and go in." . . .

Because of his talent for speaking the most outrageous lies with a straight face and for allaying doubts and misgivings by means of extravagant flattery, Reynard not only gains vindication before the king but wins honors and preferments at court as well. The following chapter concludes the book.

How Reynard Left Court Laden with Honors and Certain of the King's Favor
[Book IV, chapter 17]

Reynard thanked the king politely and said: "Gracious lord, I thank you most humbly for the great honor you have done me. You will see that I shall know how to show myself appreciative."

All this time Isegrim [the wolf who had warned the king against

Reynard and was brutally assaulted by the fox] was lying on the ground, more dead than alive. His friends went up to him, among them his wife Gieremuth, Bruin the bear, his children, servants, and relatives. They put him on a bier and carried him away, covering him with straw to keep him warm. They examined his wounds, of which they counted twenty-six. Physicians came and bandaged his sores, giving him tonics to drink. They put an herb in his ear, which made him sneeze, front and back. . . . He slept a little, but not long. What agitated him most was the thought of how he had been so ignominiously vanquished and had suffered shame and scorn along with his defeat. His wife stood beside him, disconsolate. Her sadness was manifold, for not only had Reynard brought disgrace after disgrace on her, he had also attacked Isegrim's brother and so cruelly damaged him that the poor wretch was beside himself with agony.

Reynard, for his part, took much pleasure in all this as he sat feasting with his friends while preparing to quit the king's court. The king himself furnished him with a stately escort to send him on his way with a token of his goodwill.

"Reynard," the king said, "come back soon." Reynard kneeled before him and answered, "I thank you, my lord, with all my heart. I also thank my gracious lady the queen, as well as your council. God preserve you all in good health. I love you, as you deserve to be loved. If it please you, my lord, I shall now be off to see my wife and dear children, who have been in great anxiety over me."

"By all means," the king said. "Be of good cheer and travel on." And hearing many such kind words, and certain of the king's goodwill, Reynard went on his way.

And from this we see that all the creatures of the tribe of Reynard are beloved and respected of princes, be they spiritual or secular. It is Reynard and his ilk who give the word in the councils of our rulers, for his kind is great in power and grows daily in influence.

He who has not learned Reynard's craft is not made for this

world and his advice is not heeded. But with the aid of the art of which Reynard is past master, success and power are within everyone's reach. For this reason our world is full of Reynards, and we find them at the pope's court no less than at the emperor's. Simon is now on the throne. Money counts, and nothing else. He who has money to give gets the benefice; he who has not does not get it. Whoever knows Reynard's cunning best is on his way to the top.

But enough of these observations. You may ask: What became of Reynard and his clan, the members of which must have numbered more than forty? I can tell you that they jumped with joy at the news of their elevation and left the king's court covered with honors. Reynard led the way, hailed as a great prince, his tail fluffed proudly, pleased as could be to see himself so marked for distinction and made member of the king's privy council. "This shall not be to my disadvantage," he thought to himself, "for now I can favor whom I will, and first and foremost I shall favor my friends. Let cunning be praised, therefore, more highly than gold."

11. *"Concerning Power Fools, or The Instability of Power": A Sermon by Johann Geiler von Kaisersberg on Sebastian Brant's Ship of Fools (1498)**

JOHANN GEILER (Kaisersberg is a town in Alsace where he was raised) was probably the most popular and influential German preacher of the later fifteenth century. Abandoning a promising academic career that had won him professorships and rectorates in theology at the Universities of Freiburg and Basel, Geiler in 1477 accepted a privately financed preacher's position in the city of Strassburg. From 1486 he preached regularly in the cathedral, speaking

---

* The text of Geiler's sermons is printed in Johann Scheible, *Das Kloster* . . . , I (Stuttgart, 1845). For a modern English translation of Sebastian Brant's *Ship of Fools* see Edwin H. Zeydel, trans., *Sebastian Brant's Ship of Fools* (with introduction and commentary, New York, 1962).

every Sunday and feast day, and daily during Lent. He also made it a habit to preach in nearby monasteries and convents, imploring the monks and nuns to adopt his suggestions for a reform of ecclesiastical life and discipline. Often referred to as "The Trumpet of Strassburg Cathedral," Geiler tirelessly pursued the main objective of his vocation as popular preacher: to change men's lives by holding up to them, on the one hand, the myriad crudities, shortcomings, and backslidings of their everyday lives and, on the other, the refining, inspiring, and liberating truths of the Gospel.

The cycle of sermons on Sebastian Brant's *Ship of Fools* exemplifies Geiler's objective and method. Given in public in 1498, these homilies on Brant's popular rhymes (the *Ship of Fools* had been published in Basel in 1494) urged his listeners to take corrective action by means of recognition of, and revulsion from, the countless big and little faults and vices illustrated for them in the preacher's vivid and meticulously detailed image of the individual and his society (see also No. 30 below). Widely copied, printed, and translated, the sermons on the *Ship of Fools* exerted an impact far beyond the immediate audiences to whom Geiler spoke and established his reputation as social critic and moral reformer to the German nation.

The Fifty-Sixth Brood of Fools

The fifty-sixth brood of fools is that of power-mad fools, that is to say, of fools who place all their hopes and ambitions on the attainment of power. They may be recognized by the following bells on their caps:

The first bell of the power fool is the contempt and scorn he feels for his subjects. O you power fool! Why do you disdain your subject—as though he were not as good a man as you? Were you not fashioned out of the very same clay of which the meanest of your subjects is also made? Or are you composed of more precious stuff? Were you baptised in Malmsey wine instead of water? Do both you and your subject not pray to the same God as your common father? Why, then, do you despise and scorn a man who is poorer and meaner than you in station? In truth you should not do this; you should love your neighbor as you love yourself. Beware, therefore, of holding your subject in contempt. Remember that you and he belong to the same family.

The second bell of the power fool is his inclination to exalt himself and rise to heights of splendor. O you blind mole of a power fool! Why do you pile up great mounds of earth to raise yourself to eminence, making your name glamorous in the world, building large houses with other men's labor, storing up riches for no other purpose than to be regarded mighty and magnificent? Look behind you. Do you see Jesus Christ standing there as a gardener with His hoe, waiting for you to scrape up clumps of earth? As soon as you imagine yourself secure and begin to dig, He catches you with his hoe, pulls you out of your hole, and hacks your head off. See, therefore, that you do not exalt yourself to too great a height, for when you think you are safest, you will find yourself in the greatest danger.

The third bell of the power fool is his oppressive exploitation of his subjects through tributes, taxes, and numberless other chicaneries with which he plagues his subjects day and night. O you stupid power fool! Do you think God has given the sword into your hands so that you may hurt and kill your subjects when you ought to protect and guard them? To be sure, some princes and lords are mild and merciful by nature, but even they are turned oppressive by the flatterers and whisperers among their courtiers, who instigate cruel oppression of land and people. Not a few princes, on the other hand, are by nature inclined to tyranny, and such a ruler, even if he has mild and merciful councillors, refuses to heed them and does not retain them long, favoring instead advisors with tyrannous characters akin to his own. History proves that the reign of such a tyrant cannot endure. No realm ruled by a tyrant is able to maintain itself.

The fourth bell of the power fool is his boastfulness concerning his power and the foolish pleasure he takes in it. Here we see the true folly of the power fool, for he has great joy of his power, whereas he ought to be in despair from the burden of it. Powerful lords are frivolous men by nature, and human affairs are of little concern to them. They take pleasure in reducing their subjects to misery; they strut about with bright eyes and in excellent spirits, as if the earth itself must shake beneath their steps. O you power-mad fool! Do you know why your spirits are high? God our Lord suffers you to rule on earth for your own harm and destruction, not for your pleasure and glory. For if God had wanted men to exercise earthly sovereignty for useful and good purposes, he surely would have granted such sovereignty to his disciples, who were dear to him and were good men, though poor as church mice. But he did not wish his disciples to have earthly authority. And for this reason you should not boast of your power and your authority or take pleasure in the possession of them. Instead you should grieve for the burden and the responsibility of your authority, and implore God to grant you grace to let you use your power well. When you do this, your power will not inflict pain and unhappiness on you but will lead to your benefit and salvation.

The fifth bell of the power fool is his vain expectation of long-lasting rule and dominion. Such a fool imagines that his power, sovereignty, honor, wealth, pleasure, and gratification will endure forever and that he will always be ruling over the world. O you world-ambitious fool! How you are deceived! There will come a time when fortune turns against you, and your empire will collapse in the twinkling of an eye. Do you really imagine that your authority and power will last for all time? It will not, that is for certain. Mightier kingdoms than yours have gone to ruin! What has become of the Assyrians, the Medes, the Persians, the Athenians, the Romans, the Macedonians? Did they not all end in destruction? Were they not all reduced to nothing? And you imagine that your realm, yours alone of all the great states of the world, will last forever! You are, in truth, grievously deluded. How many kings and emperors have been hanged or proscribed or cruelly slain? How many monarchs have fallen from riches to misery, how many were exiled from their lands and must live out their days in disgrace and penury? Do you not believe me when I say that nothing on this earth is constant? Take my advice, study the many examples which show how nothing in this world can endure, and do not rely on your own power. Place all your hope and trust and faith in God, for it is God alone who offers you a kingdom that will last throughout eternity.

12. *The Insolence of Ecclesiastical Princes* (c. 1450)*

IN THE SUMMER OF 1449 the Archbishop and Elector of Mainz, Dieter von Erbach, joined by eighty-six other princes and lords, declared war upon the imperial city of Hall in Swabia because it had refused to render compensation for some property taken from him. Far from being an isolated occurrence, this feud was in fact a symptom of the advanced political disintegration of the empire under Frederick III (1440–93). Other symptoms were the formation of urban, electoral, and princely leagues and the frequently violent struggle of southern German cities to maintain themselves against marauding nobles. This political context, which was the setting of the bishop's war, is, however, missing from the picture of ecclesiastical cupidity and greed offered by Ulrich Wiest, author of the following rhymes, as his contribution to the mounting criticism of the German Church. Wiest was a master singer and head of the singing school in Augsburg. His poem, though written only for members of the school, gained wide popularity in the later fifteenth century.

> O God, I call upon you in my grief;
> Wrecked lies the Christian ship upon the reef;
> Come to our aid, grant us relief.
> Show us again, O God, your saving grace;

---

* "Der geistlichen Fürsten Hoffart," printed in Fritz Kern, ed., *Deutsche Volkslieder des Mittelalters*, 2nd ed. (Berlin, n.d.), 369–72.

Not ours the guilt for bloody sword and mace
With which the bishops take the warrior's place.
Have patience with us. Recollect that you
Yourself called out, when mortal pain you knew,
"Forgive them, God, they know not what they do."

Poor guileless Christian folk are innocent;
As victims in this war their blood is spent,
Contritely their unknowing sins repent.
But prelates, called our Christian state to lead,
Whose piety should grace the holy creed,
They are the first in war-like word and deed.
The Prince-Bishop of Mainz loves sword and fire;
He ought to stay at home, sing in his choir,
And pray he may be spared from rack and pire.

The Bishop of Eichstätt joins him in the ranks,
While Babenberg delights in martial pranks;
Thus we who proffer alms are rendered thanks!
The faith that Fathers of our Church created,
Whose fervor centuries have not abated,
Is now, by wanton churchmen dissipated.
We plead with you, O Lord, in desperate pain;
Prognostications make it all too plain:
Vengeance will come, and all the priesthood slain.
The time draws near with frightening speed,
Concerning this all soothsayers are agreed.
His patience ending, God will intercede
To break the bishops' wicked pride and lust
By fanning men's outrage into a gust
To blow the Church itself into the dust.
The faithful don't give alms to see them spent
On vain unchristian pomp and merriment,
On lives that against God and Christ offend.
Alms pay for tournaments and pageantry,

Alms support raids on land and property,
Alms raise the means for every devilry.

With alms they gamble and they entertain;
With alms they buy, invest, and sell for gain;
With alms they hire soldiers to campaign.
With alms there's money for a splendid court;
Alms let them waste their time on games and sport;
Alms mean frivolities of every sort.
Alms buy diversions for the bishop's leisure;
Alms let him sample every wicked pleasure;
Alms fill his coffers with superfluous treasure.

Alms put the finest horses in his stable;
Alms drape him grandly in brocade and sable;
Alms bring the choicest dishes to his table.
Alms deck him out in jewels, pearls, and gold;
Alms fill his money box with wealth untold;
Alms buy more objects than his house can hold.
Alms draw a large and splendid retinue;
Only the fairest ladies in the land will do;
With Alms his mind is pampered, and his body too.

Thus alms bring on contempt for truth and right,
Greed, arrogance, voluptuous delight,
Neglect of duty, and abuse of might.
O Lord our God, attend to our woe:
Why must your faithful servants suffer so,
While envious bishops daily prouder grow?
I beg you, Lord our God, unbend their stern
And haughty hearts, affect their minds to turn
Away from pride, humility to learn.

I wish the Holy Empire strength and health.
May none of its great cities lend their wealth

> To its sworn foes. O Mary without stealth,
> Virgin and Mother, see your people's plight;
> Let this poor poem find favor in your sight,
> And help restore the empire to its might.

13. A Protest by the Bavarian Estates against the Arrogant Conduct of Their Prince (1514)*

WHILE IMPERIAL AUTHORITY in Germany continued to decline, centralization in the territories proceeded apace. It did not, however, go unopposed. The following excerpt from the records of the territorial Estates of Bavaria reveals the strength, skill and fervor of the Estates-based resistance to incipient absolutism and the arrogance with which it was practiced (cf. also Nos. 21, 22, 24, 25, and 27 below).

Albrecht IV, called "The Wise," succeeded in uniting the segments of Bavaria into one duchy. He had barely introduced a new law of primogeniture when he died in 1508, leaving two minor sons, Wilhelm aged fifteen and Ludwig, twelve. A committee of guardian-regents attended to affairs of state until Wilhelm came of age in 1511 and began to rule in his own right. A headstrong and quick-tempered youth, Duke Wilhelm showed little inclination to heed his councillors' advice, especially on matters of expenditure—a desperate issue due to large debts remaining from a recent war of succession. The need for more money compelled Wilhelm to convoke his Estates, whose leaders were bent on seizing every opportunity for turning their deliberations into instruments of legislative and administrative power. In their plan to limit the ruler's prerogatives (which was successful; Wilhelm was forced to give in to their demands) the Estates were guided by their spokesman Dietrich von Plieningen, a lawyer-statesman with humanist background (his translations of Sallust underline

* Printed in Franz von Krenner, ed., *Der Landtag im Herzogtum Baiern vom Jahre 1514* (1804), 460–75.

the points made in the speech quoted below) who had entered the
service of Albrecht around 1500. Confronting the two dukes at the
meeting of the Estates in June 1514, Plieningen read them the following lesson in proper princely conduct:

On Whit Monday, Herr Dietrich von Plieningen, knight and
doctor of laws, acting on behalf of the committee and the council,
addressed the two princes as follows:

Address of Dietrich von Plieningen
to the Two Princes

First, as concerns Your Graces' intended journey to join the
camp of His Imperial Majesty, our lords of the council and the
committee are informed that Your Graces have ordered to be
drawn up a provision list comprising a large number of horses for
your retinue.

Your Graces must know that there is at present very little money
in our treasuries and that you owe great debts to many creditors.
We stand in need of the utmost thrift in the management of
public and private expenditures, to the end that debts may be paid
off and Your Graces' pawned castles and towns redeemed. For
these reasons Your Graces' councillors and the committee faithfully advise and admonish Your Graces to avoid all excess in spending, and we also ask that you delay your departure as long as possible so that quartering and provisioning expenses may be held to the
minimum. . . .

Pertaining to our gracious lord Duke Wilhelm alone: The committee reports that Your Grace, some days ago, displayed an
unseemly, wrathful, and ungracious temper toward Your Grace's
councillors on the occasion of their appearance before Your Grace
in the matter of the salt trade. Your Grace is reported to have said,

"You have councillors who can take care of these things, and if they do wrong you have ways of calling them to account!"

Second, in the matter of Count Ulrich von Ortenburg . . . : When the councillors had given their considered opinion in accordance with their duty and their conscience, Your Grace is reported again to have flown into a rage and exclaimed, "Let me but get my hands on the councillors who advised against my desires." . . .

We are bound to say that the words employed by Your Grace on these occasions violate law, custom, and human reason. They violate law because it is illegal to harm, or threaten to harm, a man whose duty requires that he give advice and who gives that advice willingly. . . . Nor is it right and proper for a young prince to speak so wrathfully to aged and faithful councillors. . . . Such threats might fittingly be addressed to senseless young children or ignorant fools, but Your Grace's councillors are learned men from whom Your Grace might learn much, and they must not be spoken to in this manner. Many of these councillors did service under Your Grace's father, praiseworthy in memory. They are honored and respected men, dedicated to their duty and never before suspected of any wrongdoing. None of them would have countenanced such words from the Duke your father; much less are such threats and insults proper on the lips of one so young and still lacking in experience. . . .

Second, Your Grace's words violate custom because neither emperors nor princes are known ever to have dealt with their councillors in like manner. Third, they violate human reason and are inimical to Your Grace's best interests. For consider, gracious Prince, what man would wish to become a councillor, or to remain one, if Your Grace were to employ such tyrannical words against him? Councillors are a prince's treasure and life. They must be treated humanely if their heart is to be in their work. Therefore, it is our desire and advice that Your Grace henceforth refrain from speaking in unseemly and ungracious tones to your councillors, and if Your Grace should persist, we shall be obliged to place the matter before His Imperial Majesty and before the [Bavarian] Estates, with results which Your Grace might well ponder in advance. [Duke Wilhelm replied as follows: He would not settle for fewer than thirty horses for his projected journey. Concerning threats and angry words: this was done without malice. Councillors should continue to do their duty and not imagine slights and insults].

Upon receiving each prince's answer, committee and councillors went into joint session to confer and deliberate. On the Wednesday following, at eight o'clock in the morning, they [i.e., their spokesman, Dietrich von Plieningen] made reply as follows:

REPLY OF THE COMMITTEE AND THE COUNCILLORS

BOTH Your Graces having replied to the articles submitted by Your Graces' councillors, the committee and councillors have in their meeting found His Grace Duke Ludwig's answer acceptable and therefore declare themselves satisfied.

Concerning Duke Wilhelm's reply, however, they are not yet satisfied and cannot, in duty and conscience, hold back further protests to His Grace in order to save him from inevitable scorn, contempt, harm, and disgrace. They are also anxious lest His Grace claim afterwards not to have been duly warned by those whose duty it is to warn him.

Brought, therefore, by dire need to further remonstrance, the committee and councillors say as follows: They find that Duke Wilhelm displays a quarrelsome and willful disposition most unsuitable in a ruler. He is a youthful prince, qualified by neither experience nor intellect at present to govern a principality. If his lord and father Duke Albrecht, praiseworthy in memory and who for forty-two years ruled the duchy admirably, were still living, he would not be ashamed today to observe and follow his faithful countrymen's and councillors' advice.

Natural law and divine law dictate *ne innitaris prudentiae tuae,* which means "do not depend upon your own wisdom." This is a piece of advice addressed to both old and young rulers, showing them that they should not pursue the impulses of their own knowledge and reason without considering the advice of others. Princes are, of all rulers, bound most by this principle. They must govern with the aid of a council, must do no one injustice, nor allow injustice to be done to any one.

There is, furthermore, a Greek maxim, γνωθι σαυτόν, in Latin *nosce teipsum,* which means "it is the highest wisdom to know oneself." The committee and councillors wish to admonish Your Grace to take this word especially to heart, to become aware of your own nature, and, seeing that God has created Your Grace a nobly born prince and appointed you co-ruler of a great duchy, to realize the following:

Item: Your Grace is young in years, inexperienced, and not yet schooled in the methods of good government.

Item: Your Grace's duchy is deeply in debt and in need of expert counsel.

Item: Your Grace must not imagine that, young as you are, you have grown so rich in wisdom that you can rule the duchy without counsel.

Item: No prince or sovereign on earth is entitled to use his power arbitrarily and unlawfully or to oppress his subjects in any way.

Item: As Your Grace is well aware, the [Holy] Roman Emperor has signed a capitulation binding him, on oath, to respect every individual's rights, traditions, and liberties. If the emperor, the supreme secular ruler of Christendom, is duty-bound to observe this rule, how much more should Your Grace and your fellow princes, to whom has been accorded the *utile dominium,* that is to say, practical sovereignty, feel obliged to leave your subjects' rights and customs unimpaired.

Neither pope nor emperor can deprive individuals of the *ius naturale* and the *ius gentium,* the natural law and the law of nations, which are derived from and are founded upon nature itself. Should a ruler so forget himself as to offend against these rights, his subjects are not obliged to suffer his transgressions passively. *Defensio* is a right accorded to subjects by nature. They may defend themselves. Even a worm turns by natural instinct when a large animal steps on him. A man can do no less.

Princes may so wrongfully govern their territories that they lose all princely prerogatives and are reduced to mere administrators or deputies. . . . The emperor himself admits his obligation to see justice done to everyone; all the more should Your Grace be eager to do what is right. This Your Grace ought to know, and, knowing it, you will be able to recognize your own nature.

A prince is the first man in his country. He must, before all others, be endowed with the virtues and practice them, else no one is obliged to praise or honor him. . . . Take this to heart, Gracious Prince. Be diligent in the practice of virtue and act virtuously until the day of your death. No one can ever learn too much. Follow the advice of your councillors. You are not free to live by your impulse and whim, for such behavior would lead you to a bad end. History furnishes abundant examples of good and bad governance. . . . Fear of God, virtue, and honest government preserve rulers and principalities; vanity, pride, and obstinacy destroy them.

Remember also, Gracious Prince, that you have given a written promise to rule with the aid of councillors until you reach your twenty-fifth year. Neither pope nor emperor can nullify this contract. . . . Nor is it an innovation in the Duchy of Bavaria for a prince to give such written guarantees. Our people have long held the privilege of being governed with the aid and counsel of their fellow citizens, and this is a right which pertains not only to the prince's period of minority but to his entire reign, even to his venerable old age. . . .

[V]

Oppression and Exploitation: Economic

14. Usury, a Dialogue on Interest. In Which a Peasant,
a Wealthy Burgher, a Priest, and a Monk Engage in a
Disputation on Lending, and Whether the Taking
of Interest on Loans is Usury (c. 1521) *

THIS ANONYMOUS DIALOGUE, written around 1521, brings together four stock figures of late medieval popular comedy to engage in a dispute over a point of enormous concern to all segments of German society. [See also No. 25 below.] It was published as a pamphlet with a title page woodcut showing a merchant seated at his desk, counting his money, while a peasant enters, carrying a sack.

PEASANT: God's greeting to you, good burgher, I wish you a fine day!

BURGHER: And a good season to you, my dear peasant. What brings you to my house this morning?

* Von der gült: Hie kompt ein Beuerlein zu einem reichen Burger . . . , printed in Oskar Schade, ed., Satiren und Pasquille aus der Reformationszeit, II (Hanover, 1863), No. 4. Also printed in Otto Brandt, Der grosse Bauernkrieg (Jena, 1925), 22–26.

PEASANT: What brings me to you? Why, I would like to see how you spend your time.

BURGHER: How should I be spending my time? I sit here, counting my money, can't you see?

PEASANT: I do see, but would you let me stay with you for a while? I'm in the mood for a chat.

BURGHER: Why not? Sit down and chat away. What shall we talk about?

PEASANT: Tell me, burgher, who gave you so much money that you spend all your time counting it?

BURGHER: You want to know who gave me my money? I shall tell you. A peasant comes knocking at my door and asks me to lend him ten or twenty gulden. I inquire of him whether he owns a plot of good pasture land or a nice field for plowing. He says: "Yes, burgher, I have a good meadow and a fine field, worth a hundred gulden the two of them." I reply: "Excellent! Pledge your meadow and your field as collateral, and if you will undertake to pay one gulden a year as interest, you can have your loan of twenty gulden." Happy to hear the good news, the peasant replies: "I gladly give you my pledge." "But I must tell you," I rejoin, "that if ever you should fail to pay your interest on time, I will take possession of your land and make it my property." As this does not worry the peasant, he proceeds to assign his pasture and field to me as his pledge. I lend him the money, and he pays interest punctually for a year or two; then comes a bad harvest and soon he is behind in his payments. I confiscate his land, evict him, and meadow and field are mine. Thus I gain both money and property. And I do this not only with peasants but with artisans as well. If a tradesman owns a good house I lend him a sum of money on it, and before long the house belongs to me. In this way I acquire much property and wealth, which is why I spend all my time counting my money.

PEASANT: And I thought only the Jews practiced usury! Now I hear that Christians do it, too.

BURGHER: Usury? Who is talking about usury? Nobody here

practices usury. What the debtor pays is *interest*. Interest, not usury.

PEASANT: But if you were not a usurer, why would you be drawing interest money? What is interest but usury? You lend your money on collateral security and extract an annual profit from your loan, which is what a Jew does when he lends on a pledge. When the Jew does it, you call it usury; when you do it, you make a subtle distinction and call it interest.

BURGHER: Why do you go on babbling about usury? What you say does not touch me. Did not our Lord Jesus Christ command us to come to our neighbor's help when he stands in need of it?

PEASANT: Yes, but our Lord also said: "If you lend to them of whom you hope to receive, what thank have ye? For sinners also lend to sinners, to receive as much again."

BURGHER: You are a fine fellow! Should I have no gain at all of the money I lend? If so, how shall I keep my money bags filled?

PEASANT: I see that you've got nothing in your head but thoughts of money and property. And you strut about town puffing up your cheeks and sticking out your fat belly as if to say, "Out of my way, rabble, here I come." But I tell you, it's a grave sin you are committing.

BURGHER: May God put a fever on you, you scurvy peasant! How dare you mention my bloated belly! Was it the devil himself that brought you here to torment me in my own house? If it were a sin to accept interest on loans, tell me, do you think the holy priests would be doing it? Go away, in the devil's name, and leave me alone!

PEASANT: Softly now, burgher. Don't fly into a purple rage. You are like all the rich and mighty of this world. You don't like to hear the truth, and when a fellow tells you the facts of life, you turn blue. You act like a donkey trying to shake off a load of sacks. He kicks and bucks, but the sacks stay on. The usurer is stuck with his name, like it or not.

BURGHER: Let the plague come down on you! Had I only been

a little wiser, I should never have told you how I make my money. I believe the devil wants to plague me with you.

PEASANT: But why do you fall into such a fury? I've said nothing about your usury but what everyone knows of it!

BURGHER: Should I not be furious when you sit here and make my honest interest out to be usury? I ask you: If it were usury or wrongful acquisition, would the priests be taking it?

PEASANT: Now you really make me laugh. Is a priest less likely to get his feet stuck in the mud than you or I?

A Priest enters

BURGHER (*to the priest*): O my good sir, I bid you welcome. You come in the nick of time. Let me relate to you how this miserable peasant has been dealing with me. Here I sit at my table, counting my coins, and in walks this knave with the devil looking over his shoulder and asks me how it is that I have come into so much money. I tell him that I get it from annual interest payments on the loans I tender, and he insists that it's not interest at all, but usury. I answer that if it were wrong to charge interest the clergy would not be doing it. What do you say to this? Am I not right?

PRIEST: Peasant, who do you think you are, telling us that charging interest is usury? Can a man not buy what he wants with his money?

PEASANT: O I am ready to burst with laughing! How each of you scratches the other where it itches! The priest, too, lends at a profit, calls it interest, and claims that his honest money has bought it. But I know better than that. You money lenders say, "We lend so-and-so much on such-and-such a piece of collateral." How, then, can you pretend that you have bought it, when it is a pledge?

PRIEST: We priests call it an honest purchase. For priests must make a living, too, and that is why we have given ourselves permission to lend money at interest.

PEASANT: O by the Belly! By the Skin! Who gave you power to grant yourselves this permission? I have often heard that priests and merchants worship a different God than we poor people do.

We love our Lord Jesus Christ, who forbade the lending of money for profit. But nowadays it has come to this, that wherever there is a piece of property, be it field or meadow, orchard or house, it has been so encumbered with usury—though you call it interest—that nothing is freely owned any more.

BURGHER *and* PRIEST: Do you wish to ruin us by calling us usurers? We tell you it is interest, not usury!

PEASANT: Interest indeed! You baptize two children. One you name Fritz, the other John. Both are children. Now, if you ask me what are the two, I answer: they are children. It's the same with lending money at a profit. Baptize it as interest or anything else, it's still usury, whether you or the Jews do it. But we scarcely have need of the Jews any longer, seeing how well we Christians have learned their business.

A Monk *enters*

PEASANT: Why, now the circle is complete. Call a piper to play for us, and we will dance.

BURGHER: Silence, cursed peasant. As the devil brought you to my house, let the devil carry you away.

PEASANT: Easy, easy, burgher. Nothing good can come from such outbursts. If you keep on puffing so, you'll turn red and ugly. Look at this monk here; how sleek he is about the face. Your wife may take a fancy to him if you don't stop your raging.

MONK: But my good peasant, why do you speak thus?

BURGHER: Let me tell you the trouble I've been having with this wretched peasant.

PEASANT: My, you are in a state, aren't you?

BURGHER: Be silent, in the name of a thousand devils! Can I not say one word without interruption?

PEASANT: Now I'll stay mum.

BURGHER: Good monk, this morning I am sitting here at my table, counting my money, when this lout comes in, demanding to know where I got my wealth. I tell him that it comes from annual interest payments due me from the loans I have made.

Whereupon he proceeds to tell me that such taking of interest is usury. What do you say to this?

MONK: Leave him to me, my dear burgher. I know how to persuade a peasant with kind words. Peasants are stubborn creatures and resist force, but in the hands of a skilled orator they are as soft as wax.

BURGHER: On with it, monk; take the peasant away and talk to him. Neither the priest nor I could say anything to him but that he had an answer for it.

MONK (*taking the peasant aside*): My good peasant, tell me this: Why do you say interest is usury when you know that it isn't? Is it usury when a man lends his money so that he may have an income from it? I have heard that a merchant who buys goods and sells them at a profit is guilty of usury. But surely that is a different matter. The interest we charge is not usury.

PEASANT: O what a pretty comparison this is. When a merchant buys merchandise with his money, is he not obliged to travel with it, in rain and snow, through mud and mire, until he has found a customer? Has he not expended his own capital in making purchase, and does he not take such grave risks that the whole transaction might be a loss to him? Interest on lending is another matter altogether. You people do not lend a penny unless you are sure of double its value in security. And when you make a loan of twenty gulden, you draw a hundred in interest from it. I call that usury; give it any other name you wish.

MONK: Let us speak no more of these things. We have said enough.

PEASANT: Yes, for I see that you do not want to hear such things discussed openly.

MONK (*To priest and burgher*): I cannot do a thing with this peasant. There's no knocking sense into his thick head. We had better be rid of him, or this argument will go on forever. (*To peasant*) Well, now, my good peasant, we shall part company. Let us leave things as they are and say no more about them.

PEASANT: What a pity. I would have enjoyed speaking with you at greater length, but now there's an end to our disputation. I go on my way, then. Farewell, good sirs. Interest remains usury all the same. Interest indeed!

15. *Interest and Profiteering: From Johann Agricola's* Commentaries on German Proverbs (1528)*

JOHANN AGRICOLA of Eisleben in Saxony (1496–c. 1570) was an important Protestant theologian, active as preacher, disputant, and ecclesiastical administrator in Saxony and Brandenburg. At first a close friend and associate of Luther and Melanchthon, he broke with both men on the so-called antinomian controversy—the question of whether repentance and sin-consciousness were to be based upon the Gospel alone, or, as tradition demanded, upon the Mosaic Law as well. Agricola was a vigorous exponent of the antinomian, or anti-Mosaic, position. As a prolific writer and preacher, his concerns transcended formal theology and touched on many of the issues affecting his society and time. These concerns are reflected in his explanations and commentaries upon familiar German proverbs, the first collection of which appeared in 1528.

"No man ought to gain from another's loss."

TRYING TO BE RICH is avarice. Now it is not possible for one man to gain wealth without inflicting harm on another, unless he attempt it by means acceptable to God, namely, reticence, thrift, and moderation. Freidank[1] writes: God created three kinds of men: nobles, peasants, and priests. The fourth kind is the breed of usurers. Usurers flay towns, cities, villages and countryside. Peasants earn their

---

* Johann Agricola, *Dreyhundert Gemeyner Sprichwörter, der wir Deudschen uns gebrauchen und doch nicht wissen woher sie kommen* . . . (Nuremberg, 1530), Nos. 224, 225, 226.

1. Freidank is the author of a thirteenth-century didactic poem *Bescheidenheit,* or "Wisdom of Life," containing maxims on most aspects of life. Sebastian Brant edited the poem in 1508.

living by drawing on God's bounty by means of animal husbandry, cultivation, orchardry and pasturing. If God bestows His blessing on them, they do well; if he withholds His blessing, they are ruined. For this reason they cannot engage in usury. Nobles are sustained and nourished by the husbandmen, as are priests, who collect the tithe. Cornelius Tacitus had words of high praise for the Germans, for, as he writes, even the kings and princes among them worked at ploughing, sowing, and reaping.

Freidank again:

> Five kinds of winnings we may claim
> Without incurring divine blame:
> Fish, timber, honey, grass, and fruit
> Were never thought illicit loot;
> These grow profusely from the soil;
> We gather them without great toil.
> Whom God permits such gifts to win
> May take and keep them without sin.
> From gold, however, wine, and grain
> We may not without sin draw gain;
> God bids us lend such products free,
> Asking no interest, charge, or fee.

Scripture calls usury *pleonexia*, greediness, arrogance, wanting much, and having much. The name of usurer is given not only to a man who engages in usurious acts but also—as St. Paul says—to one whose thoughts and secret intentions run to growing rich. Such men face two kinds of danger. The first is that, giving much thought to increasing their wealth, they are burdened with worldly cares and haven't a calm day on earth. The other danger is that they fall into the clutches of the devil, from which follow deceit and financial and other frauds to make themselves rich and inflict suffering on innocent people. . . . I have heard of a knight in Thuringia, Hans von Weyter by name, whose father left him little in the way of a legacy; but all his life long this knight lived frugally, refraining from commerce, mining, and other activities for which he had no use, increasing his small wealth without subjecting any of his fellow men to hurt or loss. There is not another nobleman in Germany today who has grown rich without doing harm to other people. Wealth almost never comes to one without leaving others impoverished.

"I am not allowed to charge interest, for I haven't the capital."

It is the custom in Germany to demand five gulden in interest for a loan of 100 gulden. Whoever lends 100 gulden is said to have earned five additional gulden as his interest. For it is claimed that the lender's 100 gulden, had he held on to them, would have gained him a profit of five gulden or more. Now a case may arise in which a man will make a loan of a hundred gulden to an artisan or a merchant who needs money to save his good name, and the lender will have profit from the loan all his life. In this way, many a wealthy person invests in a business and keeps his money in it as long as he lives. That, too, is usury, for in this wicked use of money the lender takes no risks and stands in no danger, as he ought to do if the taking of interest were to be justified. All the danger rests with the debtor; let him do well or ill in his trade; gain or lose, he will still have to pay interest.

In the same way, many of our German cities have gone to destruction. Someone lends a city 1,000 gulden, and the entire town pledges itself to pay interest. A great fire breaks out and engulfs the town; citizens move away, the town lies idle and becomes a wilderness—and still the interest must be paid, ruined though the city may be. By means of such tricks the clergy of our cities have succeeded in acquiring enormous properties. The principal sums of the loans for which they are creditors may have been paid ten times over, but they continue to draw interest. This, surely, is usury. How much more honest and godly it would be to limit the amount of the loan to what the property on which it is lent can support; then, if failure should occur in grain or in cattle, let the creditor suffer equal loss with the debtor.

It is a fact that those who wish to grow rich from usury must first put out a sum of money called the principal. Therefore, if a man wants to ridicule his own poverty and impotence, he says "I am not permitted to charge interest, for I haven't the principal." Or one may say of many common folk, "These are not usurers, for they are poor and have no capital."

"Get ready for work," said the hangman to his helper. "Here comes a merchant; we'll soon have a swindler in our hands."

I do not know how or where this proverb originated, but I assume that it arose from the fact that usurious acts, such as buying and selling, were thought to be dishonest among our Germanic ancestors. Indeed, they were held in contempt, as they had been among all the old nations, Roman, Greek, and Hebrew. God did not allow His people, the Hebrews, to harbor merchants and hucksters among them, and Holy Scripture rebukes the Edomites and Moabites as shopkeepers and men of business. Christ himself spoke out in the Gospel against attending to the cares of the belly, which is a concern fit only for heathens. A Christian and righteous man makes do with little, as we read in Proverbs 17: "Better is a dry morsel and quietness therewith, than a house full of sacrifices with strife." And in Psalm 37: "A little that a righteous man has is better than the riches of many wicked." A heathen ventures much, embarks on far-flung enterprises, and never says "enough." And if he could lord it over the whole world, he would do so.

Now I do not doubt that there is excitement in such adventures. The devil is master of the world and holds out temptations. He who touches pitch finds it sticking to him. Solomon says that whoever seeks danger will be destroyed by danger. The wise Cato wrote that no harm attends the gaining of an income from commerce and that merchants perform a useful service while they do business without deception. Even the taking of interest is permitted, says Cato, as long as it is done honestly. The ancients followed this practice, and put it into their laws: "Let a thief be punished twice, but let a usurer be punished four times." From this law we see that the ancients detested a merchant or usurer far more than a thief. And when they wished to praise an honest man, they called him "a good husbandman" or "a good plowman." Plowmen bring forth brave, selfless heroes and valiant fighting men. Moreover, peasants, who spend their days behind the plow, have little time to give to wicked thoughts of exploitation of their fellow men. All this was said by Cato.

Among our German ancestors good faith and honesty counted for much, as I have written above. Nowadays, however, trading and bartering have brought our land to such a pass that a man, if he would save himself from ruin, is compelled to cheat, defraud, and lie to his neighbors, for he himself is deceived at every turn. Not a business is carried on without lies and fraud. Merchants feel no longer bound to their old principle: "Let your speech be 'Yes, yes; no, no.'" Their new rule is "Tell a lie, and swear an oath on it." It has become proverbial to caution: "Don't trust a dog's limp or a merchant's vow." There is not a merchant in the land who offers his wares for what they are worth; instead, he asks what he thinks the buyer will pay. Hence the saying: "When fools go to market, the huckster buys money." A merchant swears before God and all the saints that it cost him so-and-so much to acquire his wares, but all the time he is ready to sell them for half the price. Therefore, it is a grave danger to one's soul to be a merchant or shopkeeper.

In ancient Rome, where rulers and statesmen used to be summoned directly from the plow and the field, things stood well with the government. Plain, honest, hardworking farmers aspired to honor and uprightness, not to riches. But later on the publicans, tax merchants, buyers, and sellers came to power and Rome fell. In Germany we now have a merchant who has built up an enterprise the like of which has never been seen among men since the beginning of the world. I speak of Jacob Fugger, thanks to whom we Germans have a great name in the world today. The honorable and distinguished Hans von Doltsch, marshal to the Elector Frederick the Wise of Saxony, states that this Fugger, in order to conclude with the King of Portugal an agreement which would give the two of them a monopoly over the entire spice trade, sent the king a present of such munificence that it would have been thought excessive had one emperor give it to another. Before this agreement was made, spices were cheap. Now the price goes up, just as it pleases Fugger and the king.[2] But in order to avoid the appearance of controlling the price, they arrange every other year to let saffron or ginger become a little cheaper, after which they push the price up again, as if there had been a bad harvest. The old laws expressly forbade monopolies and corners, but no one heeds such laws nowadays. It is said that there is not a prince in Germany who is not in debt to Fugger. Little wonder the laws cannot touch the Fugger and that they do as they please.[3]

As far as the currency is concerned, there is so much cheating going on in our day that, if you want to get hold of good coins, you must take from your savings and pay extra for them. This cheating is the cause of the circulation of bad coins all over the land, while good currency is being bought up by the rich and kept from everyone but usurers. Big-time merchants acquire mines, take the copper or silver from them, and sell the metal for minting; then they buy up the minted coins and take them back to the mines in order to drive up the price of silver. That is the way things go, and all this affects the common man, whose flesh and blood are being

2. This accusation, though universally believed at the time, is unjust. The enormous rise in the prices of saffron and other spices was due in part to a series of bad harvests, in part to the predatory commercial policies of Manuel I of Portugal.

3. The question of monopolies had been discussed at the meetings of the Imperial Diet at Worms in 1521 and at Nuremberg in 1522–23. Though it was recommended that steps be taken against monopolists, nothing in fact was done. The Edict of Madrid issued by Charles V in 1525 left decisions and actions on monopolies to the territorial or urban government in which the alleged monopoly existed. This was a major victory for the south German mercantile houses, led by the Fugger of Augsburg, over the general anticapitalistic temper within the empire.

sucked dry by such operators. Go to any of our larger German cities, and you will see that there is not to be found anywhere a youngster who is taught the learned languages and the liberal arts. Instead, as soon as he can read and write a little German, he is sent to Frankfurt or Antwerp or Nuremberg where he is stuffed full of reckoning and drilled in the tricks of commerce. We will see soon enough what harm will come to our German lands from such blindness! Mohammed was a merchant before he became a prophet, and we all know what misfortunes he brought upon Arabia. Having once gained a hold on his people, he did not let go until he had produced the Koran and misled many souls with it. God grant that this fate be kept from us Germans. Amen.

Does anyone now teach our young people about the good old ways? Does anyone tell them how honestly our forefathers used to conduct themselves? Instead, we bend them at an early age toward luxury and greed. We accustom them to so much abundance that they fairly drown in it. Is it not bound to follow that all honesty and fear of God will vanish and that nothing will remain except what is thought expedient and profitable? And what can this produce but a general corruption of all men and all lands? Business is beneficial, said the wise Cato, but it is not honest, for no one can do business without usury. Indeed, everyone knows that merchandise is unclean and that honest people are taken in by the false claims made for it. . . .

The hangman has a job to do. He obeys his instructions, and even though only the meanest of men enter his trade nowadays, he is in truth an executor of justice and a servant of piety in that he punishes the wicked for the evil they have done and for the sorrow they have caused the godly. A usurer and dishonest merchant, on the other hand, does incalculable harm to people and country. He cheats the bad and the good in equal measure. In fact, he is quicker to deceive the pious, who have no weapons against him and who believe his false words, while his fellow rogues see through his fraud and guard themselves from injury. Thus merchants and shopkeepers are far more injurious to land and people . than is the hangman; but in saying this I do not wish to imply that each and every commercial act is dishonest. We do have need of men who offer sundry articles for display and sale and who manufacture and import what is needful to us. We must not condemn one and all without distinguishing the straight from the crooked. No one could object to a man's getting an honest return for hard work and trouble. If a merchant buys dear, he cannot be expected to sell cheap. On the other hand, should he buy cheap, let him also sell cheap, and not raise the price of his goods to serve his avarice. Undue profit means advancing one's own interests and causing the public grievous harm, an act not only dishonest but against God and nature. For it is true that we must always do as we would like others to do unto ourselves, and not otherwise.

Not that I would be able to set an absolute standard or rule over prices. It must be left to the individual to determine the fair price at which he should sell, that is to say, the price he himself has paid. Doctor Martin Luther has taught us something about fair profit in his little book on buying and selling.[4] But what I can say is this: Trade, commerce, and money dealings are highly injurious even to the merchant himself, for the world is full of bad faith, mendacity and deception, and a merchant must needs be in the thick of it. . . . If commerce has such a bad name today, it is because each merchant assumes that he can honorably charge as high a price for his goods as the market will bear. Against this false notion I wish to relate what the ancient pagans, with nothing but their good reason and their sense of honor to guide them, have concluded on this matter (and if these ancients were living now, they would point to us Christians as pagans, seeing how we act against all honor and piety). Cicero, in his *De Officiis*, asks whether a thing can be both useful and dishonorable. He concludes that whatever is honorable is also expedient, and, conversely, nothing can be useful that is not also honorable. To illustrate this principle he poses two cases. A merchant sets sail from Alexandria to transport

---

4. The reference is to Luther's tract *Von Kaufhandlung und Wucher,* published in 1524 and containing some suggestions on how ethical profit might be calculated. Luther also recommended the institution of governmental commissions to set maximum prices on commercial articles.

grain to Rhodes, where there is inflation and great need of it. He knows that other grain ships are also preparing to sail for Rhodes. The question is: Should he inform the Rhodians that an abundant supply of grain is on the way, or should he keep silent and sell his own cargo as dear as possible? The second case: A man is selling a house which he knows to be in bad repair: weak pillars, rotten foundations, and so on. He alone knows the condition, which is concealed from view. Should he tell the prospective buyer that the structure is defective, or should he keep that information from him? By revealing nothing, he would be able to sell the house at a higher price; by telling the truth, he would cause the value of his property to fall.

Cicero's answer to both questions is that the man who keeps to himself information that he ought rightfully to divulge acts against honor, for he places his own advantage above the interests of the public. A man who advances his private affairs to the disadvantage of his fellow men is neither honorable nor good, neither just nor pious. He is crafty, dishonest, untrustworthy and cunning, a financier and a self-seeking, malicious rogue.

Thus Cicero. In the old imperial laws it was decreed that all buying and selling, lending and borrowing, renting and letting must be carried on *sine dolo et malo*, without hurt and deceit. If, by using deception, a man did harm to another, that man was liable for the damage suffered by his victim. Nowadays, however, injustice has conquered justice, vice has dethroned virtue, and shame has assumed the place of honor.

16. *How the Jews Were Driven from Regensburg* (1519)*

ALTHOUGH, as has been seen, the protest against usury and profiteering was by no means directed solely at Jewish practitioners, Jews

* From *Wie die new capell zu der schönen Maria in Regensburg erstlich aufkommen ist . . .*, printed in Rochus von Liliencron, *Die historischen Volkslieder der Deutschen*, III (Leipzig, 1867), 319–25:

became convenient scapegoats whenever popular feelings ran high. Like Jewish groups almost everywhere in the empire, the Jewish settlement in Regensburg, one of the oldest Jewish communities in Germany, found itself increasingly impeded in the course of the fifteenth century. Taxes and tributes were increased, their activities curtailed, and accusations of ritual murder and other crimes abounded. Caught in the crossfire of their complex legal and financial relationship to emperor, the Duchy of Bavaria, and the city of Regensburg, the Jews maintained themselves precariously through crisis after crisis; but finally popular passions generated by the fanatical sermons of the preacher Balthasar Hubmair (who was to become a hero of Anabaptism but played an inglorious role in the Regensburg affair) rose steadily against them. In 1519 the death of Emperor Maximilian, their shaky protector, sealed their fate. They were expelled, most of their property confiscated, synagogue and cemetery razed, and a chapel dedicated to the Virgin was erected on the site of their former habitations. The chapel became a favorite place of pilgrimage and the scene of many miracles.

The anonymous popular rhyme of which a part is translated below is entitled "How the New Chapel of the Virgin in Regensburg Was Built in the Year A.D. 1519" and tells the story of the expulsion. It includes a lengthy catalogue of Jewish sins and crimes which reflects suspicions, attitudes, and resentments common in late medieval Germany. I have tried in my translation to retain the awkward rhythm and forced rhymes of the original doggerel.

The poem begins by describing the universal rejoicing at the news of the expulsion, excepting only a few citizens with a financial stake in the continued presence of Jews in the city:

> Among the Christians were a few
> Felt pity for the wretched Jew;
> These loved not God and felt no urge
> To venerate the Holy Church.
> But other men were free of blame;

Among them Thomas Fuchs I name
And Simon Schwebel; furthermore,
The worthy Caspar Amman, nor
Should Johann Portner be left out;
Of Friedrich Stüchs you've heard, no doubt;
Hans Hyrstorfer, councillor-elect,
Wolf Kitztaler, Hans Ofenbeck,
Hans Hetzer, Adam Kölner too,
And Urban Trünkel also, who
Supports the Christian cause with might;
Stefan Pösinger I cite,
Georg Saller and Erhard Fiechtmair,
Wilhelm Wieland and Wolfgang Steirer;
Last but not least Hans Reusold, clerk
To the government of Regensburg.

By murder and usury, the Jews
Had done our city grave abuse.
Stirred by laments from young and old,
By pleas from all the land, I'm told,
The council acted. Otherwise,
Had council members shut their eyes
And left the Jews in impunity
They would have wrecked our community.
May our brave councillors be blessed
For having rid us of this pest.
God's purpose was behind their action,
For our Lord feels satisfaction
Whenever Jews are driven from
A famous city in Christendom.
God heeds the cries of honest folk
Oppressed beneath the Jewish yoke.
No craftsman's income is too small
For Jews to demand it all.
He needs a suit, a pair of shoes?

Off he goes trudging to the Jews;
There he finds pewter, silver plate,
Velvet and linen stuffs, brocade,
The things that he himself not owns
Jews hold as pledges for their loans,
Or buy from highwayman and thief
To make their pile from Christian grief.
Stolen or found, cheap stuff or rare,
Look at the Jew's; you'll find it there.
He's got the cash to lend on it,
No questions asked, depend on it.
A piece worth fifty gulden when
Bought new, the Jew gets it for ten,
Holds on to it two weeks or three,
Then claims it as his property,
Converts his house into a store
With pants and coats stuffed roof to floor;
A cobbler can't sell a pair of shoes,
Townfolk buy only from the Jews.[1]

But these misdeeds, though they are cursed
By all the world, are not their worst.
A graver crime and fouler deed
Lies on this Godforsaken breed.
Obstinate, blind, faithless toward
Their patient, kind, forgiving Lord,
They've always sinned, never repent,
As we learn from the Old Testament.
The five books of Moses, the Book of Kings
Show how the Jew to his habits clings;

---

1. Curiously, nothing is said here about usury. The average interest rate
on small, short-term loans was 43 per cent in Regensburg around 1500. It
could go as high as the legal limit of 86 per cent but was in fact much lower.
Rates of 43 per cent or thereabouts were not higher than the average rate of
mark up set by merchants on the cost of luxury goods and many necessities.

They prove it to satiety:
Jews are a race without piety.
We're told by wise old Jeremiah
That they killed their prophets with sword and fire.
David, among their kings the first,
They sent to hell despised and cursed.
Moses, a demigod to Jews,
They covered with hatred and abuse.
No wonder, given such behavior,
They crucified God's son, our savior.
They're in the dark, can't see the clearing,
They'll never give their prophets hearing,
Must live forever in God's ban;
Who gives them aid is no Christian man.

Jewish malignity was foretold
by the prophet Isaiah in days of old;
And if further evidence you desire,
Ask Doctor Balthasar Hubmair
To tell you why it is that we
Treat the Jews with such hostility.
He'll waste no time convincing you
(By quoting God's own Gospel, too)
That there's no punishment too painful
For a tribe so openly disdainful
Not only of Christ, their adversary,
But of his mother, the Virgin Mary.
For a Christian there's no sin so great
As to merit a Jew's love, not his hate.
Unceasingly the Jewish swine
Scheme how to violate, malign,
Dishonor the pure Virgin Maid,
Our Christian solace, hope, and aid,
Whose son died on the cross that we
Might live in bliss eternally.

No city therefore can fare well
Until it's sent its Jews to hell.

Now listen and pay careful heed
To a horrendous, bestial deed
Of Christian blood shed without pity
By murderous Jews in our city.
It happened in Emperor Frederick's reign;
Six children they killed with dreadful pain,
Into a dungeon then they threw them
To hide the bodies, bleeding and gruesome.
But soon their crime was indicated,
All of the Jews incarcerated,
And the burghers resolved, for the Virgin's sake,
To burn the damned Jews at the stake.
But—though to tell it is a disgrace—
The Jews found help in an exalted place.
Our council spent what money it could
To keep the Jews from winning their suit,
But with the emperor to defend
Their case, the Jews won in the end.
This caused complaints and lamentations;
Citizens sent deputations
To ask why Jewish dogs who spilled
Pure Christian blood should not be killed.
As for the Jews, they caught the drift
Of things, made many a handsome gift
Where money counts; their silver and gold
Regained for them their old foothold.
The burghers would have burned the Jews,
But the emperor saw fit to refuse.
The might and glory of his crown
Served to keep Jews in our town.
Our councillors resented this intervention,
Which frustrated their good intention

Of just revenge on the blaspheming Jew
For the innocent children whom they slew.
The gold sent abroad also caused them grief;
It could have been used for poor relief.
Three years they wasted in vain appeal,
But the emperor adhered to his deal.
Nothing the councillors could say
Would change his mind; the Jews must stay.

For forty years we pressed our case
Against the murderous Jewish race.
Of money paid out, the total score
Was a hundred and thirty-five thousand gulden or more;
The city registers record it.
Our citizens could scarcely afford it,
While the Jews, who had much more to spend,
Bribed the emperor's courtiers to pretend
To Maximilian, double-tongued,
That the Jews of Regensburg had been wronged.
Money makes lies like truth appear,
And the facts were kept from the emperor's ear.
Thus matters stood, justice defied,
Until the day Maximilian died,
And God eliminated a few
Of our Jew-loving burghers, too,
Which left the Jews without a friend
Their horrid actions to defend.
That's all I'll say about them here,
Their stubborn blindness cost them dear.
We're free at last of their oppressions;
May God forgive them their transgressions.

[VI]

Urban Discontent and Unrest

17. *Trouble among the Journeymen Furriers of Strassburg**

THE FIFTEENTH CENTURY brought changes and strains to nearly all industrial pursuits in urban Europe, notably to handicrafts whose operations transcended local boundaries. Most disturbing among these changes, and most far-reaching in its economic and social consequences, was a shift in the traditional relations between masters and employees. Many causes of this shift can be identified: specialization and divisions within crafts, influx of rural artisans, preferred advancement given to masters' sons and a growing sense of exclusiveness among the masters, increasingly severe financial demands and long waiting periods imposed upon candidates for mastership, the tendency of masters to act as businessmen rather than craftsmen, and so on. By the late fifteenth century few journeymen could entertain any real hope of establishing themselves as master artisans in their craft and, thereby, as citizens of substance. They were on the way to becoming instead a class of skilled wage workers in a trade.

Organization was the journeymen's natural response to these problems. At first religious in purpose and operation, journeymen's associations quickly turned to pressing economic matters, such as

* Printed in Georg von Schanz, *Zur Geschichte der deutschen Gesellen-Verbände* (Leipzig, 1877), Nos. 28, 44, 52, 57, 63, 64, 65 and 66; and in F. J. Mone, "Zunftorganisation," *Zeitschrift für die Geschichte des Oberrheins*, XVII (1864), 30–68.

employment conditions and hiring practices. Just as quickly they were resisted by the masters and by city governments in whose councils masters were prominent. The main bones of contention were the journeymen's claim to judicial authority over their own members and their insistence on setting up permanent organizations with officers, places of congregation, and compulsory membership—clearly recognizable signs of a militant pressure group in the making.

Trouble was bound to come. The documents translated below enable us to pursue a particular course of incidents as an instance of the friction and open unrest that occurred in many crafts all over Germany toward the end of the fifteenth century. No matter what their immediate outcome, these incidents left in their wake an unsettled and inflamed social situation which contributed materially to the tense atmosphere pervading Germany in the decades before the Reformation.

1404: THE JOURNEYMEN FURRIERS OF STRASSBURG FORM AN ASSOCIATION

IN GOD'S NAME, Amen. We, Hans, von Zofingen, burgher of Strassburg [there follow forty-seven other names of men from as many towns in the empire], journeymen furriers, as well as all other workingmen and journeymen of the furrier craft in Strassburg, make known to all who read this document, or who hear it read, now or at a later time, that we have resolved to join together, and, realizing that we ourselves and all other men born into this world receive our soul, body, and life from God's grace alone, that all things in this world are corruptible, and that we must all depart from this world and return to the earth whence we came, though when and where we cannot know, and wishing, furthermore, to do praise and honor to God and Our Lady his Mother, Mary, Queen of Heaven, we have agreed upon and drawn up a body of rules as follows, and these we submit with all good intentions toward our masters Master Heinzemann Hirzfelder, Master-in-chief of our guild [the names of four other master officials follow], and the jurors and other honorable masters of the furrier's guild in Strassburg, who have approved and accepted what we have asked, namely, that we shall be allowed to present a wax candle at the Dominican church in Strassburg where we hold our funeral ceremonies and that this candle remain there in perpetuity to the honor of God and Our Lady....

[As for organization: The journeymen arranged to have two locked chests, each with two keys, and four sworn members in charge of them. Each member of the association was to contribute three Strassburg pennies at that time, and thereafter half a penny a week. Rules were made for fining members who were late or delinquent in paying fees and for taxing new members or members away traveling. The association was also enabled to have masses said and to conduct funeral processions. Surplus money could not be spent on food and drink but was to go for pious offerings. Elaborate detailed procedures were drawn up for the guidance of treasurers and other officials.]

If it should come to pass that a member grow ill or fall into bodily need, a sum of money shall, on his personal pledge, be lent to him out of the common chest, as much as the pledge is worth. ... If he has no pledge to give, a loan shall be made all the same, but it shall be limited to three shillings....

ALL JOURNEYMEN furriers moving to Strassburg subsequent to the issuing of this document, and in service at a master's workshop there, shall observe the above-mentioned rules and obligations.... Whoever refuses to comply, be he a local person or a foreigner, shall not be employed by a master here, nor shall assistants or apprentices work with him until he has paid his fees like the rest of us....

THE RELIGIOUS language of this charter and the pious functions stated as the organization's principal objective, could not conceal its character as an economic, social, and ultimately political bargaining body. The masters chose to oppose it on an issue familiar to every student of medieval corporations: *Gerichtsbarkeit*—the association's right to judge its own members and execute verdicts against them—a powerful weapon for achieving group solidarity and independence from government. Quarrels abounded; at one point the journeymen left Strassburg in a body. In 1426 the association was forcibly dissolved by the masters and its funds confiscated. More strife ensued. Ultimately a compromise was reached.

1428: The Journeymen's Organization Is Allowed to Stand

WE, the journeymen of the furrier's guild in Strassburg, make known through this letter that, having in the past, like other crafts, established a fraternity among ourselves, and, having won for it the approval of the honorable wise masters and council of Strassburg, . . . we recently went before the said masters, begging them diligently and earnestly to ask the said council to restore our fraternity to us, which the masters did. In view of this, we have sworn by our oath that we will from now on refrain from holding trials among ourselves unless two masters chosen by the guild be present to hear and to help in giving judgment. The same two masters, for their part, agree to be available to us whenever we notify the master of the guild of our desire to hold a trial. . . . We ourselves undertake to observe and comply with the above-mentioned rules. And seeing that we do not have our own seal, we have earnestly and diligently requested that the furrier guild's seal be affixed to this document so that the articles contained therein may stand affirmed.

THE MATTER did not end there. While the journeymen were eager to use their organization to improve their position through collective bargaining and action, the masters, suspicious and vigilant, were determined to prevent any erosion of their control over the craft.

Confronted by a formidable combination of economic and political power, journeymen looked abroad for help. In the middle of the fifteenth century they established contact with craft mates throughout the Upper Rhineland. There was talk of strikes, followed by outraged reactions from city governments. The magistrates of Schlettstadt, for example, complained to Strassburg in 1463 of attempts by journeymen furriers to keep members of their fraternity from taking employment with Schlettstadt masters. This sort of threat, combined with similar troubles in other crafts, compelled Strassburg, along with neighboring cities, to issue a comprehensive law governing the conduct of all journeymen and lesser artisans. The crucial article is number four, governing negotiations for employment.

1465: The *Knechteordnung*[1] of Strassburg

. . . .

1. No MASTER shall henceforth enter into any association, fraternity, league, or combination with any journeyman or other worker, nor shall journeymen and workers make any common laws or regulations except with the express approbation of masters and council of the city.

2. All employed persons, whether indentured to knights, artisans, or burghers, and all journeymen residing in this city shall, furthermore, swear an oath of obedience to masters and council, pledging themselves to advance the interest and honor of the city and do nothing to cause it harm or injury as long as they shall serve this city and reside in it. . . .

3. No journeyman or other employed person shall from now on have a common room or house,[2] nor any place, house, or garden

1. *Knecht*, in this connection, means any artisan who is not a master, referring to journeymen, skilled craftsmen hiring themselves out for paid work, and lesser workers.
2. These common rooms (*Trinkstuben*) were established by journeymen in imitation of the older and prestigious convivial clubs used as exclusive gathering places by urban patricians.

in which to congregate for talk of common affairs or negotiation on conditions of work, nor shall they be permitted to form any kind of association for banding together. . . .

4. Journeymen shall not prevent a master from employing, for whatever reason, whomever he wishes to employ, for no employed person has the right to negotiate with a master or with another journeyman concerning conditions of employment. All such negotiations shall take place before the guild and nowhere else. . . .

5. Journeymen shall hold their funeral processions on holidays only, and not on working days.

6. No journeyman or other employed person shall henceforth carry a sword, foil, or long knife, nor any other weapon save a common bread or cutting knife not to exceed one span [c. nine inches] in length. . . .

7. No three journeymen or other employed persons shall wear identical hats, coats, trousers, or other identifiable marks.

8. Whoever violates any of the above stated points or articles shall not be given work by any master in this city. . . .

9. No city that has become a signatory to these articles shall alter them in any way without prior consultation with all the other signatory cities.

IN ACCORDANCE with these provisions, the furrier's guild sought to impose new restrictive rules upon its journeymen. The two following documents exemplify the many ensuing protests against these "innovations."

1470: THE JOURNEYMEN FURRIERS OF STRASSBURG APPEAL TO THE COUNCIL FOR A REVOCATION OF RESTRICTIVE REGULATIONS

WISE AND HONORABLE, gracious, dear sirs: Be assured of our submissive and willing obedience at all times. Dear sirs, we have learned from several members of our craft that the esteemed masters of our guild have taken it upon themselves to introduce a number of innovations directed against us and against several valid and amiable agreements concluded in times past, innovations which indeed go beyond anything we, who travel far in the pursuit of our trade, have ever heard or seen. These innovations have placed heavy burdens upon us and other persons employed in our craft. . . . We therefore pray submissively that your worships may have patient regard for the matter at issue and that we journeymen be left in possession of our old traditions and customs and not be disadvantaged, brought to injury, and enraged by the masters. . . .

THE FOLLOWING letter, also dated 1470, is signed by thirty-six journeymen furriers who had left Strassburg in protest and gone to the nearby town of Hagenau. It puts the finger at the crux of the issue.

. . . WISE AND HONORABLE sirs: Concerning the recent troubles between masters and journeymen of the furrier's guild in Strassburg, we have heard that the master furriers are asking your worships to compel journeymen furriers to accept employment procedures dictated by your command and intervention, which, though customary among tailors and some other trades, are an unheard-of innovation in the furrier's craft and never before encountered in German lands. Surely you know that our craft has long possessed the liberty of negotiating its own conditions of employment. We cannot condone an infringement on this liberty, whether it be attempted in Strassburg or elsewhere. We do not doubt that your worships have due regard to this liberty of ours, which was granted to us by your forefathers and predecessors and was affirmed and sealed by the city of Strassburg itself. We feel certain that you will wish to leave us secure in our just liberties and that you will do nothing to destroy our fraternity and our freedoms. . . .

AGITATION was not confined to Strassburg but affected the entire Upper Rhine region. Letters of support came from journeymen furriers in other towns, affirming that they, too, were asking "nothing else than to be left in possession of our old charters and seals." Plans were made for a general boycott. In 1470 the journeymen furriers of Colmar wrote to their Strassburg colleagues as follows:

JOURNEYMEN: It is our view that none of you must agree to take employment or suffer to be forced to do so. If one of your members should refuse to take part in our endeavor, if he falls into our hands, we shall hold him and deal with him, according to the custom of our craft, as one who has acted against the common interests of our fraternity.

ANOTHER call to boycott came from the journeymen of Willstätt, also in 1470.

OUR FRIENDLY GREETINGS, dear journeymen of the furrier's craft in Strassburg. Dear journeymen, we pray that you now cease all work in Strassburg until your masters shall have decided to respect once again our old traditions, privileges and seals. No honest journeyman will wish to work under the conditions now prevailing. We therefore caution you against allowing yourselves to be persuaded by your masters to act contrary to the interests of all good journeymen by accepting improper and illicit conditions. A man who submits to the masters against our cause shall not be forgiven for ten or twenty years. May God help you to conduct yourselves toward us as you would wish us to behave toward you. The new order which our masters are now attempting to impose upon us is unheard of in Germany, in Latin lands, and even among the pagans.

A GENERAL CONFLAGRATION seemed on the way. Journeymen in many quarters offered moral and active support and protested to the council against the "innovations" introduced in Strassburg. Journeymen in other trades (tanners, weavers, locksmiths, etc.) were learning the lesson pointed by the furriers and, in the 1470's and 1480's, established their own fraternal organizations as the best means of protecting common interests. Attempts to implement the rigid provisions of the *Knechteordnung* seem to have failed; in the statute book of the furrier's guild the text of the law, entered in 1465, is crossed out. Instead, a series of council acts brought about a kind of compromise which left to the journeymen some initiative in the all-important matter of finding and regulating employment.

The effectiveness of collective action had thus been proven. Still, journeymen lacked any real economic security, and their fundamental grievance—the gradual foreclosure of opportunities for becoming masters—was not redressed. Continuing unrest all over Germany and the threat of more destructive disturbances in the aftermath of the knights' war and peasant rebellions (see below) finally forced the empire into intervention. Two imperial decrees in 1530 and 1548 sought to strip journeymen's associations of their gathering places, their judicial rights, and their bargaining powers. Like most other imperial laws, however, the decrees could not be enforced. Fraternities managed to survive, and with them endured the agitation and turmoil of their members' struggle for economic and social justice.

18. *Grievances and Demands of the Craft Guilds of Cologne* (1513)*

THE HISTORY of the city of Cologne may serve as an example of the tenacity of democratic tendencies in some late medieval German

* The document translated here is in the archive of the city of Cologne, *Verfassung und Verwaltung* V61, f. 224 recto–232 verso.

communities. A revolution in 1396 had removed the old patriarchal nobility from office and established a government of craft and merchant guilds. Almost at once, however, a new ruling class emerged, a self-perpetuating oligarchy of a number of guilds and families. Involved in incessant friction and frequent wars with the archbishops of Cologne (who had left the city in the late thirteenth century) and with the neighboring states of Berg and Burgundy, charged with gross peculation and abuse of office, the oligarchic council could not prevent the rise of a powerful and aggressive opposition among the lesser guilds and lower ranks of society. A rebellion in 1482 proved abortive, but unrest was endemic during the following decades. In 1513 a real revolution broke out when an internal guild quarrel led to a public brawl and gathered revolutionary momentum until the city itself was seized by the guilds. Having formed a steering committee of 178 representatives of all crafts, the guilds handed the council a list of 154 demands and grievances, the most important of which are translated below. The list was evidently compiled from suggestions originating among the rank and file. As a statement of grievances it is ill-organized and repetitious, but as a redaction of *cahiers des doléances* it is of considerable interest.

The commission managed to maintain itself against both the old council and the radical revolutionary enthusiasm of large sections of the population. It eliminated the old oligarchy, formed a new government, and passed laws altering the city's constitution in the direction of greater democratic control over governmental procedures. No permanent improvements seem, however, to have been achieved. Unrest recurred within a few years, and a new list of 184 demands presented by the guilds in 1525 cotains many of the very points pressed in 1513.

1. THE GREAT MERCHANT FIRMS and associations operating in our city should be put under surveillance to the end that our privileges, including the Golden Bull, be observed and nothing done to injure the common good.

2. The importation of luxury commodities, such as spices, gold, silver, precious stones, silk, and so on, should be regulated by new laws according to what is best for the common good.

6. Attention is to be given to the general abuse in the sale of butter, cheese, and similar products, whose prices are subject to cornering and monopolistic manipulation.

7. Let no man be chosen councillor who is related by blood or marriage to princes, lords, priors, or abbots.

13. Every cleric, secular or regular, young or old, who has committed a misdemeanor or felony against the council is to be taken to the dean of the Cathedral Chapter, who should punish the cleric as though he were a lay person.

14. No wine shops or beer taverns are to be open on holy days, for this is a practice inimical to the Mass, sermons, and divine service.

19. Each *Gaffel*[1] should elect an honest man from among its members to place the council's management of public affairs, including revenues and expenditures, under close scrutiny.

22. No burgher should be allowed to have a fellow burgher placed under the ban of excommunication, except in matters of religion and in cases where testamentary provisions are ignored.

23. Our secular courts should be reformed so that every man will have his day in court within a month's time.

24. The clergy should be made to fulfill all promises and concessions given in the past.

25. Let the clergy be asked to make a substantial loan to the city.

26. A number of mills should be built on the brooks about the city.

28. The Beguine nuns should be gathered into a few houses where they may occupy themselves with spinning and sewing until they die. Their most valuable houses should be sold.

1. *Gaffel*, originally the name of a house (*Gaffel* = *Gabel* = fork) where meetings of one of the city's many associations took place; later applied to all such houses and to the corporations themselves, specifically to guild corporations and their meeting places.

30. No further annuities should be granted to clerical and secular persons, nor are any annuities to be paid unless claimants can prove clear title to them by means of charters or letters. As many annuities as possible should be paid off in lump sums.

32. Clerical persons should from now on bear the same civic burdens as burghers.

35. Every parish should pay its pastor a fixed annual salary. In return for this the pastor shall perform his offices without making a charge. No monk shall henceforth become a parish priest.

41. The marriage sacrament shall be available free of charge at all times.

47. Let the clergy pay taxes on the wine they tap for themselves.

57. Executive judges[2] shall have keys to all immunities[3] in the city.

62. Every *Gaffel* should have a copy of the city's concordats and contracts with the clergy.

64. No priest or chaplain shall be allowed to make a testament.

74. The [two] mayors should, as their oath of office demands it, walk about the city and inspect weights and measures and observe the weighing and measuring.

75. Hospitals are to be open so that we may visit our sick.

76. Every parish is to choose as its priest and chaplain wise men who can correctly interpret and preach the word of God so that monks may stay in their monasteries and the sacraments not be bartered to the faithful for money.

77. No priest shall administer a hospital.

79. Burghers should not be required to pay taxes on grapes grown in their own vineyards in the city.

80. We suffer egregiously from the lack of governmental supervision over the sale of butter, cheese, bread, beer, and other commodities, also from the absence of any inspection of weights and

2. The "executive judge" (*Gewaltrichter*) was the bearer of the city council's executive and police authority.

3. Immunity: a place exempted from secular legal and political jurisdiction and placed under the authority of clerical officials.

measures, and from the injurious practice of speculative buying.
82. Inventories should be made of all precious objects in churches, monasteries, and convents. If a monastic house should refuse to submit to inventorizing, let it be deprived of its rights to protection.

99. Every municipal office and each *Gaffel* is to be left in unimpaired possession of its traditional documents, seals, contracts, and charters.

101. No employee or servant of the mayors or treasurers shall hold municipal office. No person is to hold two or more municipal offices simultaneously.

107. Let the council attend to the problem of real properties willed by testament to the regular clergy. Such properties are required to be sold by the monks within a year and a day, but the following subterfuge is common among them: Having taken a lay citizen as a boarder into their monasteries, they sell to him *pro forma* all properties willed to them; he, in turn, wills these properties back to them, and so on and so forth in perpetuity. In this way the monks hold on to their worldly goods, legally and permanently.

117. All registers[4] should henceforth be kept in a special room established for them.

121. Let a house for prostitutes be established and all common whores be put into it.

131. Let the council supervise through its meat-market inspectors all fresh meat sold at market, and let the inspectors pay special attention to weights and measures, of which there has lately been a great deal of abuse, especially by foreigners.

142. Some burghers have banded together to form commercial companies for the sale of food products, such as butter and cheese. These companies hurt the common man in the following way: When food stuffs from abroad are brought into the city the companies lower their prices until the foreigners have left. Then they

4. "Register" (*Schrein*): the repository and storage place for privileges, charters, the texts of laws, and other important documents.

raise the prices prohibitively, and we are obliged to buy what we need at inflated costs.

145. Let five or six public scales be put up at various points in the city so that the common man may weigh his own bread, grain, and flour, also his fish and meat.

147. Let provisions be made for the care of the poor, for this is a Christian duty.

150. The council should instruct the preachers of the four regular orders to preach nothing but the true word of God and to utter no lies or fables, rather to be silent altogether and say nothing.

153. Let a sum of money be appropriated, and a number of able and honest men appointed to hold this money, for the purpose of lending to burghers in need of money, for personal or business reasons, on their pledges and at an interest of five per cent *per annum*. In this way the wicked and unchristian Jews lurking on the outskirts of Cologne[5] may be driven from our vicinity. Any man with a sum of cash on hand may, if he wishes, add to this reserve.

5. The Jews had been expelled from the city in 1424.

[V I I]

Peasant Protest and Rebellion

19. *The Articles of the Bundschuh in the Bishopric of Speyer* (1502)*

PEASANT UNREST was constant throughout the later Middle Ages, but the last years of the fifteenth and early years of the sixteenth centuries witnessed an increase in the frequency and violence of rural rebellion in Germany. For some decades before 1500 the laced boot (*Bundschuh*) commonly worn by country people had been used as a symbol of the hardships of peasant life and for demands for rectification. As early as 1493 groups of peasants and urban artisans had rallied round the *Bundschuh* in southwestern Germany, and in 1502 a *Bundschuh* insurrection in the diocese of Speyer protested against the unpopular bishop's financial exactions. Its leader, the peasant Joss Fritz, succeeded in organizing a considerable force—it has been estimated as large as 10,000, including a contingent of unemployed *Landsknechte* (see No. 31 below)—for attacks on the city of Bruchsal and on towns and castles in the Margraviate of Baden. The objective of this *Bundschuh* was epitomized by the inscription on its flag· "God's Justice Alone," that is to say, the liberation of men and women from subjection to laws and rules made by the bishop and other ecclesiastical and secular lords. Before the attack

* Printed in Günther Franz, *Quellen zur Geschichte des Bauernkrieges* (Munich, 1963), 73–76.

on Bruchsal could be launched, however, the plan was betrayed to the authorities, who took stern repressive measures. Joss Fritz himself managed to escape. The articles below are based on confessions extracted from the more than 100 arrested members of the conspiracy.

THE FIRST ARTICLE OF THEIR CONFESSION: They said that the principal reason for their entering into this association of the *Bundschuh* was their desire to abolish every remaining yoke of servitude, and, following the example of the Swiss, to gain their liberty through the use of arms as soon as their number had grown sufficiently and they had gained confidence in their ability to win in combat.

2. They confessed that those who joined their organization must first say five paternosters with the Ave Maria, kneeling, in memory of the five principal wounds of Jesus Christ so that God might grant success to their endeavors.

3. They chose Our Lady, the Virgin Mary, and St. John as patron saints. In order to have a secret sign of recognition they decided on the following password: One conspirator asks another, "What is your name?" The other, if he belongs to the conspiracy, replies, "The priests are to blame." Oh, the sinfulness of the peasant mind! What a bane it has always been to the clergy!

4. During and after torture they confessed that it was their intention to annihilate all authority and government. They had decided that, as soon as their number had grown large enough, their bands would fall upon anyone opposed to them and kill without mercy all those who dared resist.

5. They said that they had decided to attack first the city of Bruchsal in the bishopric of Speyer, where, they boasted, half the inhabitants were sympathetic to them. Having gained Bruchsal, they planned to proceed armed against the Margraviate of Baden and devastate everything that lay in their path.

6. They had resolved to pillage monastic and ecclesiastical possessions, also the properties of the clergy, and to divide the booty

among themselves. They wished to humiliate the servants of the Church and to reduce them in number by killing and driving out as many as possible.

7. They had agreed among themselves that, once enough peasants had assembled, they were not to stay in any one spot longer than twenty-four hours following a victorious battle but to move on from place to place until they had subjected the whole country to their conspiracy.

8. Such great confidence had they in their endeavor that they took it for certain that, once the war had broken out, no subjects would resist them; they believed, on the contrary, that peasants, burghers, and townsmen would freely join their association out of the love of liberty which all men share.

9. They confessed that they had decided among themselves to come together at dawn on Friday the day before St. George's day [April 22] to launch their assault on the city of Bruchsal. And they would have succeeded in their objective, due to the number of sympathizers among the citizens, had a chance occurrence not prevented the plot from being carried out.[1]

10. They confessed that their main targets were monasteries, cathedral churches, and the clergy in general. These they intended to strip of their properties and deprive of their authority. They also resolved never again to pay a tithe, either to the clergy or to secular lords and nobility.

11. They confessed that they had decided among themselves to take by force of arms all the freedoms they desired and would henceforth refuse to tolerate any man's dominion over them. They would no longer pay interest, remit tithes or taxes, nor pay tolls or dues of any kind. They wished to be completely quit of all duties and tributes.

12. They demanded that hunting, fishing, grazing, lumbering,

---

1. One of the conspirators divulged the plans for the conquest of Bruchsal during confession. Notified by the priest, the authorities arrested the ringleaders and suppressed their followers with the usual cruel punishments: death for men and exile for women and children.

and every other thing that had become a princely prerogative be returned to the public so that a peasant might hunt and fish whenever and wherever he had a mind to, without being hindered or oppressed by anyone.

13. The peasants agreed that their band would march first of all against the Margrave of Baden, the Bishop of Speyer, and the monks and clergy in the vicinity. Whoever undertook to resist them would be killed mercilessly as a disobedient and seditious enemy of divine justice.

20. A Description of the Bundschuh in Breisgau in 1513: From Pamphilus Gengenbach's The Bundschuh*

AFTER the failure of the attempted rebellion of 1502, Joss Fritz became for a brief time the ideologue and organizer of peasant insurrections in Germany. He exploited local dissatisfaction, established contacts with artisan and burgher groups, and formulated scattered grievances into a coherent program of reform. This program demanded primary loyalty to emperor and pope, autonomy of local courts, cancellation of debts when the sum of interest payments equaled the principal, liberal hunting and fishing rights for everyone, abolition of clerical pluralism, reduction of taxes and tolls, and a proclamation of general peace with severe penalties for violators. An attempt by the movement to attack the city of Freiburg in 1513 was another failure, and many of Fritz's co-conspirators were arrested. Fritz himself escaped and spent the remainder of his life roaming about Switzerland and the upper Rhine region, preaching and organizing rebellion.

Pamphilus Gengenbach, a prolific verse writer, publicist, and printer, wrote the following accurate, but unfriendly, account of the affair in 1514.

* Pamphilus Gengenbach, *Der Bundschuh*, printed in Karl Goedeke, *Pamphilus Gengenbach* (Hanover, 1856), 23–31. The prefatory rhymes are omitted here.

[147

THE ORIGIN OF THE BUNDSCHUH: HOW IT BEGAN AND HOW IT ENDED

IT BEGAN in the year after the birth of our lord 1513, in a village called Lehen in Breisgau. A baker's assistant named Hieronimus, a native of the Adige region, and another man by the name of Joss Fritz, the ringleader and instigator of this business, were conspiring together. The two of them were thick as thieves, always talking among themselves and with other men about how they were going to organize a *Bundschuh* and bring it off successfully. They used the following device for winning supporters for their cause: Coming upon a man who seemed the right sort for their undertaking, they told him that if he promised to keep it a secret they would let him in on something sacred, honest and of great value to himself, his family, and the entire country. Many a man hearing this said that he would be glad to help as long as their cause was honest and godly. Upon this they revealed their plans, which were as follows:

It was their opinion that from now on they should not acknowledge any lord nor show obedience to any sovereign other than emperor and pope. Second, they demanded that forests, rivers, and all game and fish contained in them be free and available to all. Third, all interest payments on land were to be abolished, and no further interest was to be demanded in the future. Fourth, no priest was to hold more than one benefice. Fifth, they planned to take from the monasteries all surplus income from interest and divide it among themselves and their children. Sixth, no one was to be tried in any court other than that of his locality. Seventh, no summons, warrant, request for payment, or decree of prescription were to be accepted in the future. Eighth, the court of Rottweil[1] was to be shorn of its power. Ninth, all those who joined their

1. The imperial tribunal at Rottweil in Alsace attempted to extend its jurisdiction over towns and villages in the countryside, setting aside the authority of village courts.

cause would be left unmolested. Tenth, whoever opposed them would be put to death.

These articles, and a few others set down here in all brevity, were agreed to by the entire group. At the same time they elected a captain, a standard bearer, and a sergeant. The above-mentioned Joss Fritz was chosen captain, and Jacob Hauser standard bearer, though the latter objected, protesting that he was too poor a man to serve in such a post. Joss Fritz replied that, if their enterprise should succeed, he would soon find himself handsomely equipped. When Hauser had consented, they asked for contributions toward the purchase of a flag. They also deliberated on a secret sign or password to use when one of their band wanted to be recognized by another; the word proposed was the following: One conspirator would say, "Good fellow, what news have you to tell " To which the reply was, "The poor man never will fare well." But they did not come to a final decision on this matter.

Having done all this, Joss Fritz and the bailiff in Lehen went to Freiburg to see an artist about making them a flag. They told him to draw upon the flag a crucifix, the figures of Our Lady and of St. John, also the papal and imperial insignia, and below these a peasant couple and a boot tied with golden laces. The painter, however, took fright when he heard of the planned *Bundschuh*, suspected trouble, and would not promise to do the work at once, telling the men to return another day. To this Joss Fritz would not agree. Instead he went to another painter to whom he told the same story. The artist said, "Is it true that you are organizing a *Bundschuh?*" Joss Fritz replied, "Not so. When I was a soldier, I made a vow to have such a banner designed, and I want now to go and offer it to Our Lady in Aachen. I am a shoemaker's son; that is why there must be a boot on my flag." In this way he persuaded the artist, and the banner was made. . . .

[SOON AFTER THIS] Joss Fritz, the ringleader and instigator, joined his comrades on the Hartmatte [a secluded meadow]. They decided that they would open attack as soon as their number had reached four hundred. Before doing so, however, they wished to inform His Imperial Majesty of their undertaking, and, if the emperor offered his support, make him their sovereign and leader. If not, they planned to appeal to the Swiss for aid.

In the meantime, however, the citizens of Freiburg had been warned of what was afoot and began to guard themselves. Learning of this development, Joss Fritz recalled his comrades to the Hartmatte and informed them that their plans had been betrayed, advising them to lie low for awhile. He asked all to swear an oath of secrecy. But Margrave Philip of Baden and the city of Freiburg had already captured a few of Fritz's followers. Fritz himself, Jacob Hauser the standard bearer, and a third man decided to flee to safety, but as soon as they entered the territory of the city of Basel they were arrested and thrown into prison. Joss Fritz escaped, carrying the banner away with him, but the two other men were taken before the court in Basel. May God show them his grace and mercy, for God guards and protects all decent, pious, honest folk from wicked undertakings and grants them the wisdom to show obedience to the rightful authorities. . . .

21. *The Arme Konrad: From the Statement of Grievances Drawn Up by the Territorial Diet of Württemberg* (1514)*

THE *Arme Konrad* of Württemberg was more than a peasant rebellion. Involving members of all estates and social groups, the movement directed itself against those aspects of territorial centralization which were felt to be violations of ancient customs and traditions (cf. No. 13 above). Duke Ulrich of Württemberg had tried to rid his land of inherited debts by introducing a particularly noxious form of taxation involving the reduction of weights and measures. In May 1514 a peasant named Peter Gais threw a few of these weights into

---

* Printed in Günther Franz, ed., *Quellen zur Geschichte des Bauernkrieges* (Munich, 1963), 50–53.

the river Rems, calling on them to float to prove their legality. Groups of peasants, artisans, and burghers took up the cry of "poor Konrad" (Konrad or Kunz being a generic name for the common man), and a *Bundschuh* seemed to be in the making. Fearful of the consequences, Duke Ulrich made some concessions and called the *Landtag*, the territorial diet, into session. From the articles of grievance presented to one of the meetings of this diet, the selection below emphasizes complaints against the judicial and bureaucratic aspects of ducal centralization.

8. WE ASK that the councillors and secretaries of the chancellery be chosen from among honest, pious, knowledgeable, and competent persons who must not be related to one another by blood or friendship (as has been the custom in the past and is still at present) and who should be concerned only with advancing the honor of God and the common interest of our gracious sovereigns and their country rather than seek their own advantage as they have been doing in the past by means of the imposition of new taxes and burdens profitable to themselves but painful to the country. . . .

15. Due consideration should be given to the plague of learned lawyers that has been infesting legal business in every court in the land, the result being that the cost of litigation, which, twelve years ago, came to only a few pennies, runs nowadays to ten gulden or more. These are grievous innovations for the common man, and they ought to be brought to an end; if not, each village will, before long, need to hire one or two doctors of law to handle its judicial business.

16. Inasmuch as these learned lawyers and jurists have caused disruption and disarray among the agreements and other ancient customs and usages in our towns and villages—much to the hurt and disadvantage of the common man—there should be instituted, drawn up, and promulgated a general reformation and renovation of the laws of our land; if not, towns and villages should be left to

their wonted customs, laws and courts, as these have come down to us from ancient times, lawyers and doctors of jurisprudence notwithstanding.

17. We ask that our gracious prince and lord endow the posts of bailiff and tax collector with good salaries and appoint to these offices only honorable, God-fearing, competent, and affluent persons who are well disposed toward the common man and will administer their offices honestly, performing all their duties in their own persons and not through deputies or vicars. . . .

28. Soldiers on horseback and huntsmen should be required to proceed along roads and pathways rather than cross-country through our fields and meadows, for in riding over our land they cause great damage to crops, fruits, and other products. The destructive practices of conducting the chase and hunt across our fields ought also to cease and be forbidden.

40. Our gracious lord ought furthermore to make a law concerning wild game on our properties, especially for the summer months from Easter to autumn, when the poor man's fields and products are commonly destroyed by game and no remission is allowed him in the payment of rent and dues.

41. Item: No official in our gracious lord's chancellery accepts complaints concerning wild game or actions of the forester, nor do they undertake to rectify any of the above-mentioned abuses. Instead they refer such complaints to the foresters themselves, who are therefore in a position to act as prosecutors, witnesses, and judges all at once, much to their own advantage and to the harm of the common man.

42. Inasmuch as foresters, their assistants, and other officials have been appropriating some common lands and brooks, although these had always been free and open to all, and have proceeded to award these to whomever they please, it is our humble plea that such brooks and common lands be made free again, as they were in ancient times.

46. Recently the foresters have begun to sell the brushwood left on the ground after firewood has been collected. In former times

the poor had always been entitled to gather the brushwood, a custom less injurious to our lord's forests than the new practice, for what the foresters now sell as brushwood is better stuff than firewood used to be. This practice damages the interests of our gracious lord and infringes the rights of the poor, whereas it is of great profit to the forester.

47. In many places the foresters employ assistants and retainers, though in the old days no such sub-officials were known in the territory. Moreover, many of these assistants are disorderly persons, inclined to exploit and punish the poor. It should also be remembered that our gracious princes are obliged to remunerate these assistants with good money, which is a considerable expense and a loss to their treasury.

50. These foresters commit a further abuse in allowing pigs from other regions to be led to our acorn feeding places, much to the harm and disadvantage of the poor folk in our territory. We ask that this practice be halted and no outsiders' pigs be let into our forests....

22. Articles of the Peasants of Stühlingen and Lupfen (1525)*

THE TERRITORIAL COUNTY of Stühlingen was situated in southwestern Germany in a region of petty domains, small towns, and monastic territories. Unrest and rebellion began to occur among the rural population there in the spring of 1524. In June of that year the peasants of Stühlingen, irate over demands that they leave harvest work in order to collect snail shells on which the ladies of the manor could wind their thread, rose against their territorial and ground lord, Count Sigmund von Lupfen. The Count, who had been left in desperate financial straits by his spendthrift father and was bent on

* Printed in Günther Franz, *Quellen zur Geschichte des Bauernkrieges* (Munich, 1963), 101–23.

extracting as much revenue as possible from his subjects, turned a deaf ear to his peasants' demands. When attempts at mediation failed, the peasants organized military units, chose a captain, and sought help from the nearby city of Waldshut and from Duke Ulrich of Württemberg, who had recently been exiled from his lands by the Habsburgs and was looking for a cause to help him restore his fortunes. These events, and their consequences, led to the great peasant war of 1525.

In the end, the demands of the Stühlingen peasants were arbitrated and transferred to the Imperial Chamber Court (an extraterritorial, national appeals tribunal) for action. The list of articles below, translated with a few minor omissions, was drawn up for the justices of this high court. A detailed statement of grievances and demands, it is an excellent summary of the conditions of peasant life in western Germany at the end of the Middle Ages. Appealing on nearly every point to the "ancient traditions and customs" that were thought to have guarded village autonomy against attempts at state-building by centralizing territorial princes, peasant spokesmen pleaded for a reversal of the Count's steady encroachment on their independence and for a mitigation of the innumerable petty chicaneries, exactions, and regulations that stunted and frustrated rural existence at almost every turn. The articles are notable also for the absence of any references to the Church and the religious question. Issues in Stühlingen were practical and mundane.

1. THE COUNTS of Stühlingen and Lupfen should not imprison any resident involved in a civil action.

In the old days it was the custom and usage in the above-mentioned county to imprison no one against whom a civil action was pending, as long as the man held some property in the county and was willing to furnish surety for the matter or sum being asked of him. In recent times, however, our lords have ignored our village courts, where, according to our laws and customs, they should bring action. If they think that a man owes them something or if they suspect that someone has committed an offense, they order the bailiff to take the accused to prison and let him lie there until he has made his peace with them according to their bidding. . . .

2. No one should be tried for felony in a court other than the one with jurisdiction over his place of residence or the place where the offense was committed.

Although we have our own courts for criminal, including capital, matters and although it has been the custom up to now to try no offender in a superior court or away from the court in whose jurisdiction he committed his offense and was apprehended, our lords have introduced an innovation by transferring cases from our village courts to their superior court. This practice does us much harm, for a man who enjoys the counts' favor will not be punished in their court according to the gravity of his offense. Furthermore, it is up to us to escort the prisoner to this distant court, which is a venture requiring much trouble, pain, cost, and risk. . . .

3. Our lords confiscate both the stolen and the personal property of a condemned thief.

When a man is hanged for theft, our lords take not only the stolen goods, or as much of them as can be recovered, but his other property as well, which is a practice against all law and custom. For, according to custom, damage may not be added to damage; to act contrary to this custom is most unjust to the poor widow and orphans, who are obliged to repay the debt out of their own pockets. We request that the counts be made to realize that in the case of a condemned and executed thief the stolen property should be returned to the man from whom it was stolen and that the wife and children of the condemned man should not be done out of the remaining property, no matter how it was acquired. . . .

5. If a man snatches a stolen article from the thief, he is obliged to surrender it to the counts.

If it should happen that a man from whom something has been stolen succeeds in forcing the thief to surrender the loot, either in part or in its entirety, he is forced to hand it, that is to say, his own property recovered by him, to the counts. And if he should conceal from the counts the recovery of his property and they become aware of it, they punish him. . . .

6. What happens when a marriage partner dies and the deceased is claimed by the lord as a bondsman.

Marriage is an institution sanctioned by divine and Christian laws and is, moreover, free, so that in case of death nothing should be taken away from either of the partners. But when a man or a woman of the county takes for wife or husband a person not from the county and not bonded to the count, and the man dies and is claimed by the count as his bondsman, the count's officials come and take the best head of cattle. If the woman dies, they take her best frocks, even her wedding garments, and sometimes also a bed. In some places they also take clothes when the husband has died. It is our request that in future such exactions cease and we be no longer compelled to surrender cattle, clothes, beds, or anything else in case of death.

7. What happens when a man takes for a wife a woman not in bondage to the count.

If a man should take for wife a woman from another village who is not the property of the count, and the woman dies, the count takes the third part of the entire property without any compensation, regardless of debts remaining to be paid off and orphaned children to be raised. Sometimes he takes our cattle even though half of it may still be unpaid for. . . .

8. Marriage with a person from another county is forbidden without the count's approval.

We are further oppressed by the unchristian practice of refusing a man or woman permission to wed a person not subject to the lord. Even when this permission is granted, it is given only after a long delay. And if one of us should enter into such a marriage without permission, he is punished for it by the lord or his bailiffs. . . .

9. If our jurors give judgments displeasing to our lords' bailiffs,

they hale the jurors before the territorial court, which means that our jurors cannot judge freely.

Although our jurors have sworn an oath binding them to judge freely, fairly, and according to their true understanding of the matter brought before them, neither favoring nor disadvantaging anyone, it often happens that when a bailiff takes a matter pertaining to the count's business before one of our village courts and is displeased with the judgment given by our honorable jurors, he summons the jurors before the territorial court, claiming that they did not judge correctly in the matter and demanding that they be punished. From this practice it follows that jurors cannot be free and secure in their deliberations and that parties against whom the bailiff appears as plaintiff must always be prepared for an unjust verdict. . . .

10. We are all, young and old, summoned to court when a capital case is tried.

When a man is tried for a capital crime in the counts' court, the bailiffs round up all villagers above fourteen years of age and tell them to assist at the trial and to remain there on pain of punishment until it is ended. From this we have no benefit whatever; on the contrary, it does us much harm, for we must abandon our work and leave our houses unguarded. . . . It is our plea that the counts should cause to be summoned only one from each village to be present at court along with the judges. . . .

11. Sub-bailiffs should be appointed with the approval of the community or elected by the majority of its members.

Although it used to be the custom of the county to appoint a sub-bailiff with the knowledge and approval of the community or else to have him chosen by a majority of its members, our lords have in recent times undertaken to appoint sub-bailiffs without our knowledge and will, selecting them according to their own pleasure and taking only such men as are pleasing to them. A sub-bailiff appointed in this way is bound to wish to please the lords and their bailiffs, for if he fails to do so, he loses his office. Moreover, many men are now appointed sub-bailiffs who are not suitable for this post. . . .

12. We are forced to have our legal documents notarized by the territorial scribe [*Landschreiber*] even though territorial courts have no authority over our written business.

Our lords oblige us to have our papers, such as purchasing agreements, contracts, bills of sale, and other documents, drawn up by the territorial scribe, although the old laws give us leave to have them done and sealed at our own village courts at nominal cost. It is therefore our request that in future all documents pertaining to our affairs be written and sealed by the authority of our own courts. . . .

13. We are forced to provide carting service and other help to foreign lords and noblemen.

Although we are always willing to give aid in body and goods to our own lords, we feel sorely oppressed by our lords' demand that we journey to meet visiting foreign rulers and nobles, from which obligation we suffer heavy costs and risks. According to our old laws and customs we do not owe such service to foreigners, and it is our plea and request that our lords henceforth refrain from demanding it of us. . . .

14. We are prevented, in violation of the old customs, from gathering wood in the county's forest.

In the old days we were always free to go to the forests to fill our need of lumber and firewood. But in recent times our lords have abolished this ancient custom, and we are now no longer permitted to gather wood in the forest as of old, which is much to our harm and injury. . . .

15. Our lords and their bailiffs and retainers do their hawking and hunting on our fields without showing consideration for the condition of our crops.

We till our fields and meadows with great effort, cost, and work so as to be able to fulfill our obligations to our lords and to nourish our wives and children. In return for this our lords and their bailiffs ought to guard us and our property and protect us from harm. Instead, they ride and tramp over our meadows and fields in pursuit of the pleasure of hunting, hawking, and the chase. They do this without giving a thought to the harm and grief that come to us as we see our crops so brutally destroyed. It is our plea that our lords be made to realize that they should refrain from this destructive sport, but if they persist and we continue to suffer the ruin of our crops, they should be held accountable for the damage.

16. In violation of the old customs our lords have appropriated the brooks running through our property and given the fishing right to other persons.

Many of us have lands and meadows watered by brooks and rivers, and these we have always, according to tradition, had the right to employ for irrigating our fields and driving our mills, for it is generally accepted that water is free and common to all. But in recent years our lords have taken this right away from us and leased the waters to fishermen, who have inflicted grave damage on our properties by tearing down dams and weirs, thus making it impossible for us to use our mills and water our meadows. . . .

18. The widow and heirs of a murdered man are obliged to pay the costs of the murder trial even though the guilty party may have escaped and the widow has taken no legal action.

In our county, when a man is slain and the killer escapes and the friends and heirs of the victim do not press charges, the counts arrogate to themselves the right to initiate the trial, the costs for which must be borne by the victim's widow and children. Inasmuch as it is not right that a widow who does not press charges should bear court costs, we ask that our lords not insist in such cases that the widow or children or next of kin meet the expenses of the trial.

19. Our lords claim to be the legal heirs of all children born out of wedlock, to the exclusion of next of kin.

When an illegitimate child dies, our lords lay claim to the deceased's belongings and goods, excluding the next of kin, though this may be a brother or a sister. We wish it recognized that brother, sister, father, mother, or next of kin should inherit in such cases ahead of our lords. . . .

20. The penalty for assault used to be three or five shillings, but now this offense is treated as a felony.

The old customs hold that when a man strikes another on the face and is convicted of it, he forfeits a fine not to exceed five shillings and is tried before his own sub-bailiff or bailiff. But nowadays our lords have begun to treat the offense as a felony and transferred jurisdiction over it from our sub-bailiffs to their own officials. We ask that the old custom be restored and the offense in question be treated as nothing more than a misdemeanor and not as a felony. . . .

22. We are forced to grind our grain in distant and inconveniently located mills.

Although the county of Lupfen and Stühlingen has many mills conveniently situated to meet our needs, we are compelled to take our grain to a mill in the counts' domain at a great distance from our villages. It is our plea that we be left free to grind our grain wherever it is convenient for us. . . .

23. We do not know the origins of the interest and rents we are said to owe the counts.

Although we have for many years made annual payments of interest, dues, and rents to our lords, we confess that we do not know the origins of these payments, nor do we know for what reason we are obliged to make them, nor what obligations our lords owe us in return for them. We ask that the counts be required to inform us of the origins and causes of these interests, dues, and rents by showing us credible documents stating why we must pay them and what duties they owe us in return. . . .

24. We are aggrieved and oppressed by a great number of required services.

Over and above what we have stated so far, our lords and their bailiffs burden us with insufferable servile tasks, in the performance of which we are forced to neglect our plowing and other work so that we do not know how to nourish our wives and children. We ask to be relieved of services such as the following:

We are obliged to harvest oats, bind hemp, till and sow, plow, cut grain and cart it the threshing floor, thresh, take the grain to the manor house, mow the grass, do the haying, and take the hay to the barn; we must also repair yokes and reins, lay traps, and take captured game to the manor or from the manor to other places wherever it pleases our lord to command us to take it.

We must transport wine at our own expense from wherever his grace the count buys it . . . to Stühlingen. We must supply the manor not only with firewood but also with building lumber. We must clean the fields and cart and spread manure. When it is time for us to sow, the counts ask us to dig roots, gather mushrooms, cut juniper berries, and break barberries so that our gracious lords may enjoy their blackthorn sloe stew. Our wives and servant girls must pluck hemp and prepare it for the distaff.

We must transport grain from Schleitheim to Schaffhausen, cart oats to Stühlingen and Schaffhausen, and take grain and oats from Bondorf to Stühlingen and Schaffhausen. We have to mow and cut for the bailiff and weed the manor gardens—and this we must do three times a year. We must mind the bailiff's cattle, and, even though we are supposed to be relieved of plowing duties (in return for which freedom we give tributes in grain, hay, seed corn, and money), we are often forced to till and plow the lord's fields.

We are obliged to keep the counts' hunting dogs, which not only means an expense for us in feeding them but causes great loss of chickens and other fowl killed by the dogs. . . .

Furthermore, we have always in the past been allowed to cut sticks and hazelnut staffs for basket making, such baskets being a good source of added income for a poor man. But our lords have now forbidden this. We ask that the counts return to the old custom and let us cut sticks without interference or punishment.

26. The village of Witzen in the county of Lupfen is forbidden to keep geese and ducks.

In some villages in the county of Lupfen, among them Witzen, the villagers are forbidden to keep geese and ducks though they make good eating and are a source of income for the poor. . . .

27. When a man is burned at the stake we must furnish the wood for the pyre.

Whenever a criminal is to be burned at the stake, a number of villagers are required to furnish the wood regardless of the fact that this deprives the poor of their property.

31. The counts collect the toll, but we are the ones who build roads, paths, and bridges.

Although it is customary to levy tolls only for the purpose of building and maintaining roads and bridges, the counts of Stühlingen take the tolls for their own treasury while we are forced to expend money, pain, and labor for building roads and bridges and keeping them in good repair. . . .

32. If a man finds an article he must surrender it to the counts.

If a man inadvertently comes upon something useful or valuable he must notify the counts, and if he fails to do so, he is harshly punished for his omission.

34. A man's first trial should be before his own judge.

Although we have our own [village] courts and jurisdictions and although our rights as well as the laws of the empire demand that each man should in the first instance be tried before his own judge, we are frequently summoned before the counts' territorial courts, a practice which imposes grave burdens on us through loss of time and travel expenses. . . .

35. Concerning the "bailiff's dues."

Although we have been faithful in giving our lords all that we owe them according to the old customs and traditions, they have recently introduced an innovation by imposing an excise upon our properties, the payment of which we are forced to render annually. This excise is called "the bailiff's dues" [*Vogtrecht*], and we are much aggrieved by it. . . .

36. Our lords treat non-criminal offenses as though they were criminal offenses and cite them before the criminal court.

Although the common written law explicitly identifies offenses that are to be regarded as criminal and other offenses that are not criminal and should not come before a criminal judge, our lords are inclined to bring criminal actions against persons accused only of civil offenses. . . .

38. A man may not pour wine unless he does so throughout the year.

If a man has a barrel or two of wine and retails it for a period of two or three weeks but not for a whole year, he must pay a fine of three pounds of silver. It should be recognized that a poor man cannot afford to buy enough wine to retail it for an entire year; hence, we ask that each of us be allowed to buy and sell wine according to his ability and desire and to cease selling it whenever he wishes without fear of punishment.

39. One who leaves the county, or inherits property in the county, must pay heavy taxes.

If a man wishes to move from the county or if a man inherits something in the county and wants to remove it, he is forced to pay a heavy and unjust exit tax on everything he takes abroad. Moreover, this tax is inequitably assessed according to whether our lords are well or ill disposed toward a man. . . .

40. Concerning the forester.

Although, according to the common law, animals and wild game are free and available to everyone, we have been sorely oppressed by the imposition of a forester. If a man wishes to hunt or trap birds, foxes, rabbits, or small game, or to cut himself a stick or a piece of bark, he is now forced to pay the forester. If the forester favors him he sets a low price; if, on the other hand, he does not like a man, he charges a large sum.

41. Wild game ought to be altogether free.

We perform long and hard labor on our fields in order to raise crops (of which we are obliged to give a portion to our lords) and to make a living for ourselves and our wives and children. But much of our work is brought to nothing by the profusion in our land of wild game, which is ruinous to our crops. Though God and the common law decree that wild game, having been created to supply the common needs of mankind, may be trapped and hunted by everyone, our lords have proclaimed injunctions and heavy penalties against the snaring, trapping, hunting and catching of game. If a man violates these prohibitions and is caught, they gouge out his eyes or torture him in other ways according to the counts' or their bailiffs' pleasure. It is our plea that, by the authority of divine and common law, we be henceforth permitted to hunt, shoot, and trap all game found on our fields and properties and use it to fill our requirements. . . .

42. Concerning the game fences placed on our fields.

They have come to our fields (for which we must pay steep taxes and on which we perform hard labor) and put up game fences, though some of them are never used for anything. When, wishing to plow or rake, we undertake to remove the fence or a section of it, they punish us and, moreover, they refuse to allow us to shut the fence again, so that animals may enter freely and damage our crops. . . .

44. Concerning the bathhouse built by the community and then taken over by the counts.

Not long ago the community of Stühlingen built, at its own cost and with its own labor, a public bathhouse. . . . Recently, however, the counts illegally confiscated and expropriated this bathhouse, without offering any compensation to us, and gave it to a bathing master, who now boasts charter and seal to prove his ownership. Inasmuch as no one should be deprived of his property without legal action nor should be forced illegally to surrender what belongs to him, we ask that the bathhouse be restored to the community and the bathing master be given his leave. . . .

50. Contrary to the old customs we are forbidden to buy and sell salt.

The ancient laws and customs of Stuhlingen entitle every burgher to buy and sell whatever he wants to. Not long ago, however, the counts issued a decree and command preventing everyone but the territorial scribe from selling and retailing salt. We ask it to be recognized that this should be abolished, the ancient traditions and customs be left undisturbed, and we be permitted to buy and sell salt as we please.

52. We are forbidden to sell geese and ducks except to the manor house.

We may not buy or sell ducks and geese without the knowledge and approval of the count. We are forced to take our ducks and geese to the manor and offer them for sale there and take for them whatever the bailiffs are willing to give us.

59. Concerning bondage and serfdom.

Although by rights every man is born free and neither we nor our ancestors have been guilty of anything that should have made serfs of us, our lords claim that we are and ought to be their bondsmen and that we are obliged to do whatever they command us to do as though we were born slaves—and it may well happen in time that we will be sold like slaves. It is our strong plea and request that the counts be made to recognize that they ought to release us from serfdom and should never press another man into bondage. Apart from this plea, we pledge ourselves to act as loyal subjects, and we promise faithfully to perform all the duties we owe to our lords according to custom and tradition.

PETITION

WE RESERVE to ourselves the right to augment, reduce, or otherwise alter the above list of grievances and complaints. We ask that each and every article on our list be carefully considered with a view to examining our right and just demands. And if one or the other of our wishes, as stated in the above articles, is found not to be in accordance with a strict interpretation of the law and is therefore judged unjustified (which, however, we hope will not be the case) we ask your graces to consider not only the law in its strict sense but, in judging our claims, also to ponder the dictates of divine and natural law, of fairness, reason, and common sense so that we might be released from the above-mentioned insufferable grievances and be permitted to live our lives as honest, Godfearing men in our land and among our wives, children, belongings, and property. . . .

23. An Unsympathetic View of the Peasant Movement: From Sebastian Franck's Chronicle

"THE GREAT PEASANT REBELLION WHICH SEEMS TO BE SPREADING ALL OVER EUROPE" (1531)*

THE THEOLOGIAN and chronicler Sebastian Franck (on whom see the introduction to No. 34 below) published in 1531 this account of the peasant rebellions. His view was shared by many Protestant thinkers in the sixteenth century.

ANNO 1525, soon after the new year, there occurred a great and unheard-of insurrection of the common man throughout the Allgäu, Swabia, Bavaria, Austria, Salzburg, Styria, Württemberg, Franconia, Saxony, Thuringia, Alsace, Sicily, and many other places. Calling upon the Gospel as their justification, the common folk rose against their lords in protest against the injustices, taxes, burdens, and the general oppression under which they were forced to live. A considerable number of monasteries, cities, and castles were attacked by these people; other places were besieged, plundered, or altogether destroyed, notably those belonging to the nobility. As all rebellion must come to a bad end, however, the insurgent peasants were nearly everywhere pitifully butchered and tortured. Some say that the troops of the [Swabian] League, commanded by Captain Georg Truchsess von Waldburg, killed one hundred thousand in Allgäu and Franconia alone. Horrifying massacres occurred in many places no matter how valiantly the

* From Sebastian Franck's *Chronik, Geschichte und Zeitbuch aller* . . . *Sachen und Handlungen* . . . (Frankfurt, 1585), dclxxix–dclxxxii.

peasants fought at first, being—like madmen—heedless of the dangers facing them as they attacked castles, ransacked monasteries, swilled wine, looted treasuries, and assaulted clerics for no other purpose than, as they said, to get even with the clergy for the outrages and damages to which in the past the peasants had been subjected. While engaged in these depredations the peasants began to realize their strength and to relish the work of destruction, being certain that God stood behind them and justice was on their side.

God, however, had other things in mind. As it is not his custom to cut off evil when it raises its first shoots but instead to let wickedness grow tall, bear fruit and mature to perfection, he wished the rebellious peasantry to become joyful, audacious and reckless in their pursuit of revolution. Rejecting all offers of mediation, the peasants scorned reason and moderation and turned even more violent as the authorities tried to compromise. Their action proves the old saying: "Ask a peasant for something and you will see his belly swell; offer him a finger and he demands your hand." That is how it was with this rebellious, raving, and disorderly rabble. They brought on nothing but disruption, injustice, murder, robbery, tyranny, rape, and all other wickedness. And the worst of it was that all these outrages were committed in the name of God and His Gospel.

It was high time, then, that God should show them His cudgel, rip the masks and fools' caps from their heads, and make them realize that their war was being fought in the name of one other than His son Jesus Christ. For this reason, God decided to take away their courage and confidence, indeed to turn them into old women in the face of the enemy. Hardly one among a thousand of them managed to defend himself thereafter, and many a peasant's weapon fell unused from his trembling hands. Others tried to hold off the attacking foe by throwing their hats at the horsemen. In the end flight became their only defense, so thoroughly had God stripped them of their courage so that proof might be given of what He had caused to be written in Leviticus 26:8: "And five of you shall chase an hundred and an hundred of you shall put ten thousand to flight."

Many a decent old countryman was forced against his will and better judgment to join these rebellious bands, for it was the peasants' custom to call for contingents from neighboring villages, like princes raising a levy. And if a man was slow to heed their call, or refused to help them in their work of twisting the Gospel to fit their wicked purposes, they went after him and stole his property, or else they burned it all. Thus many a good law-abiding man was driven into insurrection.

At the outset, therefore, the peasant bands caused a big fright everywhere (and I ask all governments and authorities to reflect on God's purpose in allowing them to grow into such a force). But when it was time for God to put an end to the rebellion, they found themselves attacked from all sides, though the authorities fought reluctantly, out of dire need and desperation, not from the wish to do the peasant harm. . . . The nobles had few troops— some say there was one soldier to ten peasants; others think it was one to a hundred—and a risky business it turned out to be, trying to subdue the peasant bands. But where God is, there is victory. The Lord, eager now to see the rebellion punished, placed swords and rods into the hands of the authorities and courage into their hearts—the very weapons He had taken from the peasants He now put at the disposal of their rulers. . . . The peasants fled into the woods. Some stuck their heads into holes in the ground; others hid their eyes behind their hands trying to conceal themselves. And the killing and murdering went on without any resistance from the frightened peasants, who were butchered like sheep.

The Margrave Casimir killed a great number of peasants and beheaded and blinded many others once the rebellion had been crushed. Gruesome butchery went on everywhere. . . . In a certain place in Alsace four thousand peasants lay encamped in a village when the Duke of Lorraine arrived with an army, surrounded the village and set fire to it, burning to death all who remained within and killing those who ran out to escape the flames. . . .

All this I set down here as a warning against rebellion and to show that God has never tolerated disobedience. The Gospel teaches us to suffer oppression and injustice, not to rise up against them. It is only because this particular insurrection grew out of a protest against oppressive tithes, death duties, forced labor, tributes, interest payments, and serious grievances that I mention it here so that in future we may learn to keep our weapons sheathed and refrain from calling God's anger and our destruction upon our heads. Apart from the harm done to our souls in the recent rebellion, we have suffered untold material destruction in great numbers of cattle killed, vineyards uprooted, crops burned, and men and women impoverished and decimated by death and disease . . . so that even today [1531] we are still hurting from the consequences of this rebellion. . . . This is what happens when we rise against our Father's discipline—and what a soft and gentle discipline it is!—and seek to break the slender rod with which He sometimes punishes us, not realizing the reason for His discipline and His punishments. No wonder, then, that God turns on us with scourges and scorpions, chastising us for our own good in order to reduce us once again to obedience. If we were to remove the reason for God's discipline, He would himself break His rods and cast them into the flames. But when we seize the rods from His hands, even raising them against Him, His anger and discipline are severe. And if we object to one tyrant, God will put ten in his place. . . . This is how things have turned out in our own time. Everywhere the common man's lot is harder now than it was before the rebellion. He is oppressed more grievously today than he was in earlier years. For the rest of their days our peasants will have to bear conditions worse than those against which they protested at the time of the rebellion. . . .

Let us, therefore, be silent and patient. Let us bow our heads before God and kiss the rods with which He afflicts us, until He himself chooses to make an end of oppression and tyranny on earth, lead us out of Egypt, and slay Pharaoh without our help. All this will happen in good time when the appointed hour has come and time has run its course. . . .

[V I I I]

Grievances of the

Imperial Knights

24. *A Dialogue Spoken by Franz von Sickingen at the*
Gates of Heaven with Saint Peter and the
Knight Saint George (1523)*

T HIS ANONYMOUS SATIRICAL DIALOGUE, written shortly after
Franz von Sickingen's death in May 1523, takes a shrewd look
at conditions in the empire from the point of view of the German imperial knights, who recognized in the centralizing policies of territorial
princes and in the growing economic and political power of the
larger cities, a threat not only to their independence but to their very
existence. Hence the dialogue's venomous invective against secular
and spiritual princes, urban patricians, merchants, merchant companies, and the law courts. Speaking as the champion of the common
man, the ubiquitous victim of entrenched power and unearned
privilege, Sickingen, leader of the knights' war of 1522–23 and representative of his order's lawless truculence and quixotic struggle for
forlorn causes, rests his case on the need for a return to the social

* *Dialogus, so Franciscus von Sickingen vor des Himels Pforten mit Sant
Peter und dem Ritter Sant Jörgen gehalten. . . .* Printed in Oscar Schade,
Satiren und Pasquille aus der Reformationszeit, II (Hanover, 1863), No. 2.

and political hierarchies of the traditional empire (whose present head is badly misjudged by the author of the dialogue).
The translation is of nearly the entire dialogue, with a few insignificant cuts.

FRANZ: If the custom here is the same as at the courts of earthly princes, I shall get past this gatekeeper only by means of flattery or bribes. But let me make myself known.

SAINT PETER: Who is at the gate?

FRANZ: I am Franz von Sickingen, an authorized executor of justice!

PETER: An executor of justice? What kind of justice, pray?

FRANZ: The kind of justice one obtains on earth.

PETER: And is justice still to be found on earth?

FRANZ: Yes, or what passes as justice, and as much of it as a man can procure for himself.

PETER: Why, then, did you not remain on earth to see that justice continues to be done there? I fear you will find little employment with us in this calling.

FRANZ: I ask only for such employment as I deserve in reward for my past services and for the claims I have outstanding.

PETER: Speak of service and claims and you lose my attention. I know nothing of these matters.

FRANZ: You know nothing of these matters? How strange! We have nowadays no more zealous war lords on earth than your successors, the popes and bishops, who received from you the power to govern kingdoms, states, men, cities, and castles.

PETER: They have this power from me, you say? . . . I do not understand the meaning of your words. . . .

FRANZ: I am speaking of what is called the spiritual sword.

PETER: I know no other sword than the word of God uttered in true faith and pure love.

FRANZ: That is how the preachers say it, citing the ancient writings of the Fathers, the Gospels, and so on. But these mouldy

[171]

old documents are today of little interest to popes and bishops, who require foot soldiers, guns, and war material for their work.

PETER: Stop! About affairs of war I cannot talk with you. But here comes the knight Saint George. I shall ask him, as an expert in war, to examine you.

SAINT GEORGE: Franz, I have been told that you are pressing claims for arrears in soldier's pay and other business. Let me hear your case so that I may judge it.

FRANZ: Many a year now I have in good faith been in the service of right and justice, though at no stipulated rate of salary. And if I had my way, gladly would I continue to act in that cause.

GEORGE: On whose orders or commission did you serve?

FRANZ: A written summons was brought to me by a poor man, containing, *inter alia*, assurances that whatever a just man might do in Christian neighborly love for him and for others like him, including the least among them, would be requited and rewarded by God himself. I took this command to heart, not only helping the bearer of the order to receive justice but assisting all others who appealed to me in like manner.

GEORGE: How did you help these men to receive justice?

FRANZ: By pleading with the oppressors to lighten the burdens they had placed upon the poor to serve their own pride, covetousness, greed, and love of luxury. And if they refused, I fell upon them with force of arms until justice to the poor was done.

GEORGE: In doing so did you not usurp the place of kings, princes, and other worldly authorities, who alone may wield the sword in the cause of justice?

FRANZ: Kings and princes have other matters at heart!

GEORGE: How can they have other matters at heart when they are charged with the administration of justice?

FRANZ: Many among them have greater care for the enlargement of their kingdoms and principalities. Others serve the interests of the hunt and the chase. Still others have their sport with women.

GEORGE: Why do they crave larger territories when they can scarcely survey the lands they now call their own?

FRANZ: You do not understand. No matter how large a territory and population a prince has, he can survey it well enough to put a tax or assessment on it at least once a year without overlooking anyone, poor or rich.

GEORGE: And for what purpose do they gather in these treasures?

FRANZ: One portion of it goes to war, the major part falls to bankers and creditors, and what is left is spent on feasting, hunting, fancy dress, and other luxuries until it is time to impose a new tax.

GEORGE: You mention bankers and creditors. What are they? . . .

FRANZ: They are men who raise revenue for a ruler who cannot meet expenses out of his income.

GEORGE: And how do they raise money? By borrowing from a fellow prince?

FRANZ: No, indeed. There's not a prince in Germany who has money left for lending, save perhaps the spiritual princes, and they are not permitted to lend (except in return for pledges of land to augment the size of their ecclesiastical territories). No, money is raised by means of new or special taxes or excises, loans from wealthy merchants or companies, and pledges of castles and towns at half their real value. These and other ways of raising money have one thing in common: the financial agents themselves make the biggest profit on the transaction.

GEORGE: You talk as though you had yourself been in the lending business.

FRANZ: I had no success at it, for princes in Germany are not well disposed toward me.

GEORGE: And why not?

FRANZ: Because of my struggle in the cause of justice.

GEORGE: But are there no princes who take pleasure in justice?

FRANZ: Some do. A few others are, at least, not opposed to justice. But they are weak reeds, all of them.

GEORGE: Why so?

FRANZ: They fear that any power accruing to the authorities under the guise of implementing right and justice would be used to crush them.

GEORGE: And how is it that you, one lone man, were able to offer resistance to so many princes?

FRANZ: Because I had the support of the common people. Seeing the daily abuses of government to which their rulers subjected them, they sought a champion in me and helped me in my struggle.

GEORGE: But are you not, in fact, releasing the common people from obedience? Are you not encouraging them to reject discipline and punishment?

FRANZ: Not at all. The common man craves justice and accepts law where law is founded on honesty and enforced with fairness. Such law, however, is nowadays in short supply. All princes promise justice, but only while their taxes are being collected. Once the treasury is full, things return to normal, which means that justice goes to sleep. For what is done with hypocrisy . . .

GEORGE: What hypocrisy?

FRANZ: It is a long story, and a tiresome one to hear.

GEORGE: Nevertheless I wish to hear it!

FRANZ: I'll not bore you with ancient history but shall start in the present. First of all, as you know, there has been appointed to rule over us—not only over Christians but over all peoples—a supreme secular ruler, ... the Roman Emperor. We are fortunate in our empire to have as our sovereign an honorable, pious, knowing, and Godfearing emperor [Charles V]. His government, however, is threatened by all sorts of schemes and projects spawned by the vanity, envy, greed, and hatred of rival kings and potentates, Christian as well as pagan, who aim to detract from his might and destroy his power. Thus, day in and day out, the emperor is plagued with so many wars and battles in his hereditary lands that he must perforce neglect the internal affairs of the German nation. . . . For this reason he has appointed his brother, the Archduke of Austria [the future Ferdinand I] to be his deputy in Germany.

GEORGE: And does this archduke not love justice as well as the emperor himself?

FRANZ: Indeed he does. And inasmuch as he was taught in his youth to recognize right and truth, he observes these principles in his government.

GEORGE: If this is so, why must you undertake to meddle in the implementation of justice in the empire?

FRANZ: Because the archduke is not everywhere obeyed; in fact, only his hereditary territories are well governed.

GEORGE: And why not the empire, where he is his brother's deputy?

FRANZ: This is what I wish to explain to you. The empire has electors, princes, and counts, each of whom fancies himself an emperor in his own domain. These princes exhibit neither obedience nor sense of duty. When one prince gains power over another, he ruins him. And the cities, observing the princes' wantonness and love of luxury and knowing them to have empty pockets, enter into alliances and agreements with them, happy to be in their protection and safe from other princes. The princes, for their part, are equally pleased to enjoy the support of the cities. Their main reason for allying themselves with burghers is better to suppress the knights and other nobility in their territories—though these knights and nobles ought to be the princes' chief strength and bastion. Princes are sworn enemies to nobles, whom they treacherously force from their lands and estates, making war upon them on trivial pretexts. . . . It has come to this, now, that electors, princes, cities, and anointed prelates have, among them, taken over the best lands and populations in the empire, each of them using his privileges and his money to enlarge his holdings and prerogatives. Thus law has become the mighty man's tool for serving his own interests. Let a poor man begin litigation with prince or prelate, and he is soon browbeaten, driven from his land, or deprived of his property. If, after pressing the courts for years, he succeeds in having his case come to trial, he recognizes in those who sit in judgment over him the very hangers-on and yes-men of his opponent, the prince. No verdict is allowed to undermine the power of secular or spiritual princes. Nor can anything touch the merchant lords of our cities. Let an honorable burgher—perhaps a man sincerely dedicated to the common good—try to interfere with the operation of a business firm, and he will be harried out of house and home. Should he take legal action, he will find his adversaries sitting on the bench as jury, judge, and executioner. . . .

GEORGE: Cannot the Governing Council, instituted by the emperor and the estates, do anything about these abuses?

FRANZ: The few members of this council who are in attendance meet now in Esslingen. There they live in luxury. In the morning they eat ginger and drink spiced wine. In the afternoon they attend committee meetings.

GEORGE: What are committees?

FRANZ: Members dividing themselves into groups for attending to various kinds of business.

GEORGE: Do these committees not serve the common good?

FRANZ: In a way they do. The ablest and most learned of the members are given mandates to raise the funds needed for the Governing Council to function. The others receive supplications from the poor and transmit them to the Imperial Chamber Court. Having done this, they are free to devote themselves to the pleasures of the evening.

GEORGE: And what is this Chamber Court?

FRANZ: It works as follows: When a litigant has passed through the lower courts, as through purgatory, he enters into a kind of hell; for my view is that no soul has ever been as maltreated by the devil as a poor man is plagued by the procurators, advocates, and men of that ilk attached to the Chamber Court. In that court a man meets with such a proliferation of actions, exceptions, pleas, counter-pleas, rejoinders, replications, duplications, triplications, quadruplications, dilations, and ordinaries that there is never an end of it until his very blood and flesh have been consumed. . . . It is these chicaneries in the administration of justice that force a man who hasn't the patience to wait out the interminable delays into taking the law into his own hands through a feud or private war. And if he cannot get at his opponent personally—be it a prince or a city magistrate—he attacks the goods of their subjects. This is called "breaking the peace of the land," and when this has been committed, the Governing Council goes into action and issues a proscription. A proscription empowers a prince or a commune to go after the proscribed person, knock down his house, and ruin his crops, killing innocent subjects and leaving a trail of destruction. But if the prince himself is the offender, proscriptions and double-proscriptions are of no avail. Nothing can harm him. These and many other abuses have prompted me to become a champion of justice in the cause of the poor. In this cause I have lost my life, properties, children, and friends. I hope to find better reward in heaven.

GEORGE: Why did you not turn to the cities for support, seeing that the princes were your chief enemies?

FRANZ: It is true that I might have helped the common folk in the cities to achieve unity and purpose in redressing their grievances. But the merchants and burgher patricians who rule the towns are too wealthy, powerful, and well established to permit changes to occur.

GEORGE: Why is that?

FRANZ: Because they know that once their grip on the reins is relaxed the common folk will quickly see how they have been victimized by usury, deception, profit making, greed, self-seeking, and inflation. All these have been brought about by monopolistic merchants and mercantile associations, whose agreements and arrangements form a huge network in which are caught coins and letters of credit, spices, mining operations in silver, gold, tin, lead, brass, copper, and whatever else can be made by compounding the four elements. The ordinary man never sees a penny of the enormous profits. For this reason the monopolists feared that, had I come to power, I would have inaugurated a new order, abolishing all the merchant companies and allowing the common man to engage in free trade as he wishes. We might not then have quite so large an import trade in pomegranates, lemons, capers, olives, silk, velvet and camel-hair cloth (for the purchase of which our hard-earned money and goods have been flowing out of our country, leaving us destitute) but we would manage to live just the same, eating our own native products. . . .

GEORGE: And if merchants and companies are guilty of such abuses, why do kings and princes not punish them?

FRANZ: Punish, indeed! Did I not say just now that merchants are much too powerful to be controlled by princes? Moreover, many a princely courtier and councillor works hand in glove with these companies, persuading his sovereign that heaps of cash required for princely expenses, especially for war, can be obtained in the counting house. And your good prince, naïve as he is, believes him. Thus, though they are antagonistic toward each other, princes and merchants make common cause when it comes to sucking the blood and sweat of the common man. The prince allows merchants to proceed with their usury, deceit, price-hiking, and profiteering while the merchant consents to the imposition of higher tolls, taxes, levies, and tariffs. It's the poor man who pays for it all. . . . But to conclude: Let matters run on as they will; I am finished. The Bishop of Trier has given me my passport, and you see me here awaiting my reward. . . .

GEORGE: It is up to another man, then, to carry on your struggle, one who will sing a different tune.

FRANZ: If he has as much success as I, he'll soon be quit of his job.

GEORGE: He will do better. He is one with more power and influence than you.

FRANZ: And who might this be?

GEORGE: The Turkish emperor of Constantinople.

FRANZ: Oh, I do not believe that the Turk will gain any victories. . . . Just think. More than thirty feasts have been given at the two Imperial Diets in Nuremberg to protect us from the Turk, to say nothing of foot races, tournaments, sledding parties, fancy dress balls, and other such vital preparations. And do not forget that the Lutheran writings . . . have been ordered suppressed and innumerable religious processions held with the participation of the Holy Ghost. In sum, nothing that might contribute to an effective defense against the Turk has been left undone. But let us make an end of this. Surely I have told you enough to enable you to decide on my reward.

GEORGE: One more question. Some claim that what you have achieved has been done from motives of vanity and self-interest in hopes of gaining worldly honors and treasures, that you have inflicted injury on poor people, killed husbands and fathers, been a highway robber, and, posing as the champion of the people, performed many wicked acts.

FRANZ: As much as I have been able, I have avoided harming the poor. But making war on princes and lords is a violent business which cannot be carried on without causing some injury. As for worldly treasures, I have built houses and fortified places, the better to defend myself so that I might continue to aid the poor and help prepare a way for the suppressed teachings of the Holy Gospel. But when the time came for me to die, I regretted all my sins in a most contrite spirit. I have placed all my confidence and hopes in God, and claim no merits for my works.

SAINT PETER: A good resolution this, and now I shall unlock the gates. Enter, and may you rest in peace until you rise again to eternal salvation. Amen.

25. Complaints of the Knights of Franconia as Presented to the Estates of the Empire (1522)*

SICKINGEN'S COMPLAINTS and accusations were not fantasies. As the following selection will make clear, he and his fellow members of the knightly class saw themselves entrapped and attacked from all sides, in danger of losing not only their property and livelihood but the

* Printed in *Deutsche Reichstagsakten, Jüngere Reihe*, III (Gotha, 1901), 695–726.

privileges of their traditional social position as well. Although ignorant of the fundamental structural changes in economics and society which had ended their usefulness, the imperial knights could clearly identify the perils confronting them in the territorial bureaucracies, the law courts, and the counting houses.

Among the imperial knights of the empire (*Reichsritter*) the knights of Franconia constituted the strongest group. The Franconian *Ritterschaft* was made up of a coalition of local associations of knights in a region where no prince or other sovereign authority had so far been able to create the centralized political conditions that had elsewhere reduced the knights and their way of life to an anachronism. Facing the twin threats of territorial centralization and extension of imperial authority (Maximilian tried in 1517 to establish a "Knight's Law Code," which was to include an oath of allegiance), they decided on collective action. From 1495 on they addressed complaints and pleas to the Imperial Diets, protesting against the common penny, tolls and customs, rapacious bureaucrats, and the bewildering profusion of secular and ecclesiastical courts. At Worms in 1521, moved no doubt by the *Grievances of the German Nation* presented there (see No. 5 above), they prepared to draw up a formal petition and, to that end, met in Mergentheim, Mainz, and Schweinfurt in late 1521 and in 1522 while Swabian knights were assembling in Constance for the same purpose. At Schweinfurt in 1522 an urgent message from the Diet reached them. It warned against giving aid and comfort to Sickingen, who was gathering an army for his attack on the Archbishop of Trier. Deciding to prepare their reply as a formal statement of their grievances, they appointed a committee to frame such a document. The finished statement was sent to the Diet in January 1523.

Some extant responses to this statement of grievances[1] show that the princes were determined to keep the knights firmly in their place. In this light, and in view of the knights' insistence on their right to

1. Printed in *Deutsche Reichstagsakten, Jüngere Reihe*, III (Gotha, 1901), 697–709, notes.

armed self-help, the knights' rebellion of 1522–23 seems, in retrospect, inevitable.

I have made a selection of the most important of the knights' grievances. I have also made occasional cuts in the lumbering language in which they were set down.

Your Princely Graces, and the General Estates of the Holy Roman Empire, having invited the knights recently assembled at Schweinfurt to state their grievances, we the undersigned, acting on behalf of the counts, lords, knights, and general nobility[2] of the empire, obediently submit herewith a number of articles itemizing the injustices and oppressions burdening us in violation of law, tradition, and common justice. We pray Your Graces and Honors to accept these articles in a gracious spirit . . . and to ask yourselves whether our open protest would not be subscribed by a far greater number of nobles were they not afraid of being associated with us, for many of our brothers are in your service or are otherwise beholden to you. . . . We ask submissively and obediently that Your Graces use all possible means to bring our matter before the current session of the Diet, there to take measures to have our burdens lifted from our shoulders. . . .

The Complaints of the Nobility. First of all, Complaints against Princes and Sovereign Authorities

1. We consider it unjust that while all the other Estates of the Holy Roman Empire are wont to meet at times for deliberation and consideration of their grievances, the nobility has been prevented by certain princes and sovereign authorities from meeting and consulting together. In many German regions the knightly order can look back upon a two-hundred-year tradition of such

2. Nobility (*Adel*): the lower nobility, the knights.

meetings, and we have the charters of our ancient associations to prove it. We therefore ask that all interference with our right to association be brought to an end. Illicit and hostile conventicles or groupings are as repugnant to us as they are to the other estates; witness the *Bundschuh* and the *Arme Konrad,* which wrought as much destruction on our properties as on the lands of other estates.

2. Electors, princes, and other Estates of the Holy Roman Empire band together in leagues, secret or open as the case may be; such leagues tend to contribute to the schisms and mutual hatred within the empire, notwithstanding the custom of exempting His Imperial Majesty's prerogatives from their aims. These leagues are so powerful that no one dares apply the law to them. They can do what they want. But we, the nobility, are prevented from forming our own associations, though we must organize if we are to survive and were accustomed in the old days to do so. We therefore ask that either all leagues in the empire be abolished or else no group be deprived of the right to establish them.

3. When a prince captures a member of the nobility charged with a civil offense, he subjects him to severe and unbending penalties against which we may not defend ourselves even though the ancient laws and the customs of the empire guarantee the right of self-help to every man who feels himself wronged.[3] In this way the poor among the nobility are driven from their property and shorn of their privileges, for legal redress is not available against such mighty rulers, and rightful self-help is denied us.

6. If a member of the order of knights buys a piece of land from a peasant or a burgher, the land being taxable or subject to other duties, the purchaser is obliged to assume payment of these duties. If, on the other hand, a knight sells a plot of land that has been traditionally free of taxes, it is rendered taxable in consequence of the sale. This practice places the knight under a double disadvantage, for, in the first place, he is forced to sell at a lower price, and,

3. It was an ancient Germanic principle of justice that the offended party had the choice between self-help and going to court to initiate action.

in the second, more and more land is in this manner made taxable. . . .

7. Princes in upper Germany have introduced an unwarranted innovation. They hold on to benefices that revert to them through death or forfeiture although in their forefathers' time these had always been restored to the nobility. Ecclesiastical princes have been especially reluctant to enfeoff knights with benefices worth more than three or four hundred gulden; this is a violation of our traditions and rights. The prelates should remember that had it not been for the nobility's steadfast support of their ecclesiastical liege lords on the Lower Rhine, in Franconia, Westphalia, and around the Weser river, the territories of these lords would long ago have been conquered by their secular neighbors—as has, in fact, happened in Thuringia, Brandenburg, Pomerania, Mecklenburg, and elsewhere.

10. Many princes abuse their regalian rights to coinage by not striking enough silver coins. We are thus forced to accept foreign currencies though these are often of lower value in alloy and standard than the coins minted in the empire.

11. Shortly before his death, our gracious lord the Emperor Maximilian, of praiseworthy memory, was persuaded by three or more princes to grant them the right of imposing new tolls. Not long thereafter it was discovered that these new tolls were creating misfortunes, hardships, and inflation not only in the territories where they were being collected but in adjoining regions as well. Württemberg and Brandenburg revoked the new tolls, but other territorial princes and electors upheld them, believing that they would grow rich from them. We think that such tolls cause serious problems in all the lands on the Rhine and in Upper Germany, whose towns and regions are already crushed with taxes and duties made necessary by the bad times in which we live. . . .

12. Certain principalities compel their subjects to contribute not only the tenth part of their grapes when ripe on the vine, which is according to ancient laws and customs, but also a newly

established and illegal tenth part of the wine when it is cellared. . . .
13. Not long before our own time, in order to gain sorely needed
aid and loans of money from prelates, knights, and cities subject
to them, a number of ecclesiastical princes made, signed, and
sealed agreements containing articles by which they pledged themselves to refrain from waging war, from entering into leagues, from
concluding alliances with other princes, lords, or cities, promising
at the same time to share the duties of government with twenty-
one councillors to be elected by the above-mentioned Estates. . . .
But the descendants of these same ecclesiastical princes ignore
their ancestors' contracts with us. They ally themselves with whomever they wish; they scorn the advice of the nobility and their
elected councillors, . . . all this being obnoxious to the nobility
because it causes us injury and disadvantage. . . .

14. It has long been a custom in the lands of the German nation
—longer than is required to make it a law—that princes and liege
lords may not compel their counts, knights, and noble vassals to
serve outside and beyond the boundaries of their territories unless
the noble agrees of his own free will. Nevertheless, certain of the
princes have been asserting that those who hold benefices from
them must serve them wherever ordered to do so, far or near. . . .
We are ready, as in the old days, to respond as loyal vassals to the
call to service if and when our lords' lands are attacked or invaded.
This ancient custom should be left in force, but it must not be
extended by innovations or by unjustified demands for service
abroad.

The Nobility's Grievances against Princely Justice and Law Courts

16. Princes and their officials tend to favor their own subjects
against the claims of outsiders, who must by law sue in the courts
of the princes' territories. Such outsiders require the aid of notaries
and witnesses in bringing suit, but it is often difficult to find
notarial help, for although notaries are bound on pain of dis-

missal to serve whoever needs them, rich or poor, many of them are afraid to work for adversaries of their lords. Without notarial help it is impossible nowadays to proceed in court, and many of us must spend years waiting for our case to come to trial until, abandoning all hope, we settle the matter out of court. . . .

18. It is a malicious custom, especially in courts that do not meet weekly, to summon the accused three times before he is declared in contempt and the plaintiff allowed to proceed. In practice this means that a complaint entered in a quarterly court may take nine months to come to trial. It would be well to shorten the summoning period and to make provision for peremptory citation of an accused who fails to heed the summons unless he shows cause why he cannot appear.

19. Many princes cite before their territorial courts matters that do not belong there but should go instead before the ordinary lower tribunals of the nobility or the local authorities responsible for private matters. If a count or knight lodges a complaint against this practice, he is informed that he may have the case revoked from the territorial court, although this court should of its own accord have transferred it to a lower tribunal. . . . In this way their Graces' courts extend their jurisdiction to the detriment of the nobility, upon whose lesser authority they encroach more and more as time goes on.

22. Certain princes and other authorities have acquired a novel privilege from the Emperor Maximilian of praiseworthy memory. This privilege prevents the losing party in a suit heard before a princely court and involving a sum of less than 600 gulden from appealing to an imperial court. Several other electors and princes arbitrarily forbid appeals to courts beyond their own jurisdictions. . . . They do this in order to prevent His Imperial Majesty's deputies, officials, and Chamber Court from detecting the injustices done to knights and other unfortunate men and from helping them to what is their due. This is the cause of many a private feud and armed assault in our country.

23. Criminal courts are in even worse state than civil courts,

for princes are nowadays accustomed to appoint as judges to criminal tribunals such men as former soldiers and other simple-minded persons innocent of legal knowledge, who think a case is proved when they have extracted a confession from a prisoner under torture. Instead they ought diligently to inquire into the circumstances and background of a case, for it has often been shown that a man confesses under torture to deeds he never committed.

24. In most German principalities, criminal judges and jurors are rewarded out of the fines collected from criminals after trial. In consequence of this custom members of the nobility and their subjects are given much heavier penalties than culprits directly subject to the territorial sovereign, a practice which reduces our people to poverty and disables them from meeting their grain and rent payments and rendering other services to us. Judges and jurors should be paid a fixed salary, and assessed fines should go undivided into the prince's treasury.

25. Many princes refuse to allow appeals from criminal courts to be heard by their councillors or by other men better able to examine matters of law than unlearned, inexperienced judges. This refusal is profitable to them because criminal courts bring in a lot of money, but it causes much injustice to be done to the nobility and their subjects.

28. Criminal judges make themselves responsible for matters that do not concern them, for example, defamation, boundary disputes, bloodshed, debts, and so on—matters that are traditionally in the jurisdiction of the lower courts of the nobility. They justify this extension of their jurisdiction by citing precedent, claiming that so-and-so many years ago they had given judgment in such a case. . . . And by means of these cunning devices they divest nobles of their rights of *quasi possessio* and investitures and deprive them of their jurisdictions and authorities. . . .

31. Many criminal courts do not employ a recorder to take down proceedings and judgments. When appeals are launched from these courts, and trial records are to be made available to

the appellant, the judges simply ask the jurors to write down whatever information they recall of a case heard two or three years earlier. These recollections constitute the trial records although the jurors may have forgotten or left out the most vital details.

COMPLAINTS AGAINST THE IMPERIAL CHAMBER COURT

32. ALTHOUGH the number of assessors at the Imperial Chamber Court has been increased in order to despatch business there, several assessors' places are now vacant and have not been filled by the authorities; therefore, the humble man suing by law against a stronger adversary faces a long and slow road to justice.

33. This Chamber Court, furthermore, is likely to suspend operations for two or three years after it has completed a term of the same length of time. Practices such as this cause insufferable delays in the law. While the court makes holiday, we, whose properties and incomes have been sequestrated by a prince or some other powerful ruler, are expected to look on and refrain from taking matters forcibly into our own hands even though force has been used against us. . . .

35. Persons accused of breaking the peace are frequently cited to appear at a place three, five, or more miles away from their homes. . . . Now, it often happens that the citation does not reach the accused until after the appointed date or that the accused has ridden out on some business of his own and cannot appear in time. Still, the plaintiff can, on the delivery of this one summons, have the accused person proscribed, a practice which is a double violation of the imperial law which states that the plaintiff shall justify his complaint to the accused, and the latter, upon failing to heed the first summons, shall be cited a second time. . . .

37. If an appellant omits some small technical detail in drawing up his appeal, the Imperial Chamber Court disallows it and the appellant loses not the appeal alone but his entire case. Appeal procedures should be made uniform throughout the empire and

ought to be well publicized so that simple, uneducated men of the nobility and other estates, who have not the subtleness of learned lawyers, will not be so disadvantaged.

41. It sometimes happens that a man acting out of pure envy or malice accuses another of having broken the peace. Such an accusation, when lodged with an imperial official, is sufficient to commence proceedings even when not a scrap of proof or evidence has been offered as to where and how and why the alleged offense took place. The acceptance of such denunciations as evidence is plainly against the constitution of the Holy Roman Empire. More substantial suspicions and proof should be offered before action is taken. . . .

42. We could report many instances in which a prince or other powerful ruler has ordered a member of the nobility to desist from hunting—although the latter has enjoyed this traditional right for a long time—or else to cease fishing or lumbering. . . . The poor noble has no recourse but to comply with the injunction unless he wishes to be put into chains and beaten. Should he be compelled to defend his good right with force of arms (for a trusting man does not keep his own when a stronger is after it), he is declared in breach of peace, placed under the ban of the empire, and subjected to general persecution with the result that the stronger not only keeps what he first stole, but takes the rest of the man's property as well, an outcome which must have been his design and intention from the beginning. . . .

55. When a member of the nobility or other poor man, following years of litigation, succeeds in gaining from the Chamber Court a final judgment against a prince or other ruler—a judgment from which appeal or escape are supposedly impossible—he must litigate many more years before he wins an execution of the verdict. . . . And if a noble who has gained a judgment but cannot get it implemented should seek his friends' help in undertaking marque and reprisal, the authorities step in and keep him from rallying such support although this is not forbidden by the laws and the man who has won the judgment is too weak to gain satis-

faction by himself. All this can serve only to encourage the mighty in their contempt for the law. . . .

56. Princes and high authorities often refuse to allow the goods of persons declared proscribed by the Imperial Chamber Court or the Governing Council to be confiscated on the roads and highways of their territories. They pretend to be offering protective escort to these goods (although imperial laws interdict the escorting of proscribed goods) . . . thus cutting themselves in on the penalties imposed in the court's judgment. . . . Such actions by powerful sovereigns make it impossible for weaker and poorer men to achieve implementation of judgments given in their favor.

COMPLAINTS AGAINST THE SWABIAN LEAGUE[4]

61. THE SWABIAN LEAGUE has made ordinances that violate the common law and the empire's constitution. To wit: If the League suspects a man of having taken action against one or several of its members, its officers summon him and order him to prove his innocence or purge himself before them. They claim to be acting in the interest of peace and order and in virtue of their privileges and liberties, but the imperial constitution declares null and void all privileges that violate the imperial peace. . . .

64. Whenever the Swabian League breaks the peace, neither it nor its military leaders are placed under the ban. Poor noblemen, on the other hand, who defend themselves with arms as is their good right, are summarily condemned and thrown bleeding into hell.

66. Spokesmen for the Swabian League have been heard to say that they do not care how many complaints of breach of peace are lodged against them before imperial courts. They have a large army of soldiers, they say, . . . and need not justify their past or

4. Swabian League: an alliance of cities founded in 1376 among fourteen imperial cities in Swabia, later expanded to include cities in Franconia, the Rhineland, and Switzerland. The League's objective was self-protection against the policies of territorial princes and the depredations of knights.

future actions except to His Majesty the Emperor personally. . . .
They are now attempting, by means of representation to His Imperial Majesty in Spain and to the imperial deputy, his brother, to gain privileges exempting them from the jurisdiction of the Chamber Court and the Governing Council. If they succeed, they will have taken another step toward the destruction of law and order and common welfare in the German nation.

Indication of Other Grievances, and First Concerning the Great Merchant Associations

67. If all the evildoers in the empire were punished equally, without distinction of estate and station, we and our brother knights and nobles would gladly assist in the administration of justice, acting out of self-interest as well as out of a sense of dutiful obedience to His Majesty the Emperor and the other authorities. We see, however, that none of the grave faults and shortcomings of the empire is being discussed and acted upon at the Imperial Diets. We note that the uppermost concern of the Estates of the Empire seems to be for the persecution of the nobility and the destruction of the nobility's properties and long-held rights while appearances of legality are carefully guarded so that we are being prevented from taking matters into our own hands as a means of self-defense. Your Princely Graces will understand that this and other matters touched on above are grievous burdens for us to bear.

68. It is plain to all that the mighty merchant companies in Germany—with their monopolies, combinations, and pricing agreements—have been causing trouble and injury to nearly all subjects and all Estates of the Holy Roman Empire. These companies eliminate the small businessman whose wares we could buy more cheaply; they engage in usury by bilking the country of annual interest far beyond their expenses and justifiable profits; they pay little in taxation compared to the other estates and make few loans or other contributions toward the abolition of the grievances of our common fatherland, the Holy Roman Empire.

70. Merchant companies are responsible for a nuisance of which

everyone in the empire now complains, namely, the shortage of minted and unminted silver, copper, and gold. They send our precious metals across the Adriatic to the Turks, an unchristian thing to do and a violation of imperial laws. The result is that we have not enough money in the empire to defend ourselves against the Turk and other enemies to our nation.

71. While engaged in ruining the common good these companies make one and all inhabitants of the empire the victims of their usurious greed by pegging the prices not only of spices but also of other commodities and goods . . . so that—as several of them have openly confessed—they are able to turn a capital of 100 gulden into a profit of 40, 50 and even 80 gulden. These men defraud the German nation of more money in one year than bandits and robber barons can do in a decade. And yet they do not like to be called thieves but wish instead to be known as honorable citizens!

73. For these reasons we ask Your Princely Graces to consider well the harm the merchant companies are doing to our society and to order a restriction of their activities in accordance with the common law and the constitution of the empire. We know that these companies have lent large sums of money to numerous princes—at considerable interest—to enable these rulers to carry on their wars. We know also that some princes invest their revenues with these companies, that expensive gifts are made to courtiers and councillors, and that even marriage alliances between princely houses and merchant lords are not unknown. All this is done in the hope of turning sovereign rulers into friends and dependents and to prevent them from attacking the companies' position and practices, leaving them unmolested to carry on their mischief.

A COMPLAINT AGAINST THE CLERGY OF THE EMPIRE

74. AT WORMS not long ago a number of serious grievances were brought to His Imperial Majesty's attention, to wit, how His Holiness the Pope and his prelates and courtiers within and with-

out the German nation place heavy burdens upon the empire, burdens so oppressive that we can no longer bear them. Nothing has so far come of these complaints. No action has been taken. We the nobility, counts, and knights therefore request as men concerned with the common welfare of the German nation that the grievances presented at Worms be brought up for discussion and be acted upon in the interest of redressing the shortcomings and faults mentioned therein. When we shall come to feel that the governing authorities are moved by a concern for the common welfare of the nation, when we believe that electors and princes pursue their aims in an equitable and unbiased spirit instead of persecuting us and depriving us of our livelihood, then we shall gladly offer our lives and our belongings to the common cause and undertake, as our forefathers used to do, to act at all times with dutiful obedience and loyal submissiveness.

Several of the counts, lords and knights.

26. The Life of a German Knight as Seen by Ulrich von Hutten (1518)*

In order to dispel romantic notions of the life of a German knight in the late Middle Ages, it is well to include in this anthology Ulrich von Hutten's description of his own circumstances.

Hutten had entered the service of the Archbishop-Elector of Mainz in 1517. About a year later he recorded his reflections on court life in the dialogue *Aula*, where he painted a rather somber picture of the courtier's career while defending his decision to embark on it. One of the readers of this dialogue was the Nuremberg patrician Willibald Pirckheimer, a man who, eighteen years Hutten's senior (Hutten was thirty at the time), could look back on a rich store of political and diplomatic experiences at the great courts of the age.

* Printed in Eduard Böcking, ed., *Ulrich von Hutten: Schriften*, I (Leipzig, 1859), 195–217. The translated passages occur on pp. 201–203.

Pirckheimer judged the dialogue "immature." Hutten was foolish, he implied, to have entered courtly service at all; better that he give it up, return to his castle, and devote himself to his studies.

Hutten's reply to Pirckheimer is a long letter, usually entitled *Epistola vitae suae rationem exponens*, sent on October 25, 1518. It sets out to justify not only Hutten's service with the archbishop but his entire life, claiming that political action is not incompatible with literary labors and pointing to Pirckheimer's own career as a demonstration of how a busy life may be combined with devotion to scholarship. Besides, Hutten continues, when Pirckheimer advised withdrawal into the study he must have had his own luxurious town house in mind. Consider, by contrast, Hutten's surroundings:

Do YOU KNOW what sort of place it is to which you ask me to return? Do not make the mistake of equating your own situation with mine. You city people, who lead comfortable, placid, easygoing lives, seem to think that a man in my position can find peace and quiet in his country retreat. Are you so ignorant of the turmoil and insecurity to which my sort is subject? Do not imagine that your life has anything in common with mine. Even if our estates were large enough to support us and our patrimonies ample, there are many troubles that deprive our minds of peace. Our days are spent in the fields, in the woods, and in fortified strongholds. We lease our land to a few starveling peasants who barely manage to scratch a living from it. From such paupers we draw our revenues, an income hardly worth the labor spent on it. To increase our revenues would require enormous effort and unremitting diligence.

Most of us are, moreover, in a position of dependence on some prince to whom our hope of safety is attached. Left to ourselves we would be at everyone's mercy, but under princely protection we still live in constant apprehension. Indeed, whenever I leave my house I face danger. If I fall into the hands of those who are at war with my overlord, they seize me and carry me away. If my luck is bad I lose half my patrimony in ransom. . . . No wonder we must spend large sums on horses and arms and employ retainers at great expense to ourselves. I cannot travel a mile from my home without putting on armor. I dare not even go hunting or fishing except clad in iron. Not a day passes without some dispute or altercation breaking out among our retainers. Often it is nothing more than a contention among stewards, but every quarrel must be approached with caution, for if I respond aggressively to a wrong done to one of my men, I may find myself embroiled in war while submission or concessions lay me open to extortion and a thousand new injuries springing from the first. And, remember, these quarrels arise not among foreign rivals but among neighbors, relatives, and even brothers.

Such, then, are our rural delights; such is our leisure and our serene peace. The stone structures in which we live, whether they stand on a hill or in the plain, are built for defense, not comfort. Girded by moats and walls, they are narrow and crowded inside, pigs and cows competing with men for space, dark rooms crammed with guns, pitch, sulphur, and other materials of war. The stench of gun powder hangs in the air mixed with the smell of dogs and excrement and other such pleasant odors. Knights and retainers go to and fro, among them thieves and highway robbers, for our houses are open to all, and how can we tell one armed man from another? There is a constant din of sheep bleating, cows lowing, dogs barking, men working in the fields, and the squeaks and creakings of carts and wagons. Wolves can be heard howling in the woods beyond the fields.

Each day is filled with anxiety over what the morrow might bring—worrisome trouble, perhaps, or tempests. We must think about digging and ploughing, pruning the vines, planting trees, irrigating the meadows, sowing, spreading manure, cutting hay, reaping the grain, threshing, and picking the grapes. Let the harvest fail, and we suffer terrible privation, with poverty, confusion, sickness, misery all around us. Is it to this kind of life, then, that you are inviting me to return? Shall I leave court for an existence which is anything but the calm haven you city people image? Do you really think that peace and tranquility await me in my tower? And if you do not think so, what strange twist of your mind has led you to offer me such advice? . . .

[IX]

Protests against the Spread of

Roman Law and Jurisprudence

27. Protests against the Roman Law in Bavaria and Württemberg 1471–1521

THE INTRODUCTION OF ROMAN LEGAL THOUGHT and procedure in late medieval Europe is an important chapter not only in the history of law but in the development of the modern state as well. Soon recognized as a threat to the autonomy of the regional, class, professional, and local groups and bodies of which medieval corporate society consisted, Roman jurisprudence was vigorously opposed wherever "ancient traditions and customs confirmed by charters, seals, and liberties" had secured a measure of independence from power-building and, usually, ruthless sovereigns and their agents. Academically trained lawyers and jurists were the most effective of these agents, and from the middle of the fifteenth century onward they played an ever-increasing role in princely councils and bureaucracies as well as in courts of law. As chancellors, diplomats, advisers, consultants, and writers of memoranda on public affairs, lawyers gained enormous prestige and considerable influence on the conduct of politics. Attached to territorial courts, they evinced little sympathy for the bewildering profusion of local traditions, customs, statutes, and privileges, which violated their sense of legal tidiness and their loyalty to a central source of right and power. The fact that centralizing princes found their ablest spokesmen among lawyers with degrees from foreign universities was not lost on those who protested against concentration of power. That is why fifteenth-century lists of grievances contain so many complaints about the destructive practices of "foreign" jurists and the "alien law" introduced by them. (See, for example, above No. 21 and No. 25, articles 16–31) Professional lawyers had been unknown in Germany during the high Middle Ages. Law and jurisdiction had rested in the hands of popular jurors and respected local men. The new law and the alien lawyers who brought it in were thus held responsible for "innovations" considered abhorrent and bewildering in theory, costly and time-consuming in practice.

The few selections translated below give a mere sampling of the great number of widely scattered protests against the penetration of Roman law and Roman lawyers into German territories. Bavaria may serve as an example. Charters of Liberties (*Freiheitsbriefe*) had, as early as the fourteenth century, assured citizens of the right of being directly governed and judged by indigenous and, usually, local officials. Ludwig the Bavarian, for instance, promised in the late 1330's that "no foreigner will ever be appointed over the land, and every man's rights and privileges will remain untouched." His sons confirmed

that we and our successors intend to dismiss all foreign officials who do not stem from our land; also, that positions at court and in the administration will henceforth be filled by men who hail from the country; finally, that no foreigner will ever again be appointed as a judge on our courts.

These guarantees, frequently reiterated in later generations, formed the "tradition" upon which late fifteenth- and early sixteenth-century spokesmen for territorial estates based their opposition to "innovations."

FROM BAVARIAN GRIEVANCES AND PETITIONS PRESENTED AT THE TERRITORIAL DIET OF LANDSHUT (1471)*

. . . THE ESTATES GENERAL implore Your Grace to issue orders to the effect that only sensible and honest men, natives of our country familiar with its customs, shall be appointed to official posts and judgeships so that our ancient freedoms and usages may not be impaired.

Gracious Lord, concerning law and judicial process, let it be said that the members of the Estates General feel themselves sorely oppressed by the present condition of our territorial and princely courts which are not now in the administration of the proper persons. We cannot afford to hire advocates to plead our cases for us because orators and lawyers charge exorbitant fees for their services. . . . Therefore, Gracious Lord, all your subjects, spiritual and secular, noble and common, rich and poor, are today grievously injured as we never were in the days of your ancestors. . . .

FROM THE PETITION OF BAVARIAN KNIGHTS (1497)

. . . A notable infringement on our common privileges has taken place. Territorial and princely courts are no longer administrated, as they were in the old days, by men of the local nobility but have instead come into the power of academic jurists who know nothing about the laws by which we have a right to be judged. And these foreigners make new laws every day, law that were unknown to our ancestors and are abhorrent to the traditions and customs of our country. Your Grace should know that such innovations will bring great disadvantage and oppression to the land.

* Printed in Franz von Krenner, ed., *Baierische Landtags-Handlungen* (Munich, 1804 ff.), VII, 263f.; XVI, 122f.; XVII, 10of.

FROM THE GRIEVANCES OF THE ESTATE OF WÜRTTEMBERG (1514)*

ANOTHER INSTANCE of opposition is provided by events in the Duchy of Württemberg. There, as elsewhere in Germany, the late fifteenth and early sixteenth centuries witnessed angry altercations between territorial estates and princes. In Württemberg, as in Bavaria (cf. No. 13 above), the matter at issue was partly the conduct of the ruler and partly the whole network of abuses from which subjects were suffering or believed themselves to be suffering. Duke Ulrich of Württemberg was a mercurial young man with expensive tastes and an appetite for fame and excitement. Seeing his turbulent reign threatened by exhausted treasuries and revolts (among the latter the *Arme Konrad,* cf. No. 21 above), he convoked the Estates of Württemberg in the summer of 1514, demanding money and promising attention to the many complaints itemized in the Estates' list of grievances: ruthless and insolent officials, incompetent parish priests, extension of princely power at the expense of urban self-government, lax morals at court. Points 9–17 of the thirty-two articles of grievance touch on lawyers and legally trained officials.

9. WE ASK that the chancellery be staffed by honest, pious, knowledgeable, and skilled persons who must not be related to each other by friendship or blood.

10. Councillors and chancellery personnel should be natives of our land, not foreigners.

11. If a matter under consideration touches your subjects, no doctor of law should be consulted or allowed to give his opinion on it.

15. Only honorable, decent, informed men taken from the

---

* Printed in Christian Friderich Sattler, *Geschichte des Herzogthums Würtemberg,* I (Ulm, 1769), 159–64.

nobility and the Estates should be named to the prince's court of law [*Hofgericht*]. None of them should be a doctor of law . . . so that judgments will be given in accordance with our ancient traditions and usages, and subjects be not bewildered by learned legal procedures.

16. We ask that due consideration be given to the plague of lawyers who have been invading the courts of our land, bringing with them their learned juristic procedures. Because of these lawyers, we, who must have recourse to the law, face costs of up to ten gulden per case where, twelve years ago, we paid no more than ten pence. We deem this a grievous innovation in our territory and a heavy burden on its inhabitants. If an end is not made of it soon, there will come a time when every village is forced to employ a legist or two to make certain that justice is done.

17. Considering the disruption brought by these doctors [of law] to old traditions and usages in our towns and villages, and in view of the injury done by this disruption to the lives and interests of poor subjects, we think it necessary that a common and general legal reform be undertaken and promulgated to the end that, the efforts of lawyers notwithstanding, towns and villages be left in possession of their ancient courts, procedures, and customs as they had them in the old days.

From Johann Eberlin von Günzburg's XV Bundsgenossen (1521)*

Johann Eberlin was a prolific preacher and pamphleteer whose writings ventilated the great issues agitating the early years of the sixteenth century, among them social and religious grievances and appeals for reform. His translation of Tacitus' *Germania* appeared in 1526. The *XV Bundsgenossen* (Confederates), a series of short leaflets published in Basel in 1521, contain, among other topical matters,

* Printed in *Neudrucke deutscher Literaturwerke des 16. und 17. Jahrhunderts*, Nos. 139–41 (Halle, 1896), 127–28.

the Utopian tale "Wolfaria," with proposed reform statutes, including the following ones on law and lawyers.

CONCERNING LAW AND STATUTES

LET NO MAN be allowed to own property in a district and enjoy citizen rights there unless he can give proof of his knowledge of the common customs and laws of the place.

Imperial [Roman] and canon law are declared abolished.

Every man should know the common law of the land. Right and Wrong is what everyone knows.

We will permit no more jurists and advocates in our country. If a man has business in a court of law and cannot speak for himself, let his nearest neighbor speak for him.

POPULAR VERSES

POPULAR VERSES reflected the prevalent sentiment against alien law. The following lines, written about 1470, are from a lengthy poem on the evils of the age by Hans von Westernach, a Bavarian nobleman and topical rhymster.*

> A profession has gained the upper hand
> And caused much uproar in the land:
> I speak of jurists and doctors of law;
> A more harmful lot you never saw.
>
> They've got a book they call the "Decretal";
> Teaches them to bully and wheedle.
> To twist its sense they're not at a loss;
> Just write a comment or add on a gloss.

* Hans von Westernach, *Ein Straflied*, printed in Rochus von Liliencron, *Die historischen Volkslieder der Deutschen*, I (Leipzig, 1865), 560.

We would not today be plagued by this sort
Did they not enjoy our princes' support.
Much misery has come into our land
Since the lawyer became the ruler's right hand.

SEBASTIAN BRANT, in the *Ship of Fools* (see above, No. 11), agrees.*

No use to try and litigate
Unless you've got an advocate,
Whose clever cavils will disguise
The truth from judge and jury's eyes.
Such men are masters of delay,
While you their wage and costs defray
So that your total bill might come
To more than the disputed sum.

28. *From Ulrich von Hutten's* The Robbers (1521)**

THE MOST VIOLENT, sweeping, and indiscriminate assault on lawyers
came from the pen of Ulrich von Hutten. His dialogue *The Robbers*
is the fourth in a series of Latin dialogues written in 1520–21 while
he was staying with his friend Franz von Sickingen (Cf. Nos. 8
and 24 above) at the latter's castle. Hutten defends his own class,
the knights, against the usual accusation that they are nothing more
than a pack of highway robbers, and he portrays in ascending order
of destructiveness the activities of four kinds of predators at large in
German society: impoverished petty nobles, profiteering merchants,
clerks and lawyers, and the clergy. His excoriation of lawyers takes up
nearly one fifth of the discussion. My translation of the relevant
passages telescopes the arguments somewhat.

* Sebastian Brant, *Das Narrenschiff* (Basel, 1494), No. 71.
** Printed in Eduard Böcking, ed., *Ulrich von Hutten, Schriften*, IV (Leipzig, 1860), 363–406. The translated passages occur on pp. 378–86.

MERCHANT: And whom do you take to be the third species of robbers in Germany?

SICKINGEN: Why, clerks and jurists, of course, a breed of men growing more rapacious as the scope of their activities widens. Wherever you encounter them—at princely courts, in municipal councils and assemblies, at public and private deliberations, in war and in peace—you see them engaged in the business of robbing the public. As makers of statutes and law codes they are the brain of all that happens nowadays. No state can be governed without their help. They establish and alter governments as it pleases them.

HUTTEN: These are the men to whom the good old Emperor Maximilian was so beholden that all his royal power went into their hands. . . . They held the key to his treasuries; his revenues were in their pockets . . . ; in time of war money flowed into their coffers, and not a penny could be spared for the soldiers who did the fighting. While they guided affairs of state, the emperor was forced to abandon sieges, evade battles or acknowledge defeat, let his armies go ragged and hungry, leave allies in the lurch, and look on helplessly as his cities were conquered. . . . And their reward for all this treachery? To be raised to the estate of nobles and even of princes. . . .

SICKINGEN: I used to refer to these marauders as Germany's calamity and to the time of their ascendancy as the age of misery. For when did things ever look gloomier for our country than when these people manipulated the reins of government? Sad to relate, they appear to be gaining the same kind of control over our present ruler Charles.

HUTTEN: Yes, the signs point to this, and, like you, I grieve over our country's misfortunes. . . . The edict against Luther is a sorry beginning to Charles' reign.

SICKINGEN: But Charles is not the author of this edict. It was forced upon him by clerks and scoundrels in the pay of Rome.

HUTTEN: This is the time, then, to wrench him from the evil influence of these malignant advisers. . . . Once the emperor has torn himself from their clutches other princes will follow suit, and the power of that entire breed of wretched scribblers will have come to an end. . . . Then no decent prince will wish to put up with a chancellor who invents new constitutions and statutes by copying them out of his law books. . . . Is it not true that, when their memoranda and drafts are examined in the light of day, they give evidence of a malevolent disposition at work?

SICKINGEN: Indeed they do. There is no injustice of which they are not capable. Laws, decrees, injunctions are mere articles of trade for them. . . .

HUTTEN: A lucrative trade, indeed. They forge signatures and purloin seals. They go about in splendid dress, puffed up and proud but mortally afraid of being found out as the empty windbags they are. That is why they show such hostility toward scholars and men of letters, whom they rightly suspect of seeing through them. Frightened of having their ignorance revealed, they banish scholars and poets from the prince's presence.

SICKINGEN: It is just as you say. . . . But let us speak of jurists now. Are they a lesser plague on our land than their colleagues the clerks?

HUTTEN: By no means. In fact, they are worse. For, notwithstanding their stupidity, they enjoy among common men the reputation of possessing profound learning, and, indeed, they hold themselves to be the very superlatives of erudition as they parade their art of hair splitting and their virtuosity in the science of turning all things inside out, causing chaos and corruption wherever they plead or argue. Is there anything in our time to equal the arrogance of these pettifogging lawyers?

SICKINGEN: No other class of men is so bloated with self-importance.

HUTTEN: If our princes had but a spark of insight into the quibbling chicaneries of these wretches, the entire school of Bartolists would soon be doomed. But the whole world is having the wool pulled over its eyes, and the lawyers' sophistic axioms are now preferred to the noblest of arts. No discipline stands in higher dignity today than theirs. Their profession alone, they claim, has plucked the flower of wisdom. All others are mere weeds.

SICKINGEN: And yet there is not a speck of intelligence in what they say and write.

HUTTEN: How right you are! What kind of art can it be, what sort of discipline, which rests upon nothing more than idle chatter? Can you call it an art when they defraud honest men and bend the law with cunning twists of phrase, this way or that, until it means the opposite of what it was intended to mean, corrupting honesty and decency? Can you respect a science that awards its highest honors to the most accomplished liars and tricksters?

SICKINGEN: Unfortunately, only few among our compatriots know this. How could the layman decide whether a lawyer is learned or ignorant? One thing alone is clear: they are, all of them, a wicked and baneful lot. . . . Our forefathers had no knowledge of such parasites. I have asked old men and women to search their memories for evidence of lawyers and jurists, but they tell me that in their parents' time no such profession was known in Germany. The invasion of Roman legists wearing their red hats is a recent phenomenon. But as things are going now, they are not far from inundating us with their numbers. Still, the tide may be turning. People may be losing patience with legal sophistries and chicaneries. At Worms not long ago I listened with a crowd of spectators as several of these hairsplitters gave an interminable harangue on the rights and wrongs of a certain case, saying nothing at all and twisting themselves into countless intricacies, distinctions, and subterfuges as they discussed irrelevant trivia. Emerging at last from beneath a mountain of law books, exhausted and sweating from mental strain, they muttered lengthy conclusions which we had no choice but to accept, for they were able to point to a thousand proofs in their worm-eaten tomes though we knew in our hearts that they were but absurd drivel.

HUTTEN: Yes, it takes great ingenuity to confuse right and wrong so thoroughly that no one can tell them apart. They devote all their cunning to demonstrating that the most crooked of actions can be shown to be straight and holy while honest deeds are condemned as malignant.

SICKINGEN: But their main interest lies in discovering whether, in drawing up a deed or contract, a man has omitted a word or a comma. "Ha!" they shout triumphantly, "he has invalidated his case." Conscience has no voice with this sort. It is words that decide whether a man is to be declared guilty or innocent. Honesty means nothing to them. They ruin a man by contriving a case of lies and trivia against him. . . .

HUTTEN: Much of the fault for this lies with the huge pile of books they have accumulated.

SICKINGEN: No doubt, for these contain the substance of the pettifogging punctilia with which they befuddle the best of judges. . . . To them argument is fitting the law to the case. For, they ask, what glory is there in winning an honest argument? Fame in jurisprudence comes from winning when you haven't a legal leg to stand on. As a sculptor's hand forms the soft wax, these men twist, knead, and bend the law to their advantage. No tyrant could rule our nation more oppressively than these rascally administrators of justice who now lord it over us. . . . I should rejoice, therefore, if the entire breed of lawyers, every last man of them, were to be abolished in one swift blow.

HUTTEN: A good idea. Let them be deported to Plato's Republic or to that newly discovered island of Utopia. We have suffered their tyranny long enough, and not their legal tyranny only; I speak also of their effect on literature, for it is because of their activities that truly meritorious efforts are rarely rewarded now. Wherever a council or diet meets, it is the red hats who sit on the front benches and set the tone of proceedings while honestly learned men are pushed to the rear. . . .

SICKINGEN: No controversy can be settled, no issue aired without the presence of one of these Solons to give his piece of advice. They have succeeded in driving the nobility out of princely courts. They alone rule the roost at court. . . . Why do we set so little store by our own ideas of right and wrong? Why hand the disposition of our public and private affairs to these men, who are the worst of scoundrels?

HUTTEN: Because it is the will of destiny that Germany fall

into misery. How else can you explain the confidence which we Germans have misplaced in these malicious and corrupt men who would sell their very souls for money? It is the punishment of heaven imposed on us. . . . We conclude, then, that jurists are highly destructive robbers in our country.

MERCHANT: They surely are, for other robbers steal only material goods, while lawyers carry off justice, destroy laws, exploit the unfortunate until their very veins are sucked dry, and sow strife and dissension wherever they show their faces. . . .

HUTTEN: And should we continue to tolerate such people in our midst? Let us instead emulate our forefathers, those brave warriors who, having won their great victory over the Romans and restored liberty to their country, struck at all enemies without distinction but saved their most violent vengeance for Roman advocates. Whenever one of these ranters fell into their hands, they cut out his tongue, sewed up his lips, and said to him: "Now, viper, will you cease hissing?"

MERCHANT: Would God that all Germans heeded your admonition. . . .

SICKINGEN: God grant they may do it.

[X]

Time and Society out of Joint

---

29. *"Let Everyone Conduct Himself According to His Estate": From Johann Agricola's* Commentaries on German Proverbs (1528) *

*A*MONG THE INNUMERABLE CONTEMPORARY COMPLAINTS on the trend of German society in the late Middle Ages, one stands out by the frequency and urgency with which it was raised. Fifteenth- and sixteenth-century reformers were firmly committed to medieval social principles, particularly to the twin ideas of estate and calling, i.e., the proper standing assigned to a man in society and the duties and responsibilities attendant upon this standing, to whose performance he was summoned. If time and society were out of joint, it was because the natural and divine order of social relationships and duties had been broken by human self-seeking and ambition. A return to "order" was seen as the only solution to the many bewildering problems besetting mankind.

On Johann Agricola and his collection of proverbs, see the introduction to No. 15 above.

A PERSON'S ESTATE is his calling, his profession, his way of life. Princes and magistrates must ensure that their subjects live in

---

* "Ein yeder sol sich halten nach seinem Stande," Johann Agricola, *Dreyhundert Gemeyner Sprichworter* . . . (Nuremberg, 1530), No. 259.

mutual peace and perform their appointed tasks; they must also punish the wicked and protect the pious. The performance of this duty earns rulers their titles of *liberales, munifici, benefici,* and gracious lords. They are addressed by these titles because of their obligation to display grace and beneficence to their peoples. Those who govern otherwise are called tyrants.

Aged people should comport themselves in a seemly way. A calm and measured manner suits them best because the young should learn from them. When an old man sports the mannerisms of a youngster, he is not acting according to his estate. In the same way, a rich man ought to offer help and support to his fellow citizens; he should act kindly and with consideration toward all; he should fear God and remember that his wealth has been granted him for no other purpose than to share it with those less fortunate than he. Solomon says: "The people curse him who holds back grain, but a blessing is on the head of him who sells it." Merchants should be honest and act in good faith; they ought not to attempt to gain unfair advantages over others. Wives should obey their husbands and not seek to dominate them; they must manage the home efficiently. Husbands, for their part, should treat their wives with consideration and occasionally close an eye to their faults. Servants ought to work diligently at all times, not just while they are observed.

In external matters each estate ought to conduct itself according to its place as far as apparel, food, drink, carriage, demeanor, deportment, words, and actions are concerned. For this reason a prince must be more nobly clad than a count, a burgher should walk about more modestly than a knight, and old men should not by their garments be mistaken for young men, nor a middle-aged matron for a young girl. Our Lord wishes people to conform to rule in external matters no less than in their thoughts. Each must do what is right and proper for one of his estate and order. If this is not done we shall become no better than beasts and irrational animals. We ought all to be dismayed by the general disappearance of modesty and honor from our modern society. Though we boast of being Christians, none of us keeps himself according to his estate, high or low. What the burgher has the peasant wants too, while the burgher apes the nobleman and the nobleman the prince. There is so much ostentation about us, such lavish display and wanton splendor, that we shall soon be brought to our knees by the weight of it all. We live so crudely nowadays, so brutishly, without measure or retraint! Not that wicked people did not exist in former times, but I cannot believe that men have ever before lived in such flagrant disregard of faith and virtue or have held justice in such contempt.

Princes are obliged by their calling to govern fairly and prevent unrest and rebellion in their realms, but nowadays they neglect their duties. The peasants, seeing court offices go to dishonest and self-seeking flatterers, conspire with one another, form war bands and raise an insurrection, which they would not do had the nobles been mindful of their estate and their obligations. Preachers must teach us how the blood of Christ delivers men from the laws of sin, death, and the devil, but they should also caution us to act in all outward matters with due obedience and submission to the authorities. But what preacher nowadays remembers his office? Instead he misleads innocent folk into believing that they are, or ought to be, outwardly free in body and belongings and that they can strike dead anyone who denies them license. This is the cause of the bloodshed we see all around us. Would that we kept to what our Lord Jesus Christ has ordained for us with his flesh and blood. But we have forgotten it all. Each of us forgetting his own estate, we teach and act against the doctrines of Christ. . . . This is the cause of confusion in our lives and the sectarianism and civil strife evident everywhere in Germany nowadays. If each man lived according to his estate, we should have peace in the land.

30. *"Gluttony and Drunkenness": A Sermon by Johann Geiler von Kaisersberg on Sebastian Brant's Ship of Fools (1498)**

THE ONE NATIONAL VICE admitted even by the most unrestrained of patriots was the well-known German indulgence in uninhibited eating and drinking. The gross food habits of Germany were described by most visitors to the country and furnished social critics and moral preachers with an inexhaustible store of warnings and admonitions. Among the latter, the outstanding practitioner was Johann Geiler von Kaisersberg, on whom see the introduction to No. 11 above. His public sermons on Sebastian Brant's *Ship of Fools* were given in 1498.

OF GLUTTONS, GUZZLERS, BELLY STOKERS, GORGERS, TOSSPOTS, BOOZERS, SOUSEHEADS, GREEDY GUTS, AND WINE SPONGERS

THE SIXTEENTH BROOD OF FOOLS

THE SIXTEENTH BROOD of fools is that of gluttons, guzzlers, food crammers, sots, and drunkards, whom you may recognize by the following bells on their caps.

The first bell of the gluttonous fool is the numbness and confusion of his mind. For gluttony and gormandizing cause damp vapors to rise to the head, and these fumes disarray the mind, causing deafness and loss of sense. Nothing is more ruinous to reason than overindulgence in food and drink, for as blindness is the daughter of lust, folly is the child of gluttony.

The second bell of the gluttonous fool is the futility of pleasure. It is the custom of drunkards and gluttons, when they are in their cups, to give themselves over to fantasies. One man is moved to

---

* Printed in Johann Scheible, *Das Kloster* . . . , I (Stuttgart, 1845).

anger, another put into an antic mood, and a third filled with hope or fear; in sum, when a man is drunk there are many ways of playing the fool. What is more, gluttonous fools feel compelled to rave about their fantasies. One man deems himself the cleverest among a dozen tipplers and proceeds to give lectures on the Holy Scripture and sing Psalms, claiming to be the most pious and learned of the company. A second man boasts of his riches. A third tells a tale of stupendous feats of strength. A fourth weeps hot tears over his drunken misery or other vices committed long ago. A fifth brags of his prowess with women. A sixth regales you with descriptions of his collection of relics. A seventh plays with fire. An eighth offers to sell you all he has for half its value. A ninth reveals his innermost secrets. A tenth stretches out on the bench and snores like a horse. An eleventh shouts like a medicine hawker. A twelfth, having filled himself up like a barrel, spews it all forth again. And these twelve acts are the habits of all drunkards.

The third bell of drunkards and gluttons is the noise they make while drinking, for carousing loosens the tongue and brings a man to shame and embarrassment. . . .

The fourth bell is salacious and unchaste talk accompanied by boisterous laughing and rude behavior, which is proof of the loss of reason and good sense caused by gluttony.

The fifth bell is uncleanliness, such as vomiting and other filth, brought on by overeating and drinking.

The sixth bell is the glutton's inclination to eat and drink at strange and unusual hours. Many a glutton has hardly awakened in the morning before he resumes what he interrupted the previous evening, stuffing himself out of habit, without desire or pleasure.

The seventh bell is the passion to let no moment go by without eating or drinking. Many a glutton never stops gorging himself all day long, a habit which is unwholesome and unnatural, for every bite taken beyond the two daily meals is too much.

The eighth bell is the glutton's wish to eat only rare delicacies and precious morsels. . . .

The ninth bell is his appetite for exotic and unfamiliar foods, there being many gluttons who expend all their ingenuity on the invention of new and marvelous dishes for no other reason than to gratify their voluptuousness.

The tenth bell is to waste enormous sums of money on meals, of which custom we have an example in Cleopatra, who once spent the value of a precious stone worth thousands of gulden on a single banquet.

The eleventh bell is to give lavish parties at which expensive food and wines are consumed; this serves no purpose other than to destroy body and soul.

The twelfth bell is to put great effort and industry into the preparation of meals. Some men use up all their time and skill in the discovery of new ways of serving food, preparing it soft or hard, warm or cold, stewed or roasted, peppered or salted, and spiced with caraway or cloves or sugar—there are so many methods that I cannot describe them all. Such fools ought not merely to be reprimanded; they should also be ridiculed and scorned, for they have no other aim in life than to tease the appetite and indulge the belly.

The thirteenth bell is to overeat and overdrink, that is to say, to eat more than the body can hold. Overindulgence is sorely injurious to men. For just as crops are damaged by torrential rains, men are hurt by taking in more food than they can digest.

The fourteenth bell is to eat greedily, as some gluttons do who bolt their food as though it were about to be snatched from their plate.

The fifteenth bell is to cut bread improperly by trimming off the crust, leaving the soft part to go to waste.

The sixteenth bell is to sit at table with arms and elbow above the board, gesticulating and waving the hands in the air as though putting on a carnival show.

The seventeenth bell is to move about the table with hands and eyes. Some men sit at table looking from one place to another, shouting wildly, crumbling bread, spilling wine, tugging at the cloth—in short, acting like a soldier besieging a town and wondering where to attack it first. Such fools cannot decide where to begin their assault on the meal and which of the foods laid out on the table to dig into first.

The eighteenth bell is to lose oneself in the contemplation of the dishes placed on the table. Some men sit forever gazing at the delicacies brought in for each course, unable to take their eyes off them for a moment. And this is a discourteous thing for guests to do, particularly for young men, who ought to sit at table with heads and eyes lowered, nonetheless paying attention to what is being put before them.

The nineteenth bell is to soil the table by making a mess at one's place. Some men eat like pigs, heaping their spoons and knives with more food than they can carry, spilling half of it, and making a pool on the tablecloth—a crude and filthy thing to do.

The twentieth bell is to rinse one's fingers in the wine cup in order to save oneself the trouble of washing them later.

The twenty-first bell is to wipe a greasy hand on one's clothes before reaching out for more food.

The twenty-second bell is to fish about in every dish on the table. Some fools poke their crust of bread into each bowl, or they scrape the dish with their hands in order to get at the last specks of food sticking to its side. . . .

The twenty-third bell is to dip a half-eaten morsel back into the dish for more gravy so that another man feasting from the same dish will get his neighbor's spit to eat along with the meat.

The twenty-fourth bell is to stuff the food way back into the throat with one's fingers, filling the gorge as though it were a sausage skin.

The twenty-fifth bell is to use one's teeth as though they were a knife to cut and tear food.

The twenty-sixth bell is to employ the mouth to sharpen a piece of bread to a fine point in order to eat a soft-boiled egg with it.

The twenty-seventh bell is to drink so lustily that one's glass will break to pieces. . . .

The twenty-eighth bell is to keep drinking until water streams from one's eyes.

The twenty-ninth bell is to drink so much and so fast that wine runs down one's cheeks and stains one's shirt.

The thirtieth bell is to drink such a huge draft that one loses one's breath and fairly chokes to death.

These, in brief, are the bells by which you may recognize gluttonous fools. The holy books are full of instructive examples indicating how the vice of gluttony has always been punished by God, for which reason I need not here explain and describe it in greater detail.

31. *The Nuisance of Undisciplined Mercenary Soldiers: From Sebastian Franck's* Chronicle (1531)*

A CIVIC AFFLICTION of a particularly obnoxious character was the social havoc created by itinerant mercenary soldiers (*Landsknechte*). Many writers commented on the deplorable influence exerted by these elements. Sebastian Franck, on whom see the introduction to No. 34 below, regarded them as both symptom and cause of much that was wrong with Germany in his time.

CONCERNING THE ARRIVAL OF TWO PLAGUES IN GERMANY IN THE TIME OF EMPEROR MAXIMILIAN. TO WIT: THE TERRIBLE AFFLICTION CALLED "THE FRENCH DISEASE" AND THE DESTRUCTIVE LANDSKNECHTE

IN THE YEAR 1495, while Emperor Maximilian was campaigning against the Venetians and the King of France, the *Landsknechte* brought a dreadful and destructive plague called "the French disease" from France into Germany. They named it "the French disease" because it was in France that this disease had first struck them. And to this day the affliction has kept its original name.

That same emperor's reign also witnessed the arrival of that

* Sebastian Franck, *Chronica* . . . (Frankfurt, 1585), dcii-dciiii.

useless breed of men called *Landsknechte*, a plague upon our land which invades us uncalled for and uninvited, seeking and causing war and visiting misfortune upon us all. *Landsknechte* are not citizens who respond to their lord's call to war. Such citizens are proper soldiers and loyal militiamen. They do what they are obliged to do out of a sense of duty and obedience, not for gain. For *Landsknechte*, on the other hand, I find no excuse or justification, seeing that they are an unchristian, cursed tribe whose trade consists of gouging, stabbing, pillaging, burning, murdering, gambling, drinking, whoring, blaspheming, willfully killing husbands and fathers, persecuting peasants in war and peace, stripping fields, and demanding tributes. They are harmful not only to others but also to themselves. In truth, they are a plague and pestilence on the entire world.

In the old days if men were forced to resort to war—the ancient Romans, for example—they left their honest toil for a time and served selflessly, satisfied with their soldier's pay. When the war was over, they returned to their work. Nowadays, however, things have gone so far that each and every *Landsknecht* acts as though he had sworn an oath never to do another day's honest work in his life. We are forced to maintain and support these people in their military finery in wartime and in peace so that we ought to weep every time an artisan or peasant abandons his work to go to war, for what can he turn into but an idler and a drifter? Princes and lords ought to give their mercenaries the choice of either going to work or leaving the country so that under the pressure of work they may cease instigating wars.

Landsknechte are a useless tribe, no better than monks and priests. In war not one among them is satisfied with his pay, but— as I have said—they stab and hack and blaspheme, whore, gamble, murder, burn, rob, and make widows and orphans—these are their skills and their pleasures. He who is keenest and brashest in this kind of work is considered the best among them; he commands the rest and draws double pay. . . .

When the war has ended and they return home with their booty and blood money, they consider it their duty to initiate others into the joys of loafing. They strut about the city, of no use to anyone but tavern keepers. Some of them, less lucky than most in the conquest of war booty, set themselves up as beggars although they are strapping fellows in fine health and well able to do a good day's work. Thus they are a burden to the honest working man, living off the sweat of his brow and the blood in his veins. . . . Others among them, grown rich with booty, loll all day in the taverns, drink and carouse until they have spent every penny, brag about their great exploits, entertain the yokels with fantastic yarns, and thus keep honest men away from work and induce them to follow their way of life. In this manner each tempts the other, and the world is filled with soldiers and loafers. In former days every family wanted to have a priest among its members, but nowadays no father is happy without one or two *Landsknechte* in every generation.

When the drinking and gambling has used up the money brought home from war, it is the peasantry's turn to pay up. . . . Other people's misery is the *Landsknecht's* greatest fortune. But there he deludes himself, for he does not merely waste money and goods; he loses his soul as well though he may have won the whole world with his wars. . . . I say nothing here of his short life (Who has ever seen an old *Landsknecht?*). . . . In truth *Landsknechte* seem to be a miserable breed of men whose lives ought to be the objects of pity rather than resentment. How can we be astonished at high prices and scarcity of money in the land, seeing that so many men in our towns are lounging about, drinking, and wasting time? . . .

In the old days a prince could make war only with his own people, or else he asked a neighboring lord to come to his aid with additional troops. Soldiers did not then offer themselves for hire like whores on market day. . . . War in those days were simple and short; they involved few men on either side and began and ended honestly. Nowadays, with *Landsknechte* being employed everywhere, wars involve thousands of men as each prince tries to build a bigger and stronger army than his neighbor. It costs more nowadays to prepare for war than it used to require in the old days to fight and conclude one. There is an old saying: If thieves could not sell their loot, there would be less stealing. In the same way if there were no *Landsknechte,* we would surely have fewer wars. Princes would have to conduct their campaigns with hundreds of men where now they lead thousands into war. Wars would be shorter, too, for *Landsknechte* tend to prolong campaigns, peace being hateful to them. And thus the whole land is exhausted until neither peasant nor prince has any money left. . . . For these reasons *Landsknechte* are of use neither to the world nor to God, not even to themselves. I wish to God that they might see the truth and desist from their wicked trade, . . . though I fear that my wish is uttered in vain, . . . for a world that does not want to see the light needs to be chastised by such a scourge as the *Landsknechte.* God help us, amen!

32. *Religious and Social Upheaval: The Drummer of Niklashausen* (1476)*

VIOLENCE, religious and social, was always just beneath the surface of events. Occasionally it erupted, as in the famous series of incidents described in the following selection.

Hans Böhm, the "drummer (or piper) of Niklashausen," was one of many lay preachers who showed the influence of the preaching of St. John of Capistrano in Germany. Niklashausen is a village in Franconia. The account translated here is from Georg Widman's *Chronika,* written 1544–50.

IN THE YEAR of our Lord 1476 there came to the village of Niklashausen in the County of Wertheim on the Tauber River a

* From the edition of Georg Widman's *Chronika* in *Württembergische Geschichtsquellen,* VI (Stuttgart, 1904), 216–20.

cowherd and drum player who preached violently against the government and the clergy, also against pointed shoes, slashed sleeves, and long hair. He also claimed that water, pasture, and wood ought to be held in common by all and that tolls and escort payments should be abolished. The whole country, he said, was mired in sin and wantonness, and, unless our people were ready to do penance and change their wicked ways, God would let all Germany go to destruction. This vision, he said, was revealed to him by the Virgin Mary, who appeared in a radiant light one Saturday night as he sat guarding his cattle. It was the Virgin, he said, who commanded him to preach.

Thus it came to pass that great numbers of people went to Niklashausen to pray in the Church of Our Lady there. All Germany seemed to be in commotion. Stable boys ran from their horses, taking away the bridles. Reapers left their reaping, carrying their scythes. Women ceased haying, coming with their rakes. Wives left husbands, husbands wives. As it happened, the grape harvest had been excellent and abundant, and wine was cheap that year. Taverns were set up in the fields and on the roads about Niklashausen to ply the pilgrims with food and drink. At night the pilgrims slept in village barns and in the open fields, men and women helter skelter and some improper goings-on, you may be sure.

So great was the crush that the drummer, who was then staying in a farm house, stuck his head out of a window in the roof so that the crowd might see him and hear him preach. And some say that a Franciscan monk was seen standing at his back, prompting him as he spoke. When his sermon had ended, the pilgrims began to bewail their sins though it may be that it was really the drink in them causing their misery. They cut the long points off their shoes (pointed shoes being then in fashion) and trimmed their hair, and it seemed as though a dozen carts would not suffice to haul away the hair and shoes being discarded that day, to say nothing of embroidered kerchiefs, robes, doublets, and other female and male adornments. Many men and women took off all their clothes and left them in the church, going away naked except for their shifts. Before they had travelled a mile from Niklashausen, however, with the noise and the wine abating in their heads, they began to regret having abandoned their clothing. And an incredible amount of money was donated by these pilgrims, also wax and wax candles stuck like hedgehogs with coins of neighboring cities and regions.

The drummer wore on his head a kind of cap with tufts on it. A few among the people who could reach him tore these tufts from his cap, believing them to have the power to cure ills and ease pain. Women in labor swore that application of one of these tufts to the belly guaranteed a safe delivery. Wherever the drummer went, people touched his hands and his staff, thinking these to be capable of wonderful cures.

There were also some who sought their own advantage in the simple folk's faith in miraculous signs. These attempted to make money out of the general excitement. For instance, in the valley of the Fischach there dwelled a pig sticker and his wife, both of whom liked to drink. Though the woman was in perfect health, her husband bound her with a rope to his horse as if she were lame and unable to walk a step. In this way they rode to Niklashausen, where the man begged the milling crowd to fall silent so that he might explain the cause of his pilgrimage. From all around they came running to hear the news. He announced that his wife had for years been lame in all her limbs, and no medicine could help her. Then one night she had heard a voice bidding her go to Niklashausen and pledge to the Church of Our Lady there a gift of as many pounds of wax as she weighed herself. If she were to do so, the voice said, she would be cured. The woman replied to the voice, "I cannot make this vow because I have not the means to buy such a quantity of wax." But the voice instructed her to proceed with the vow and go on to Niklashausen, where a great crowd of pilgrims, seeing a miracle performed on her, would help her toward the purchase of the wax. "And now, dear wife," said the man, turning to the woman, "if the Holy Mother of God has really made you well, leap from your horse and go into the church to offer thanks to the Virgin." Saying this, he pulled the loop of the rope, and his wife jumped off the horse and ran into the church. Then the pig sticker removed his hat and begged the crowd to help with contributions for the wax which he had promised to buy. They were poor devils, he said, and without the aid of others would not be able to keep their vows. And everyone present tossed a coin into the hat until it was full. Thus the pig sticker and his wife returned to their home and had plenty of money for wine.

This drummer preached so vehemently against the priests that the pilgrims of Niklashausen made up a special song, which they chanted along with their other hymns. It went:

> O God in Heaven, on you we call,
> Kyrie eleison,
> Help us seize our priests and kill them all,
> Kyrie eleison.[1]

One Saturday the drummer announced to the public that all who wished to honor and support Our Lady should assemble in Niklashausen on the following Saturday and bring their weapons. Upon their arrival he would tell them what Our Lady had in mind for them to do. Hearing rumors of this gathering, the Bishop of Würzburg, Rudolf von Scherenberg, suspecting that trouble was likely to come of it and afraid of the misuse such rebellious peasants would make of the Gospel, decided not to wait until the following Saturday. He ordered armed retainers to go at once to Niklashausen to arrest the drummer and his chief henchmen and take them to Würzburg to be thrown into prison. On the appointed Saturday great crowds converged on Niklashausen. When they learned that the drummer, whom they called "Our Lady's

---

1. Wir wollen's Gott vom Himmel klagen,
     Kyrie eleison,
   Dass wir die Pfaffen nit zu tod sollen schlagen,
     Kyrie eleison.

Emissary," had been put in chains, they started at once for Würzburg, brandishing clubs, sticks, banners, candles—anything that came to hand—and intending to ask the bishop for the release of "Our Lady's Emissary." They planned to say to the bishop that if he refused their request, his prison tower would fall of its own accord and "Our Lady's Emissary" would go forth from it unhurt. As they approached Our Lady's Mountain,[2] they were stopped by a troop of armed men from the city, who questioned them about their intentions. They said that they wished only to have "Our Lady's Emissary" released to them. If this were not done, they declared themselves prepared to besiege the prison and remove him by force. While the soldiers sought to calm the rabid populace, some in the mob attacked them with clubs and other weapons, an action which so infuriated the soldiers that they struck back, leaving many a bloody head. As the mob advanced to Our Lady's Mountain, the bishop ordered cannons to be aimed from the ramparts and fired to kill. The bishops's councillors, however, felt pity for the poor wretches and saw to it that the cannons were pointed safely above the heads of the crowd. But this seemed only to increase the stubbornness of the mob. They said, "Our Lady will protect us from harm. You cannot hurt us." Hearing these words, the soldiers charged the crowd, killing and wounding many, for they wished to teach them a lesson about the harm that could be done to them. Many people were captured; in Würzburg the towers and dungeons were filled to overflowing. Later, however, most were pardoned. Only the drummer and two or three others were burned at the stake, and their ashes thrown into the Main River so that no superstitious cult might be made of them. All the same, a few of the faithful succeeded one night in digging up some soil from the spot where the drummer had been burned. They carried this to their homes and treasured it as a sacred relic.

2. The *Frauenberg*, a rocky hill across the Main River, on which the residence of the Bishop of Würzburg was situated.

[X I]

Prospects for the Future

33. *Sebastian Brant on the Inevitable Fall of the Holy Roman Empire* (1504)*

EBASTIAN BRANT (1458–1521), the author of the gloomy rumi-
nations translated below, is best known for his *Ship of Fools*,
a long verse chronicle of the vices, delusions, and excesses to which
mankind is prone (see introduction to No. 11 above). He was also
a writer on legal subjects, a prolific poet—especially of Latin devo-
tional verses—and a zealous political publicist with a self-imposed
mission to advance the cause of restoring political and social stability
to the Holy Roman Empire. Frequently despondent, particularly
over the state of the empire, he sometimes gave vent to a foreboding
pessimism which was widespread among literate people in his time.
His unhappy speculations lose none of their poignancy for their
self-pitying bathos and the rhetorical catch phrases in which they are
conveyed. The following letter is an example of this strain in Brant's,
and his contemporaries', thought. It is addressed to the Augsburg
humanist Konrad Peutinger and is dated July, 1504.

. . . As to your expressions of sadness concerning the
disorderly state of Germany and the dissensions which are now

* Printed in Erich König, ed., *Konrad Peutingers Briefwechsel* (Munich, 1923), 32–36.

dividing our compatriots, let me say that I used to be as unhappy as you are about these calamities. Now, however, I have very nearly ceased grieving; or perhaps I have gone beyond grief, for it has become clear to me that the web of fate must be approaching its inexorable completion. Ours is the destiny of all empires and all human societies: fate being well disposed they prosper; fate wishing them ill they decline and fall into ruin. The poet Lucan describes what happened to Rome:

> It was the chain of jealous fate and the speedy fall which no eminence can escape; it was the grievous collapse of excessive weight. . . . Great things came crashing down upon themselves; such is the limit of growth ordained by heaven for success. Nor did Fortune lend her grudge to any foreign nations to use against the people that ruled the earth and sea. The doom of Rome was due to Rome herself.

My opinions on this subject cannot have been concealed from you. Did I not, a decade ago, predict in general terms, and explicitly in my *Ship of Fools*, that there can be no constancy in human affairs?[1] I foretold, too, the dreadful conjunction of Saturn, Mars, and Jupiter in Cancer [occurring on October 2, 1503]; and what I said then came true soon enough, for whether the stars really do determine earthly events, as many authorities claim, or have no influence on us at all, as Pico della Mirandola insists, I was, alas, only too correct in my prognostications, having written:

> No unity is left in our land, no peace, no law, no friendship. Like lions we prowl on each other; we rob and plunder like wolves. Our bitter internal conflicts fill me with fear and shame. In such disorder and rivalry kingdoms and empires lose their grip on power as their dominion passes to other states. Thus we shall lose our imperium. Divided kingdoms must fall. They lay themselves open to conquest by foreign enemies; they are ready to have the yoke put upon them. Stars and the fates indicate that this will be our lot. But no one

1. See Edwin H. Zeydel, tr., *The Ship of Fools of Sebastian Brant* (N.Y., 1944), No. 99, "Of the Decline of the Faith," especially pp. 318–19.

believes that the day of our destruction is imminent. Grieve, Germany; the time is at hand. Our scepter will be torn from us.

These sentiments and others of the same kind I uttered, though I would not then have believed it had someone told me that my forebodings would so soon become events. Why should we be surprised at the reversal of fortunes taking place in our time? There is no escape from the destiny of empires. What Rome experienced in ancient times is coming to pass in Germany today. "If a tree fall toward the south, or toward the north, in the place where the tree falleth, there shall it be." Thus Ecclesiastes [11: 3]. Like all other empires we shall go down the path to extinction. Assyrians lost their power to Persians, Medes gave way to Greeks, Greeks to Romans, and the Romans to us. Like all the other peoples we will disappear from the stage of history when fate gives us the cue. No one can doubt it. Each empire is fashioned from the ruins of its predecessor. Every age, says Seneca, has come to grief, and grief will come to all the ages of the future.

There was a time when we could rightly claim of our empire that it was lord and master over the world. Now, however, our society has become a haven for every kind of folly and vice. Caution has turned to passion, industry to torpor, and the behavior of our fellow beings furnishes examples of every variety of human frailty. Nor will things get better; no, they will grow worse, for—as many distinguished writers have foretold and as the outline of events makes plain—we will become more wicked, men being by nature inclined to vice and self-destruction. Do you doubt that our end will be the same as the end of all the kingdoms and empires that went before us and all those that are still to come: dust, ashes, a scattering of rubble, a mere name? Nothing lasts in human affairs except the immortal soul. Great enterprises vanish without trace, deeds falter, and edifices fall to pieces. Discord, dissension, pretense, and civil struggle are manifestations of the turmoil that accompanies the end of empires. Other kingdoms have been destroyed in like manner; minor differences notwithstanding, our extinction, too, is imminent. And why, indeed, should Germany be exempt from fate, seeing that the world itself is mortal and its days numbered? The heavens are rushing toward their destruction; earth, mountains, and seas are in turmoil; all things return to the nothingness whence they originated:

> For that which once came from earth to earth returns back again, and what fell from the borders of ether, that is again brought back and the regions of heaven again receive it.

Thus Lucretius. Horace, too, reminds us of the ubiquitousness of death and extinction:

> Earth is going through her changes, and, with slackening force, the rivers flow past their banks.

"Sovereignty is transferred from nation to nation," says Ecclesiasticus [10: 8].

Is there any wonder, then, that our society is thrown into wars and civil strife? Like headstrong children who learn nothing without the rod we seek war in peace, and peace in war. We sometimes escape harm, but we never know true peace; for even in the absence of conflict we suffer from political disorder, bad laws, shifting morals, covert hatreds and envy, and open tyranny. How often in this country of ours have we seen wicked rulers wrecking the peace and order of the land! How often have our towns and our citizens been ruined by strife! Armor is more suitable to us than the toga; we are safer on the open field than in the bed chamber. We dance to the trumpet, not the pipe. Caesar's saying "For the strong man there is no safer place than war" applies to the abuse of peace in our land. Lucan, the poet, rightly foretold the character of civil affairs in Germany when he wrote:

> It is useless to pray for peace. When peace comes, a tyrant will come with it.

Greed, envy, wrath, and pride—these are the four enemies of peace among us. If they were driven from our society, we might at last have real peace. But as things are, we cannot preserve our cities from chaos . . . for the vices that dwell in them. And this was noted long ago by the satirist Juvenal, the chronicler of the dissipation of Rome's ancient virtues:

> We are now suffering the calamities of long peace. Luxury, more deadly than any foe, has laid her hand upon us and avenges a conquered world.

Our German ancestors considered a lengthy period of peace odious to virtue. War, however, was thought to be inimical to vice. If peace means the prevalence of civil strife, loose morals, open fraud and rapine, and free rein given to pleasures—why, then, is peace preferable to war? To conclude in a word: Rarely peace without vice unless it is the peace sent by heaven. . . .

34. Sebastian Franck on the Incurable Folly of Mankind (1534)*

SEBASTIAN FRANCK, who lived from 1499 to 1542, was one of the most interesting and most tragic figures of the age of the Reformation in Germany. Though early attracted by Luther's words and writings, he quickly became disillusioned with the institutions and doctrines of established Lutheranism. Influenced by Anabaptist and spiritualist sources, he turned toward an independent faith which he elaborated in a series of theological, historical, and geographical writings and which he advanced as a "fourth" Protestant religion against Lutherans, Zwinglians, and Anabaptists. Opposed to every rule, ceremony, and formulation that suppressed or limited the pure spiritual substance of Christianity and convinced that the Protestant principle of scriptural authority had made of the Bible a "paper pope," Franck addressed his books to that small scattering of true Christians and truly devout members of other religions who constituted the *ecclesia*

* From Sebastian Franck, . . . *Weltbuch* . . . *Warhafftige Beschreibunge aller theil der Welt* . . . (Frankfurt, 1567), xxxvii recto–xxxix verso.

spiritualis in an obtuse and corrupt world hastening toward its end. Wherever he settled to ply his trade of printer or to make a living as a soap maker, Franck met with suspicion and hostility. The publication of his *Chronicle* in Strassburg in 1531 caused his expulsion from that city. His *Weltbuch,* or *Book of the World,* was printed in Tübingen in 1534; from there he went to Esslingen, Ulm, Basel, and Frankfurt, persecuted everywhere as an "Anabaptist" propagandist and a subversive influence. Toward the end of his life he returned to Basel where he was allowed to remain until his death.

Such experiences were scarcely conducive to an optimistic attitude toward history and society, and Franck's books are filled with explicit descriptions of, and acerbic comments on, the blind folly of men's actions (see also Nos. 23 and 31 above). The chapter translated below is a characteristic example of Franck's judgment on the direction of human affairs in his time.

Concerning the Congenital and Innate Folly of the Unstable, Fickle Rabble called The Common Man and of His Traits, Nature, and Character

My *Chronicle and History of the World* brings together a great mass of evidence concerning the nature and disposition of the common man throughout the ages. It shows how the pagans used to blame all their misfortunes on the Christians although Cyprian makes it perfectly clear that wickedness in the world has no cause other than the idolatry and false worship which fills our lives, . . . how the heathens put the guilt onto the Jews, in short, how it is always the innocent lamb drinking from the brook downstream that is accused of fouling the water by the wolf standing in it up to his neck upstream.

History books are filled with the madness of the filthy, raving, rebellious, fickle, many-headed rabble. Pythagoras taught us that we must not walk along the common path, nor ought we to think as the great mass does. The common rabble is called a many-headed monster and compared to the seven-headed beast mentioned in Revelation 12 and 17 because it is never at one with itself, except in uttering lies, doing evil, contradicting truth, raging about the earth without sense or direction, and blindly following where its leaders take it.

Now, Moses was one who discovered what a nasty, ignorant, many-headed animal the rabble really is. See Exodus 17, Numbers 20, and elsewhere. The chronicles contain countless stories of popular tumult and agitation. Passions govern men—including men who teach us how to subdue the passions and who imagine that they are above the world and its tumult. Everywhere the majority sets the rules; each individual takes his opinions from those around him and from the masters who lord it over him. The religion of the prince is also the religion of his people. A Lutheran prince governs Lutheran subjects. Bohemians are Hussites because Hussism is the religion in Bohemia. Italians and Spaniards obey the pope and the emperor because such is the faith of their leaders. Moravia produces Anabaptists because Baptism is common coinage there now. Few men can give reasons for holding a faith other than that they are following the crowd, custom, and authority. . . . Let a prince die and another ascend with a new religion, and the mob will go along with him, this way or that, without reason or sense. . . . Men are eager to please those above them; whose bread they eat, his song they sing. . . .

I have long been wondering why this is so. I think the reason is that truth can make no impression on the mob because the mob seeks and demands lies and craves to be deceived and ruled by falsehoods. For the masses one must play the kind of tune to which they like to dance, as Plato realized, when he taught that truth can make no headway against the wild, untamed mob. Nor is it safe, in view of the ignorance of the masses, to proclaim true opinions about God to them: witness the Prophets, Christ, and the Apostles, who lost their lives in doing so, as did numerous pious, honest, and wise pagans, among them Socrates, Anaxagoras, and Diagoras, who ventured to denounce the rabble for its idolatry and false gods. Moreover, the common folk love innovations. Being fickle, men want something new every day. No matter how greedily they covet a thing, once they have got it they quickly tire of it and wish to have it replaced. All the history books record this trait of the rabble. No matter how avidly men go after a thing, if you leave them alone they will soon abandon it for something else. . . . In short, whatever the childish masses set their minds on is sacred to them; they believe it and chase after it. When misfortune befalls them, they blame it on their adversaries. Papists accuse Lutherans, Lutherans point to papists, *Schwärmer* attack Anabaptists, and so on. Thus the mad rabble rages on, drawing its every intention and opinion from the Gospel, as we discovered during the peasant rebellion of recent memory, never considering alternate views except as heresies to be put down.

I explain all this in such detail because I wish men to recognize the many-headed beast of the mob for what it is and not imagine it to be pious, wise, thoughtful, and capable of good judgment but, rather, mad and senseless as it is in reality. We do ourselves great injury when we believe the world to be filled with good Christians or the common man to be pious and possessed of wisdom. If we show ourselves ignorant of the true disposition of the mob, we only display our own foolishness. The ancients were shrewder about such things. They—particularly those among the old Greeks and Romans who had political responsibilities—could see more deeply into the heart of their fellow creatures. They saw the common man as he is: neither capable nor willing to do what is good and right. And this is proved to us also in the experiences of Jesus Christ and the Apostles; would anyone claim that they were well received in the world?

In short, the swarm of common men sticks to whatever it touches. A wise man moves out of its way as he would to avoid a staggering drunkard. . . .

More now about the nature of the unstable, fickle rabble, particularly about the trouble it gives to the authorities. Let us take a look at history and see how the mob has always tended to attribute its own maliciousness to its superiors. The Old Testament tells us how Aaron and Moses and, after them, the judges and kings had their difficulties with the Israelites. See, for instance, the rebellion of Korah, Numbers 16, or see how the pious Gideon fared. Did Jephthah benefit from his benevolence? Did Moses, Samuel, and David reap the reward of their faithfulness? What they reaped was ingratitude, insurrection, envy, and hatred. The more magnanimous the rulers, the more wicked the people. . . . Scripture is one long record of the mad rabble's noisome rebelliousness, and Josephus and all the other chroniclers and historians tell the same story. Being clever hypocrites, men put on benign faces, but their actions show that there has never been anything other than wickedness in their hearts. . . . To a good king they pretend to be good; let a prince be a Lutheran, and the land is full of good Christians, each trying to outdo the other in acts of piety. But let the prince die and be replaced by a Nero, and your Christians will disappear like flies in winter. . . . The Gospel shows also that the followers of Jesus Christ were moved more by curiosity and self-interest than by love and understanding. See John 6, for example. Thus turmoil remains in the world and the world remains in turmoil. . . .

Now, since that is the way of the common man, and inasmuch as we ought to praise what he dislikes and beware of that of which he approves—which is to say, his praise signifies disgrace, and his insult is deemed an honor (as Christ himself teaches us in Luke 6:26)—it is incumbent upon us always to avoid the way of the mob. . . . What the world loves is abhorrent to God. To the rabble belong also those who emulate persons—be they princes, scholars, or peasants—who spend their lives in the pursuit of wealth, honor, power, and similar worldly treasures, not knowing the nature of true riches, such as wisdom, piety, morality, pleasure, honor, and nobility. . . . For this reason St. Paul warns us not to be eager to

[231]

please men; . . . he who finds approval in the sight of men is not a servant of God (Galatians 1). Therefore, we conclude, to please God one must arouse the displeasure of the mob. Hence, all those who gain their support from the mob—false prophets, for example, who boast that they appeal to the masses and draw a huge audience —belong to the devil's synagogue.

You may note that even though the seven-headed monster, the rabble, is forever mischievous and lying, it is accustomed to submit peaceably and hypocritically to Godfearing monarchs, under whose rule it pretends to have great zeal for the pursuit of piety. But let a Nero come to power, and people will quickly return to their true nature and be as blood-thirsty and cruel as that dreadful tyrant was himself. . . . The history books will prove to you that the mob thinks and acts, or pretends to think and act, as the ruler does. Under Domitian it fell upon the Christians, each member eager to outdo the other in persecuting them. Then, under Constantine, Christians multiplied like flies in the summer. With the King of England the whole country suddenly turned Christian, a veritable rain of Christians fell upon England at that time. Thus, the unstable, childish rabble veers this way or that, believing without question or sense, what it is told to believe.

This, then, is the portrait of the common man, *Herr Omnes*, painted in his own colors. Let it be a warning to you in sharpening your judgment. Flee from this many-headed monster as fast and as far as your legs can carry you. . . . If you inquire of me: Are there not a great many pious men left on earth? I answer: Do you not believe what Jesus and the prophets said, that no one is truly pious, save real Christians, who are not men at all, who are a breed set apart from men, true children of God, created of God and not of men, given life by the Word and not by corruptible human seed, born of the spirit and not through the will of the flesh? These alone, the children of truth and light, to whom all things are clean, are capable of doing good works. To the others, to the mob and rabble, nothing is clean. Impure in mind and conscience, they pretend to know God but instead deny him in every action, being incapable of doing good works. For what clean thing can come from an unclean? . . . Rightly, therefore, Scripture warns us to beware of men, neither to trust them nor to believe in them. . . .

35. Reform and Redemption: From the Book of One Hundred Chapters and Forty Statutes (c. 1500)*

THE TRACT of which a few passages are translated below is not only the strangest manifestation of the medieval reform idea; it is also one of the most curious literary relics of late fifteenth-century Germany. Its anonymous author—he is usually referred to as the "Upper Rhenish Revolutionary," but except for the geographical designation this is a misnomer—was a pamphleteer and reform preacher active in the late decades of the fifteenth and early years of the sixteenth centuries. He seems to have spent his time pointing out the failings of German society and urging the need for speedy reform. According to his own testimony he submitted numerous proposals to rulers and councils. His ideas have much in common with those of the so-called *Reformation of the Emperor Sigismund* (See No. 1 above); despite his occasionally inflammatory language he is an essentially conservative thinker. But to a much greater extent than the *Reformatio Sigismundi* his treatise is a farrago of the fears, hopes, memories, suspicions, sympathies, and interests pressing upon the minds of spectators to the late medieval scene. Indeed, the book can serve as a synopsis, albeit a distorted one, of notions and ideas circulating in Germany on the eve of the Reformation as these have been illustrated in the selections of this anthology: the longing for religious and moral restoration, virulent anticlericalism, fascination with the ancient historical past, the desire for a reconstituted empire mixed with

* Printed in Gerhard Zschäbitz and Annelore Franke, *Das Buch der Hundert Kapitel Und der Vierzig Statuten des sogenannten Oberrheinischen Revolutionärs* (Berlin, 1967). The translated excerpts occur on pp. 181–3; 218–19; 237; 247–8; 258–9; 273–4; 313–15; 341–3; 368–78; 526–9.

a sometimes extravagant Germanic nationalism, astrology, Joachimite and other prophecies, apocalyptic forebodings and messianic anticipations, the tendency to blur the distinction between Christian and pagan traditions, rejection of all modernist trends in politics and society, the whole catalogue of German complaints and protests, and the ever-present undercurrent of social violence. Reform and redemption—political as well as religious—were closely associated ideas in Germany. In this treatise they are inseparable.

The writer probably compiled his treatise (surviving in only one manuscript copy, which may be the work of one who heard him preach) in the years 1489–1510. As a piece of writing it is a chaotic production: ill-organized and repetitious, moving from sentence to sentence as if by free association. The "revolutionary," however, was evidently an intelligent and informed observer of his time. He knew what was wrong even if his idiosyncratic points of view and proposals for solutions strike us as weird. It is impossible to cull a representative selection of chapters from this very long book, nor can a few sample passages illustrate the fantastic thought structure of the whole. But the following chapters—much abbreviated and linked by bracketed connecting synopses—may suggest something of the high-strung and agitated tone of a work which, though it had little impact on events, is more representative of the temper of its time than many modern scholars like to think.

PREFACE

In a.d. 1490 I wrote this book of a hundred chapters and forty statutes.[1]

Michael, archangel and worthy messenger of Almighty God, appeared to this pious man and made revelations to him as follows: God has grown impatient and angry with sinning mankind, who break God's commandments without fear or contrition. Thinking

1. The preface was written about 1509 after the composition of the body of the work.

themselves immune from civic penalities, men violate all the laws of their society. Adultery is licit, blasphemers are respected, the usurer has the law on his side, murderers sit in the judgment seat, and the plunderer of the church has become the very shepherd of the house of worship.

Having issued these warnings, Michael commanded the pious man to form an association of honestly-born married folk, men and women who hold marriage in faithful respect. They are to be distinguished from the rest of mankind by a yellow cross worn on their garments. Leading this band, Michael proposes to set out to reestablish a firm Christian faith on earth so that the words of our Savior may be fulfilled: "There shall be one flock, one shepherd." None but pious married men and women may accomplish this aim, for the sacraments are not efficacious except upon honest married people. All good things have their beginnings in marriage.

The archangel also quoted Revelation 9: 1: "And I saw a star fallen from heaven to earth; and he was given the key to the shaft of the bottomless pit." Sins are proliferating. The power of evil has teeth like the teeth of scorpions with which to torture men until they fall into despair and crave release in death. These are the words of John, writer of the Apocalypse, cursing mankind. And Michael says further: "A great portent appeared in heaven, a woman clothed with the sun." The woman wore eagle's wings and she alighted upon the wasteland of the world, there to give birth to a son who will rule the nations with a rod of iron. And he will do battle against the Turks, who are the children of the antichrist, until they are brought to the fear of God.

I observe how three unclean men, the pope, the emperor, and the king of France, will wake the dragon—that is to say, the Turk—from his sleep.[2] Gruesome wars will be waged, and thousands will die. And God will cause stones to fall from the sky, and these will destroy us with fire and blood. We read in Revelation [11:4]:

2. A reference to the League of Cambrai, 1508, concluded by the three sovereigns named against Venice.

"These are the two olive trees and the two candlesticks standing before the lord of the earth."

Whoever wants to join in punishing the wicked, let him take the yellow cross and raise his voice in songs of praise: "Great and wonderful are thy deeds, O Lord God the Almighty. Just and true are thy ways. Who shall not fear and glorify thy name, O Lord? For thou alone art holy." . . . God has said: "Let no one go into the temple unless he has first cleansed himself of the seven deadly sins." And the archangel said further that only they are priests who keep God's commandments and are brothers in Christ. Those who call themselves priests but lead not the priestly life make a mockery of Christ's passion. A priest saying mass while in a state of sinfulness is a very torturer of Christ. Therefore, purify yourselves and your garments so that no sin may remain clinging to you. With such a band of men will I challenge the entire world.

[More prefatory material and programmatic assertions outlining the author's historical and religious purposes. The first chiliads[3] of world history and their rulers. Noah and his sons. Japhet inherits Europe.]

Chapter 7: How a Roman Emperor Shall Rule over All Europe

I speak of Europe, Japhet's inheritance, and now governed by the mighty and unconquerable King Maximilian. I speak of Europe in praise of the German nation. The following twenty chapters tell of the kings who have reigned in German lands, and after that I shall say something of the children of Israel and their monarchs. . . . Then, in chapter 40, I come to the origins of Rome and the destruction of Troy and Jerusalem, not failing to mention

3. The author's historical scheme is determined by great astronomical conjunctions, each of which inaugurates a historical period called a chiliad, whose beginning is marked by the rise of a great man: Seth, Japhet, Alexander, Justinian, etc. The opening of the eighth chiliad is expected shortly. It will be inaugurated by the messianic Emperor Frederick.

what the pious, mighty, unconquerable Germans have accomplished and how they defeated the Gauls, that is to say, the French, who were slaves to the Germans.

In chapter 46 I come to the foundation of our faith, to the victorious Virgin Mary, born of Jesse, who conceived Jesus, who gave us the New Testament. . . . And in the following forty-three chapters I tell how a humble man shall arise and conquer the whole world with a tiny band of helpers, bringing to pass the prediction of Jesus that there shall be one faith in the world, one shepherd, and one ruler.

[Various European rulers, including Semiramis and her son Tribeta, who went to Germany and founded Trier.]

Chapter 16: The City of Trier, and How It Was Constructed[4]

THE great German city of Trier, when it was first built, had four gates. One faced east and was called the Black Gate in honor of the planet Saturn. Whenever the people of Trier lost a battle, they returned by this gate. The second gate faced west, in honor of Mars, and in front of this gate lay an open space where the military arts were taught. When they won a battle, the people went in procession through this gate. . . . They also were the first to build a capitol, which is a place where wise men sit in judgment.

In the middle of the city stood a great temple in honor of Jupiter or Jove. For this reason we Germans are called "Jovinici," which is to say, "pious Christians." Facing the great statue of Jupiter in the temple they raised a suspended statue of Mercury, a god they revered as an intercessor between men and the heavens. This statue of Mercury was made of iron, and the dome of the temple

---

4. The city of Trier is the center of a strange but persistent body of legends, according to which Trier was founded, long before Rome, by Tribeta, son of the Assyrian king Ninus, as a paradigmatic community with model institutions and laws. These laws are the *Forty Statutes* appended to the *Book of One Hundred Chapters.*

was a huge magnet so that, when it was moved into the temple, the statue was drawn upward by magnetic force and floated free within the building. . . .

The city was surrounded by a number of thick walls, towers, and strong points. These were later converted into churches and monasteries. The citizens also built an aquaduct to transport water from the mountains into the city. This structure was a mile in length and built entirely of marble. They also installed drains to flush the population's waste into the Mosel river so that no pollution could remain within the city.

[Various other rulers. Reflections on marriage, oaths, etc.]

CHAPTER 21: THE ORIGINS OF THE LATIN LANGUAGE

THE ruinous Latin language has long been a destroyer of that unity of peoples which prevailed when France, the Roman Empire, and Spain were still governed by the Kings of Trier, that is to say, when these three kingdoms were ruled and civilized by the Germans. Even now the French could be restored to obedience and tribute to our emperor if we first reformed ourselves and our society. . . .

The three languages, French, Latin, and Spanish, were invented by an exiled Trojan named Latinus. His purpose was to throw men into confusion by preventing them from understanding one another's speech. He therefore constructed from the rules of Greek grammar a written language, and he called it Latin as it is still called in our day. . . . Latin does not, therefore, stem from the tower of Babel. It was invented by an exiled Greek.

The Latins also made a law code called *ius quiritum militare*. This code teaches what is mine and what is thine. Now it is the law of the monks, who connive day and night how they might bring the treasures of the world into their clutches. Law is employed by the rich to break society apart; Scripture and the chronicles have taught this to me. An emperor is a lord anointed by God. He should never permit transgressions against the common good to go unpunished, for the following reason: the emperor is lord over the world. Monks have sworn poverty and contempt for the world. A monk with half a penny in his pocket is not worth half a penny. . . . And if a priest misappropriates as much as a penny of his benefice, giving it to his concubine or children, he renders himself subject to secular judgment as though he were a common church robber. Pious priests ought to have enough to eat and a dry roof over their heads, but what they own beyond this is not theirs; it should go to the sick and the poor. And what is most important, no priest should take money for saying mass or giving the sacraments. . . .

[Thoughts on the imperial escutcheon. The duties of knights. Law and justice. Alexander the Great.]

CHAPTER 26: THE BIRTH AND ORIGINS OF ALEXANDER THE GREAT

ALEXANDER THE GREAT was a native German, born in the western part of the empire. Most of the poets tell lies about him, for the Greek writers begrudge us Germans the honor of claiming Alexander as our own. Latin historians disagree with one another. Some say Alexander was born in Pannonia. Theophilus claims Apollo was his father; on the other hand, Orosius thinks his father was Philip of Macedonia. . . . Still others believe that he was a natural son of Nectanebos of Egypt. . . . The Latin language did not exist in Alexander's time, as Aristotle, Alexander's teacher, indicates clearly in his books, where he proves that Latin is not one of the seventy-two original tongues. . . .

I have already described how Alexander drove the grasping Jews into the mountains of Gilboa, where he chained them with irons so strong that no fire could melt them. . . . At Worms some time ago I proposed a scheme for abolishing usury. . . . My idea was to end it by applying the written divine law to it. I also promised to deliver an excess of ten tons of minted gold to the emperor. Is it not disgraceful to see how our judges, who should represent the power and anger of God against usury, let themselves be bribed to recognize usury as legal and right? The worldly goods of such judges should be confiscated and they themselves driven out of the land. Who has heard of thievery greater than that of the usurer? A man lends me twenty gulden. In the first year they earn interest of one gulden, in the second year a gulden and three kreuzer, in the third year a gulden and six kreuzer, and so forth and so on. Never a holiday for the twenty gulden; they go on earning night and day. . . . And no one quotes Leviticus 25! Even the priests do not refer to this sort of thing as usury though they know well enough what it is. . . .

Chapter 31: Concerning the Monks, Their Beliefs, and Their Vows

Emperors should hold no property of their own but may draw their income from the common treasury. Theirs should be the fifth part of offerings made to God. The sovereign of a country should pledge faith and duty to his people before they swear allegiance to him. In the same way husbands receive the vows of their wives before they give their own, and priests give vows before being ordained. Many monks have to spend a year on probation before being allowed to give their vows.

Neither monks nor nuns existed before the birth of Christ nor for eight hundred years afterwards. In those days there were temple servants and priests but no monks. The Gospel warns us to "beware of false prophets, who come to you in sheep's clothing but inwardly are ravenous wolves" and who exploit and destroy the earth. . . . Taking vows means maintaining chastity and turning away from the world. Monks and nuns should have nothing to do with the world. Those who break their vows are perjurors and damned persons.

When a monk hears of a pious man with property to bequeath, he dogs his footsteps day and night, waiting to grasp it all for his

order. The monk imagines himself good and holy, but he is in fact
cursed and despised as a transgressor of his vows, a perjuror cut off
from the community of saints and beyond the mercy of God. He
knows he will never go to heaven; this is why he is so eager to
prevent the rest of us from going there. . . .

[The Hebrews. The Romans. Germanic tribal history.]

CHAPTER 47: CONCERNING THE NEW TESTAMENT, AND WHY JESUS, OUR SAVIOR, WAS SENT BY GOD TO THE CHILDREN OF ISRAEL

I HAVE explained above how the Germans used in ancient times
to be called "Jovinici," meaning pious Christians. As long as we
honored Jove and kept the commandments of Trier, we remained
Christians. . . . Astronomers tell us that the hour of Jesus' birth
saw Jupiter standing in the middle of the heavens and the Virgin
ascendant while the sun stood in the sign of Capricorn but Mars
in the Ram, which indicated a short life. . . .

Jesus said: "All punishment comes from sin." Sin is effort contrary to the will of God. Sin extinguishes the grace of God, and
where there is no grace there can be no mercy. Whoever, therefore, is in a state of sin must first do penance. Through penance he
may gain God's mercy and thus reenter the state of grace. . . .

You may recognize sin by six characteristics. One is despair of
God and His ways. Another is the envy and cunning of ecclesiastics
who swear an oath against one of God's own commandments. The
Holy Sacrament of Matrimony is God's way of making one flesh
out of two. Those who vow chastity and despise the Holy Sacrament of Matrimony lead the devil's life. . . . God wanted his son
born in holy wedlock, for marriage is sacred and is consummated
without sin. . . . But if a nun has a child, let her be buried alive and
the baby starve to death. . . .

[The sacraments. Divine grace. The clerical estate and what it may
do and not do. Alms and tithes.]

CHAPTER 55: THE POPE IS INFERIOR IN POWER
TO THE EMPEROR

As the emperor is lord over the whole world, our mighty sovereign and prince Maximilian is a lord above all other lords. All countries of the world should be subject to him. Imperial law derives directly from God. God gave the emperor a two-edged sword to signify his rule over both estates, spiritual and secular. . . . The emperor should examine each pope to determine whether he is worthy of being successor to St. Peter. He may sequestrate spiritual properties and fortunes in order to advance the common weal. . . . An emperor should live modestly, for poverty is more becoming to him than are riches. He is called the first among knights [*Ritter*], meaning the first judge [*Richter*], a power given him by God. The Bible tells of kings who fought and struggled in the common interest. . . . When the emperor sees the Roman Church guilty of corruption and incompetence, he should intervene to set things straight. Failing to do this makes him a destroyer of the Church, for excessive leniency is inimical to justice. . . .

The emperor is lord over the world. He is like the eagle. Whoever opposes him falls into grave sin, for emperors are the blessed of God. Esther speaks to God: "You are the God of Abraham. Lord have mercy on us, help us defeat our enemies. Smite those who are not with us." Popes pile up huge revenues by proclaiming jubilee years, and they set out to tyrannize the Christian faith. . . . Against these popes the Emperor Frederick or the Emperor Henry has written: "When a holy man destroys holy things, he should be stripped of his holiness." . . . We Christians, born of Japhet, were holy Jovinici, that is to say, pious Christians, for we honored Jupiter, and Jesus did all his miracles on Thursday in Latin *dies Jovis*. . . . I have read that, when we changed Thursday into Sunday, we forfeited much territory in the Orient to the pagans and lost our western lands to the Gauls. And Jerusalem was retaken by the Jews. It is all the fault of the clergy.

Chapter 56: The Great Conjunction of the Sun, Jupiter, and Saturn in the Sign of the Ram

Justinian, a great and mighty emperor, was born in the city of Trier at the time of the great conjunction of Saturn, Jupiter, and the sun in Ram. He was a wise and learned man, who condensed many laws into one code of twelve books. His heart enclosed all human rights and laws. There is nothing in his writings to suggest that the popes have the right to crown emperors. He did say, however, that no province should be served by more than sixty-five clergymen. . . .

Kings should adhere to the written law. Paul writes: "The virtue of law is to command. But justice is knowing how to keep the law." Cicero: "Holy law means doing divine things and allowing no injustice to endure." It is likely, therefore, that the Germans were the first people to keep the law when they were the rulers of Greece. Latin peoples are descended from the Gauls, who used to be slaves to the Germans. Every man was then the judge of his fellow man. But as wickedness increased, trained judges had to be appointed and were later confirmed by the excellent Emperor Charles the Great. Nowadays all laws are upside down. He who can do wicked things never fails to do them. . . .

[More thoughts on laws. The conquest of Jerusalem. Habsburgs and Burgundians.]

Chapter 62–63: Concerning the Future King Frederick Whose Reign Will, with the Help of God, Commence the Eighth Chiliad and Who Will Establish One Shepherd, One Fold, and One Faith throughout the World

In the chapters above, I have taken note of the events of past chiliads. Now I wish to indicate what is going to come to pass in the eighth chiliad beginning in 1500. Great changes always occur at times of great conjunctions. In the impending great conjunction a comet will appear in Cancer while the sun stands in the sign of the Ram and Saturn and Jupiter are also in Cancer. Saturn, on account of its slow motion, is a harbinger of great things, while the sun in its fourth aspect signifies disintegration in worldly affairs and major transformations among rulers and laws. Cancer, a truthful sign, governs mutations and reformations in the estates of society. . . . Peasants will rise against their masters. . . . Mars in his own house at the time of the lunar eclipse in 1509 signifies great changes, and with change will come much bloodshed and a terrible heat wave. As the sun will pass close to Mars, Mars being lord of knights and the sun being lord of kings, the common man will strip lords and kings of their titles and dignities. Mars passing close to the sun indicates that peasants will attempt to slay their kings.

FREDERICK

Our future king is sent us by God. He is great in wisdom but small in power, not rich but endowed with reason, strict in giving judgment, loving justice and hating those who transgress the written law. He is a knight of righteousness, and all other knights will declare him their king and crown him with a chaplet of oak leaves. . . . He will deal with usurers according to the instructions in Leviticus 25. He will protect the land, emancipate the peasantry, nourish the poor, and guard widows and orphans. Jesus our Savior has said: "A wise man will come from the north and go into all lands," by which He meant the heart of Europe, the Rhineland between Bingen and Basel. And he will bear upon his breast a yellow cross as a sign of his mission to abolish evil and reestablish the good.

The Cumaean Sibyl says: "He will reform and discipline both estates." Saint Bridget of Sweden writes: "Be of good cheer. A pious man will enter into the garden of the Virgin," by which she means the Black Forest and Alsace. And Jesus said: "Greater works than these will he do," that is to say, he will make of all the nations one people united in one faith, and will subject three kings to his power, and the earth will be strewn with the slain bodies of his enemies. . . .

Is it not high time for common men to raise to the throne one like themselves so that an end might be made of the depredations of the priests? God and the law will be on his side. All kingdoms will join him, but the first will be the people of the blessed land, which is Alsace, a country where all things are in abundance. . . . Jesus Christ has told us that his father's house belongs to those who obey His will, not to those who live off the sweat of the poor man's brow. For this reason Jesus bids us punish the priests, saying "Make them subservient to the people, bid them do what I have done, not to be served but to serve." Drive from our temples all those who commit sacrilege. I refer to the priests who consume with their concubines the common people's offerings. . . . The Emperor Sigismund once told the Council of Basel that priests who waste offerings are nothing more than thieves and robbers. No priest should have more than one benefice, and his income should not exceed the tenth part of the offering, for a priest who has more than the bare necessities of life stifles the love of God. He is no longer a servant of God, but a disciple of the devil. Better one pious priest than eleven thousand useless ones as Emperor Sigismund used to say. . . .

THE NEW KING'S APPEARANCE, AND WHY HE IS CALLED FREDERICK

Many have written about the emperor to come. I have heard him called a peacemaker to the world and an abolisher of the power of the wicked. He will know the written Divine Law, and he will reform those who are are ignorant of it, not with severity but with justice. . . .

Some say the new sovereign will be a prophet, and not wrongly, for his lawmaking will derive from the customs of past ages. Many think he will be a priest. This, too, is true, for he will teach the truth and lead his people to the path of righteousness. Several claim he will be a holy man. True again, for he will hate evil and keep the Divine Law ever before his eyes, and this will make him holy. Still others say he will be a knight, which is also true, as he will make peace and allow the common man to cultivate the soil in tranquillity.

I also find that he will be a wise man of humble origins. . . . And his name [*Friedrich*] means Man of God, Lover of Right, Bringer of Peace—for where justice does not dwell there can be no peace. Hence Friedrich—rich in peace [*Frieden*]. For this reason he will be crowned with an oaken chaplet, like a knight. He will bear the yellow cross on his breast and lead a vast throng of men to reconquer the Holy Land. . . .

Take the cross and prove your knighthood against the infidels. Contend with words and fight with deeds! Do as Jesus our Savior commanded you to do; go through the world proclaiming the Gospel and baptizing unbelievers in His name. And those who do not wish to be baptized are not Christians according the Scripture. Kill them all, and let them be baptized in their own blood. The Cornelian law directed that men who injure their fellow beings must be punished, for which reason no straighter path to divine grace exists than to remain steadfast in your Christian faith. . . .

[The "Forty Statutes of Trier" follow.]

THE FORTIETH STATUTE: CONCERNING THE ESTATE OF THE SUPREME SOVEREIGN

This fortieth statute pertains to the emperor and to his subjects, the pope, knights, and vassals. The emperor is lord over the world, king over all other kings. He wields power above all other powers. And his empire has its name from God alone. . . .

An emperor must at all times be armed, ready to fight evil and defend the common good. . . . For this reason he may not burden the common weal with tolls, taxes, duties, and so on, and he must

maintain honest coinage and let no wickedness go unpunished. . . .
He is knight and judge over the whole world. . . . The laws are
written in his heart. His rule on earth is like the reign of God. God
has said: "I have given the mighty power to rule in the world." He
must lead the disobedient to obedience and abolish adultery. . . .

I beg all mighty and serene princes and lords to accept this work
of mine not in anger but as a token of my simple nature. . . . O you
learned men with your fat benefices, O you wealthy persons growing rich on usury and other income ground from the poor! Let this
book be a mirror for the study of your own reflections. I urge all
Christians born in Jesus Christ to take the yellow cross of his
confession and to look to the passion which our savior suffered on
the Holy Cross on Good Friday for us and for us alone. And even
as He himself went through hell and entered paradise, so shall we
gain salvation, providing we keep his comandments. . . . Amen.

Strauss, Gerald, 1922–   comp.
  Manifestations of discontent in Germany on the eve of
the Reformation; a collection of documents selected, translated, and introduced, by Gerald Strauss.   Bloomington,
Indiana University Press ₍1971₎

  xxiii, 247 p.   22 cm. $9.50

  1. Germany—History—Frederick III, 1440–1493—Sources. 2. Germany — History — Maximilian I, 1493–1519 — Sources. 3. Reformation—Germany—History.   I. Title.

DD174.S87   943′.03   75–135014
ISBN 0–253–33670–8   MARC

Library of Congress   71 ₍4₎